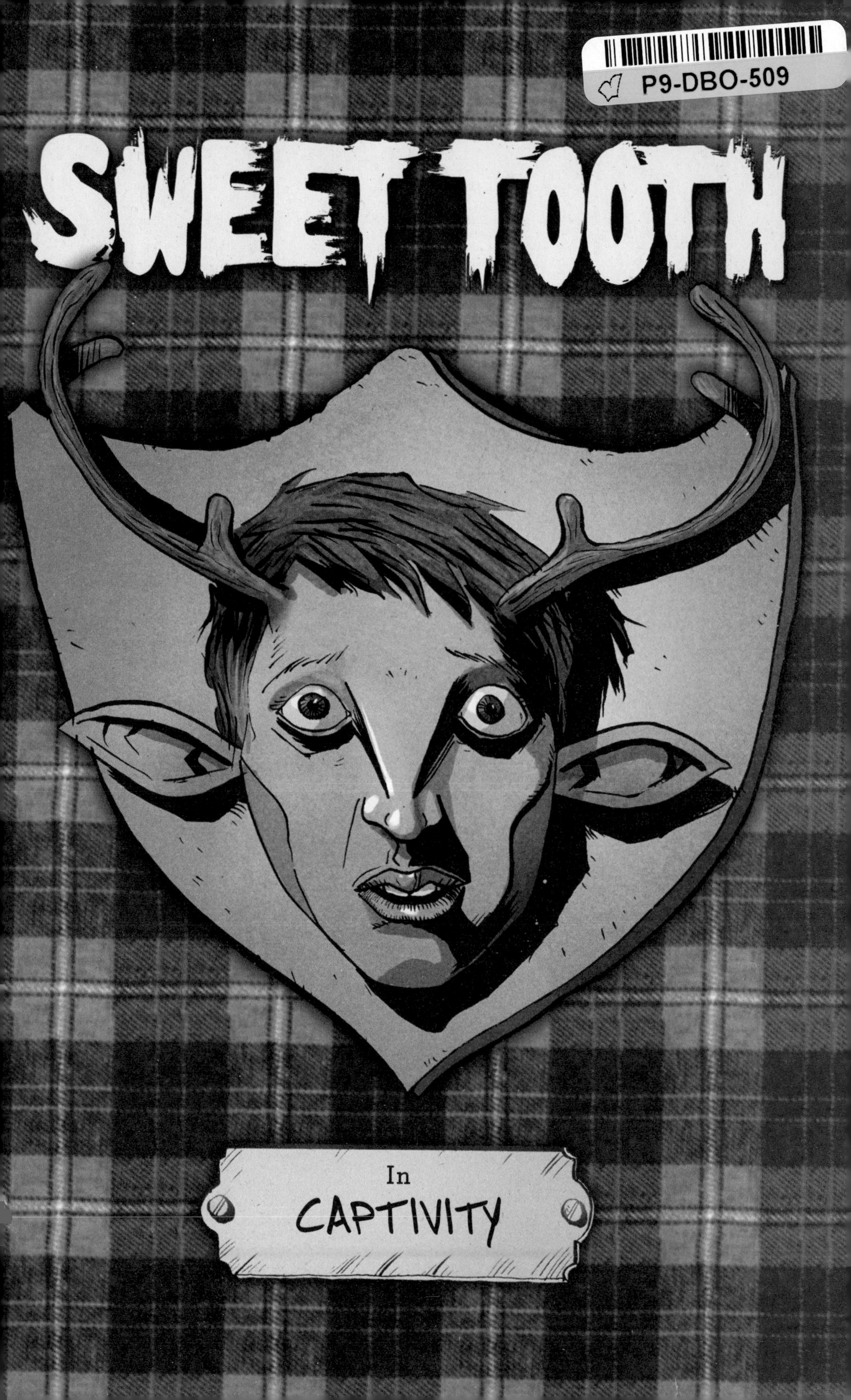
SWEET TOOTH
In
CAPTIVITY

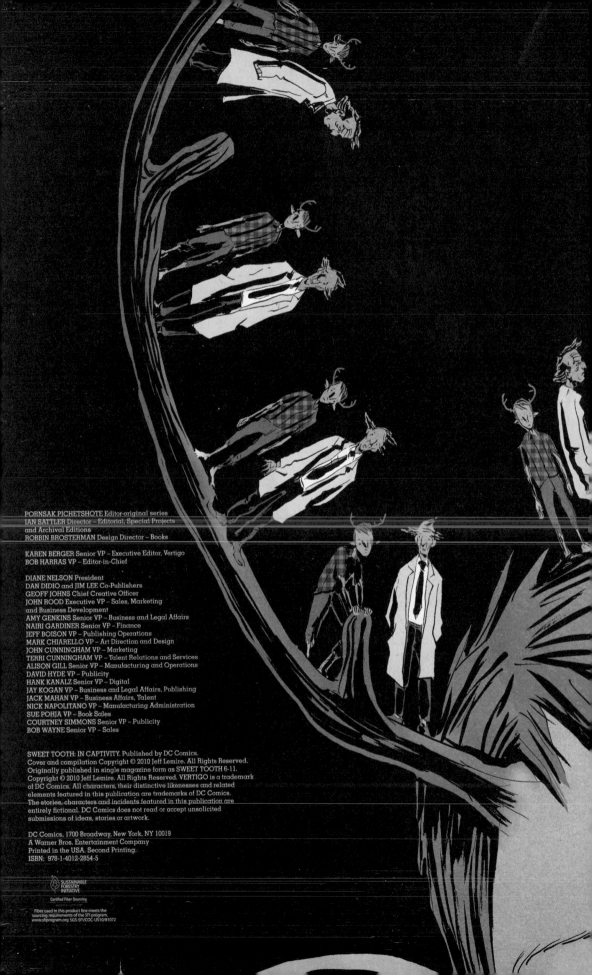

PORNSAK PICHETSHOTE Editor-original series
IAN SATTLER Director – Editorial, Special Projects
and Archival Editions
ROBBIN BROSTERMAN Design Director – Books

KAREN BERGER Senior VP – Executive Editor, Vertigo
BOB HARRAS VP – Editor-in-Chief

DIANE NELSON President
DAN DIDIO and JIM LEE Co-Publishers
GEOFF JOHNS Chief Creative Officer
JOHN ROOD Executive VP – Sales, Marketing
and Business Development
AMY GENKINS Senior VP – Business and Legal Affairs
NAIRI GARDINER Senior VP – Finance
JEFF BOISON VP – Publishing Operations
MARK CHIARELLO VP – Art Direction and Design
JOHN CUNNINGHAM VP – Marketing
TERRI CUNNINGHAM VP – Talent Relations and Services
ALISON GILL Senior VP – Manufacturing and Operations
DAVID HYDE VP – Publicity
HANK KANALZ Senior VP – Digital
JAY KOGAN VP – Business and Legal Affairs, Publishing
JACK MAHAN VP – Business Affairs, Talent
NICK NAPOLITANO VP – Manufacturing Administration
SUE POHJA VP – Book Sales
COURTNEY SIMMONS Senior VP – Publicity
BOB WAYNE Senior VP – Sales

SWEET TOOTH

IN CAPTIVITY

JEFF LEMIRE
story & art

JOSE VILLARRUBIA
colors

PAT BROSSEAU
letters

SWEET TOOTH
created by Jeff Lemire

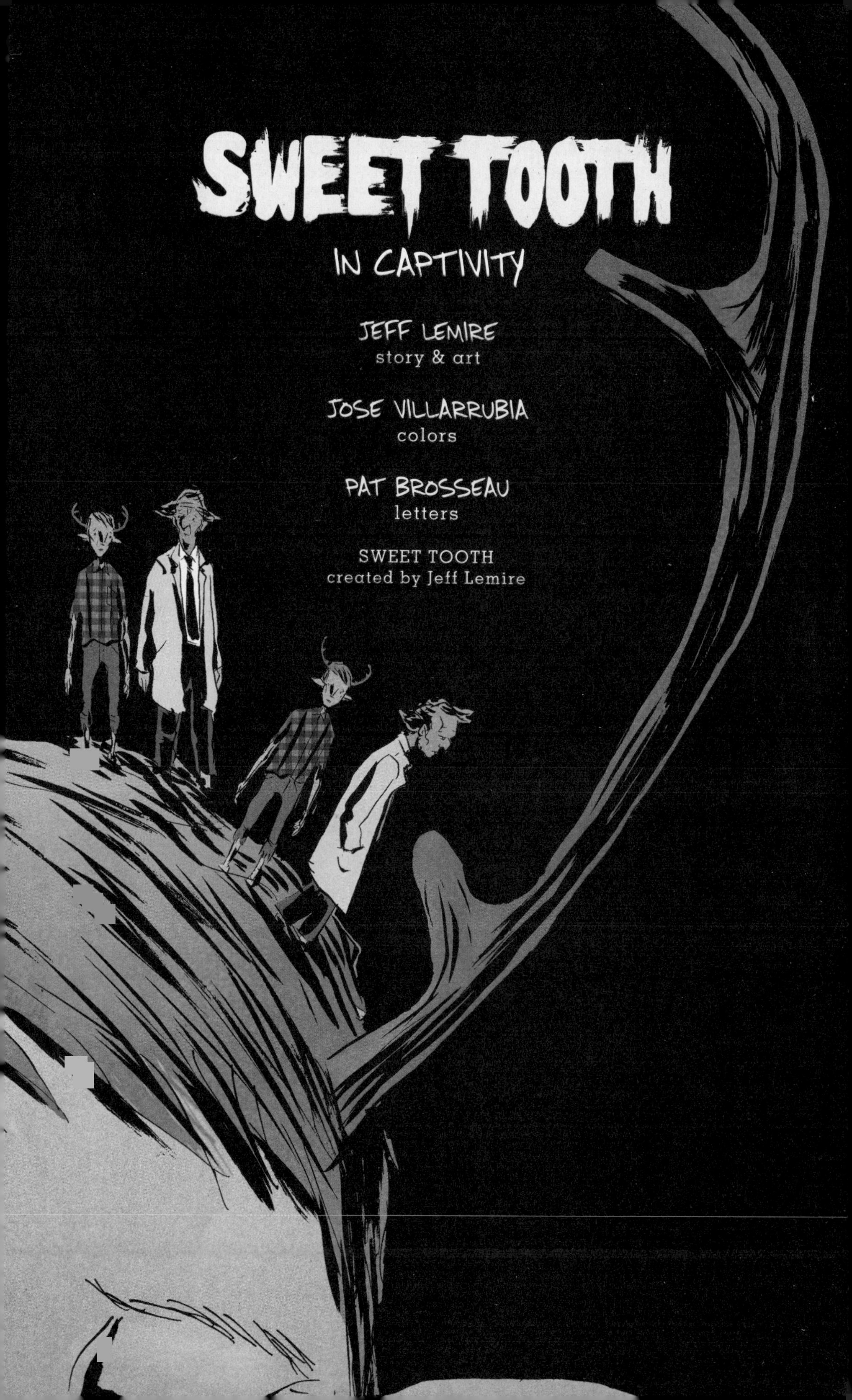

PREVIOUSLY

A decade ago, a horrible disease raged across the world like a forest fire, killing billions. Even more mysterious is that the only children born since are a new breed of human/animal hybrids.

GUS is one such hybrid. A young boy with a sweet soul, a sweeter tooth – and the features of a deer. He has lived his entire life in isolation, deep in a forest sanctuary with his father, a kind but zealous man who has taught Gus that the world beyond the trees is evil and sinful, a place he should never enter. But Gus's father also succumbs to the plague, and the boy is left alone. When two vicious bounty hunters invade Gus's forest, it's only the intervention of a hulking, violent drifter named JEPPERD that saves him. Jepperd promises to lead Gus to "The Preserve," a rumored safe haven for hybrid children, sending the two on a journey across a dangerous post-apocalyptic America. Along the way, Gus dreams of an innocent cartoon deer named DANDI who seems to hint at a prophetic knowledge of the future, and Jepperd saves BECKY and LUCY, two prostitutes who were beaten by domineering pimps.

Despite the man's violent demeanor, Gus quickly finds a substitute for his dead father in Jepperd. But when they finally arrive at their destination, the fabled "Preserve," the drifter reveals his true motivation: he sells Gus to a concentration camp for hybrid children in exchange for a beguiling form of payment... an old duffel bag whose contents are still unknown...

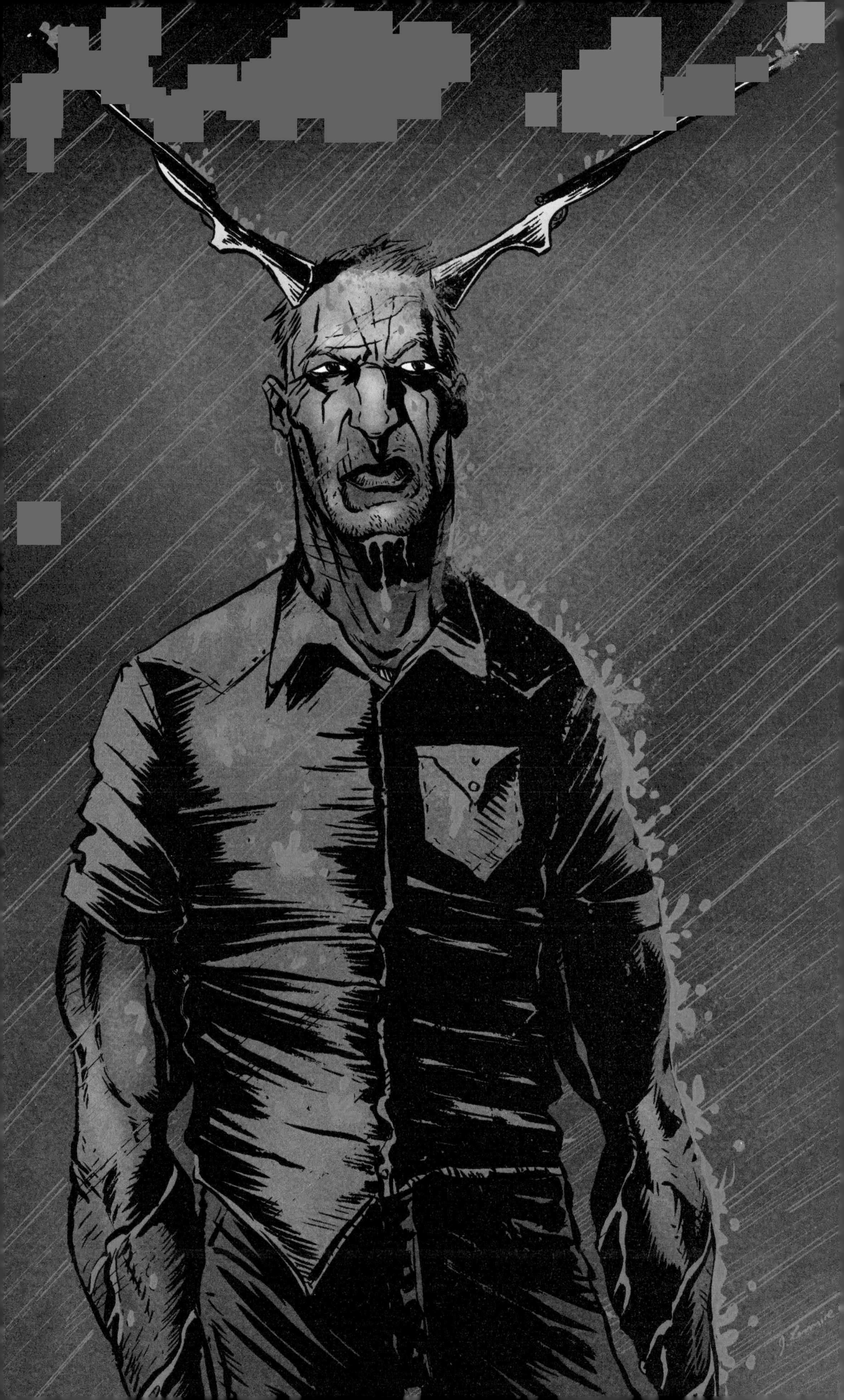

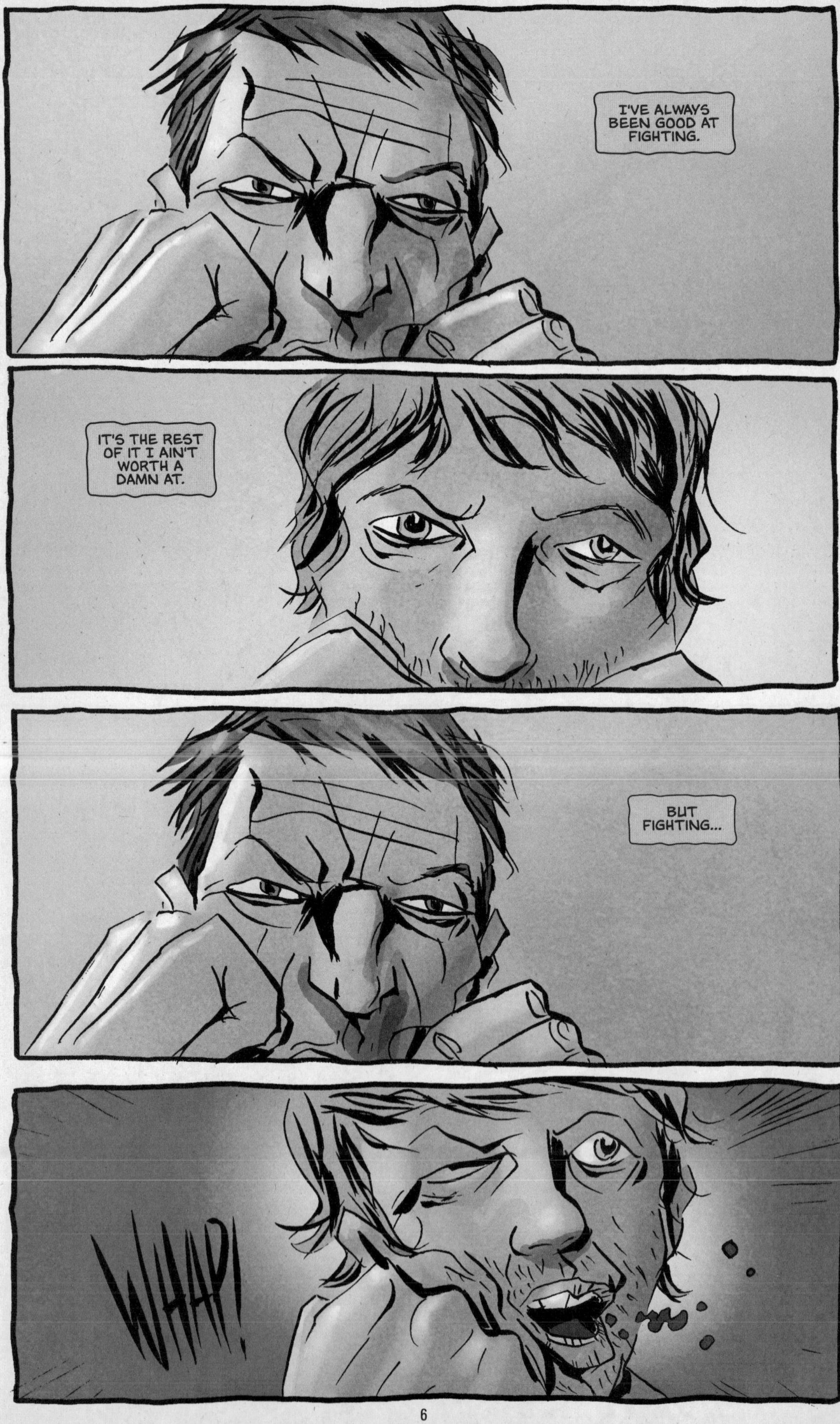
I'VE ALWAYS BEEN GOOD AT FIGHTING.
IT'S THE REST OF IT I AIN'T WORTH A DAMN AT.
BUT FIGHTING...
WHAP!

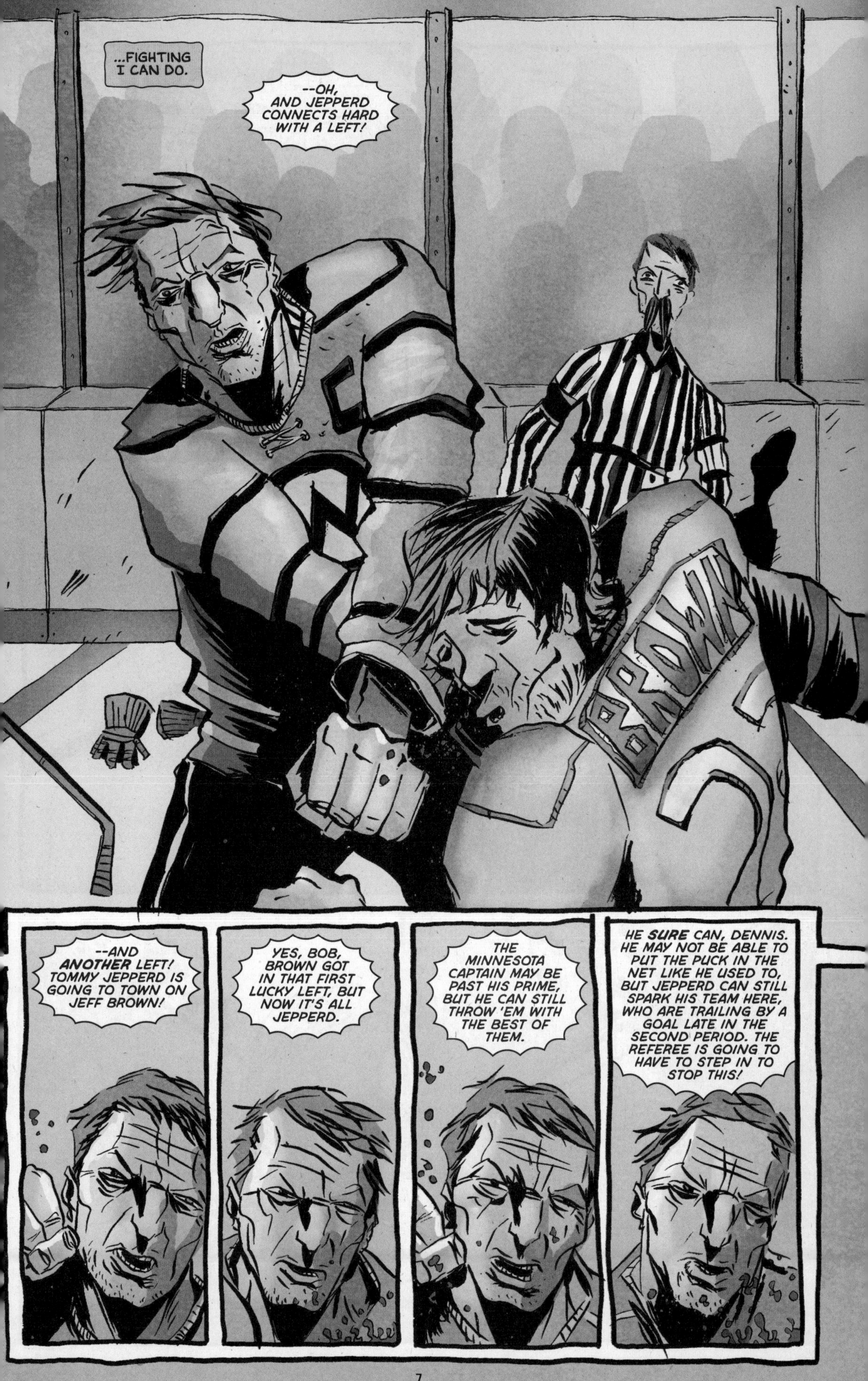
...FIGHTING I CAN DO.
--OH, AND JEPPERD CONNECTS HARD WITH A LEFT!
BROWN
--AND ANOTHER LEFT! TOMMY JEPPERD IS GOING TO TOWN ON JEFF BROWN!
YES, BOB, BROWN GOT IN THAT FIRST LUCKY LEFT, BUT NOW IT'S ALL JEPPERD.
THE MINNESOTA CAPTAIN MAY BE PAST HIS PRIME, BUT HE CAN STILL THROW 'EM WITH THE BEST OF THEM.
HE SURE CAN, DENNIS. HE MAY NOT BE ABLE TO PUT THE PUCK IN THE NET LIKE HE USED TO, BUT JEPPERD CAN STILL SPARK HIS TEAM HERE, WHO ARE TRAILING BY A GOAL LATE IN THE SECOND PERIOD. THE REFEREE IS GOING TO HAVE TO STEP IN TO STOP THIS!

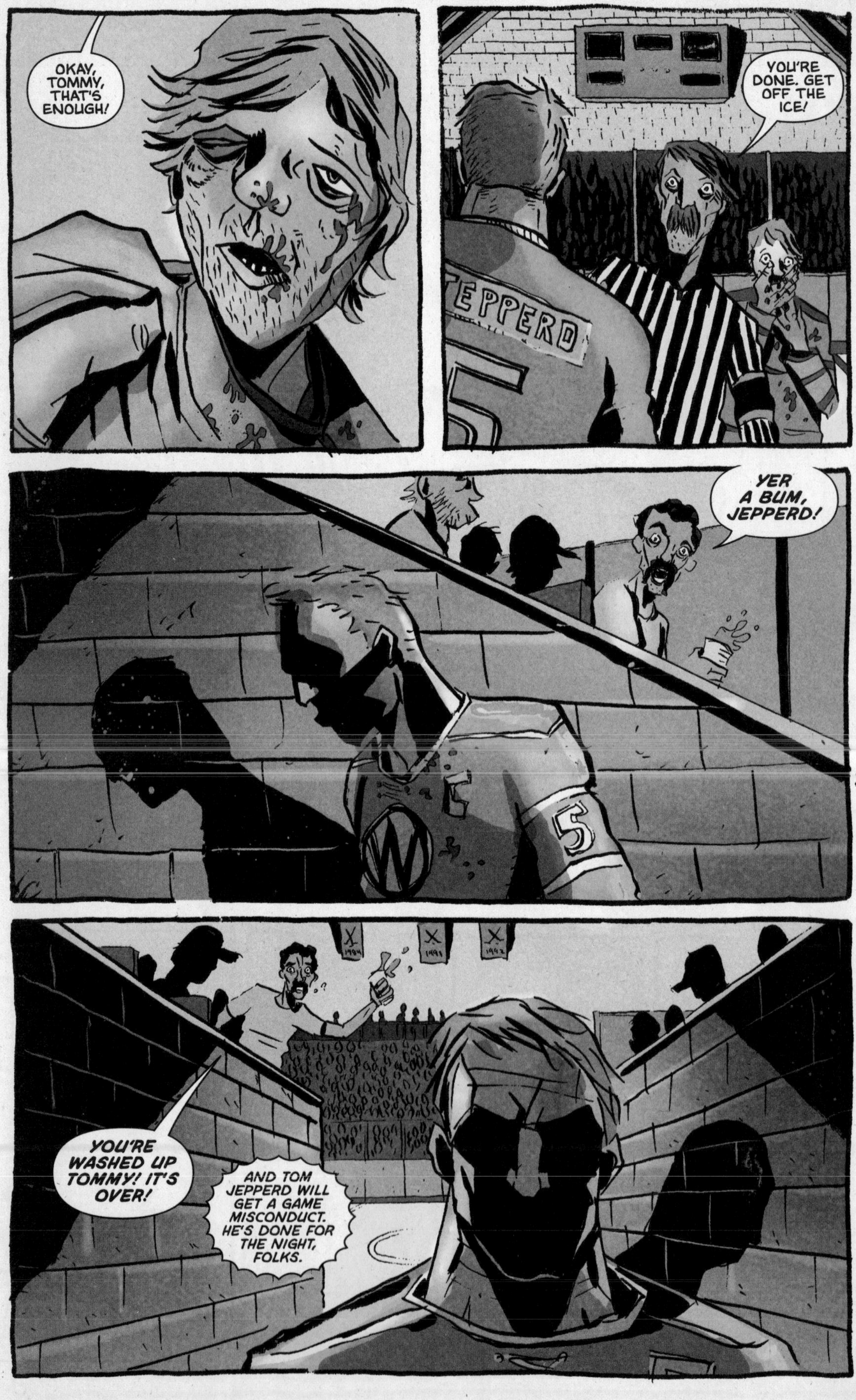
OKAY, TOMMY, THAT'S ENOUGH!
YOU'RE DONE. GET OFF THE ICE!
JEPPERD
5
YER A BUM, JEPPERD!
5
YOU'RE WASHED UP TOMMY! IT'S OVER!
AND TOM JEPPERD WILL GET A GAME MISCONDUCT. HE'S DONE FOR THE NIGHT, FOLKS.

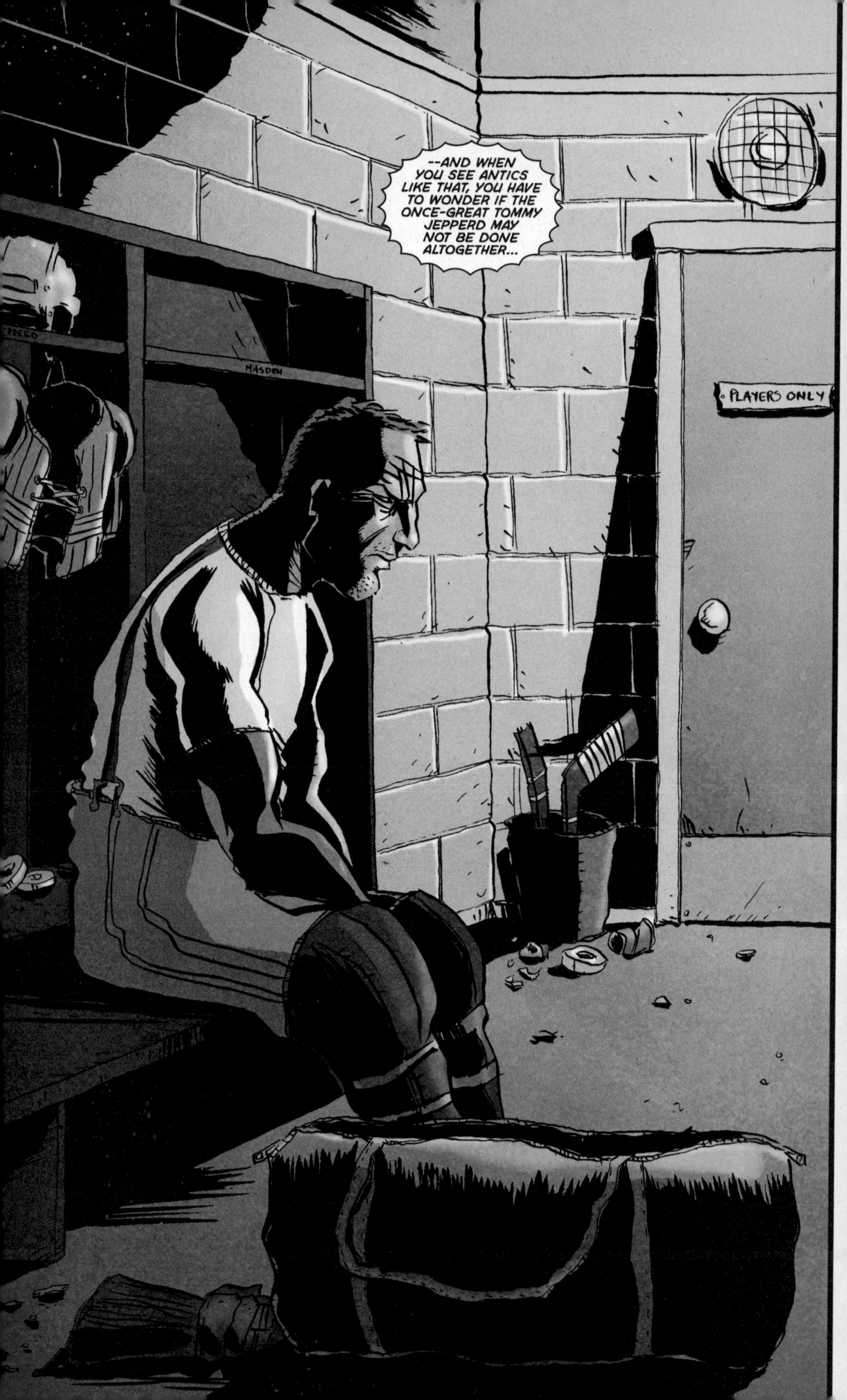
--AND WHEN YOU SEE ANTICS LIKE THAT, YOU HAVE TO WONDER IF THE ONCE-GREAT TOMMY JEPPERD MAY NOT BE DONE ALTOGETHER...
MADSEN
PLAYERS ONLY

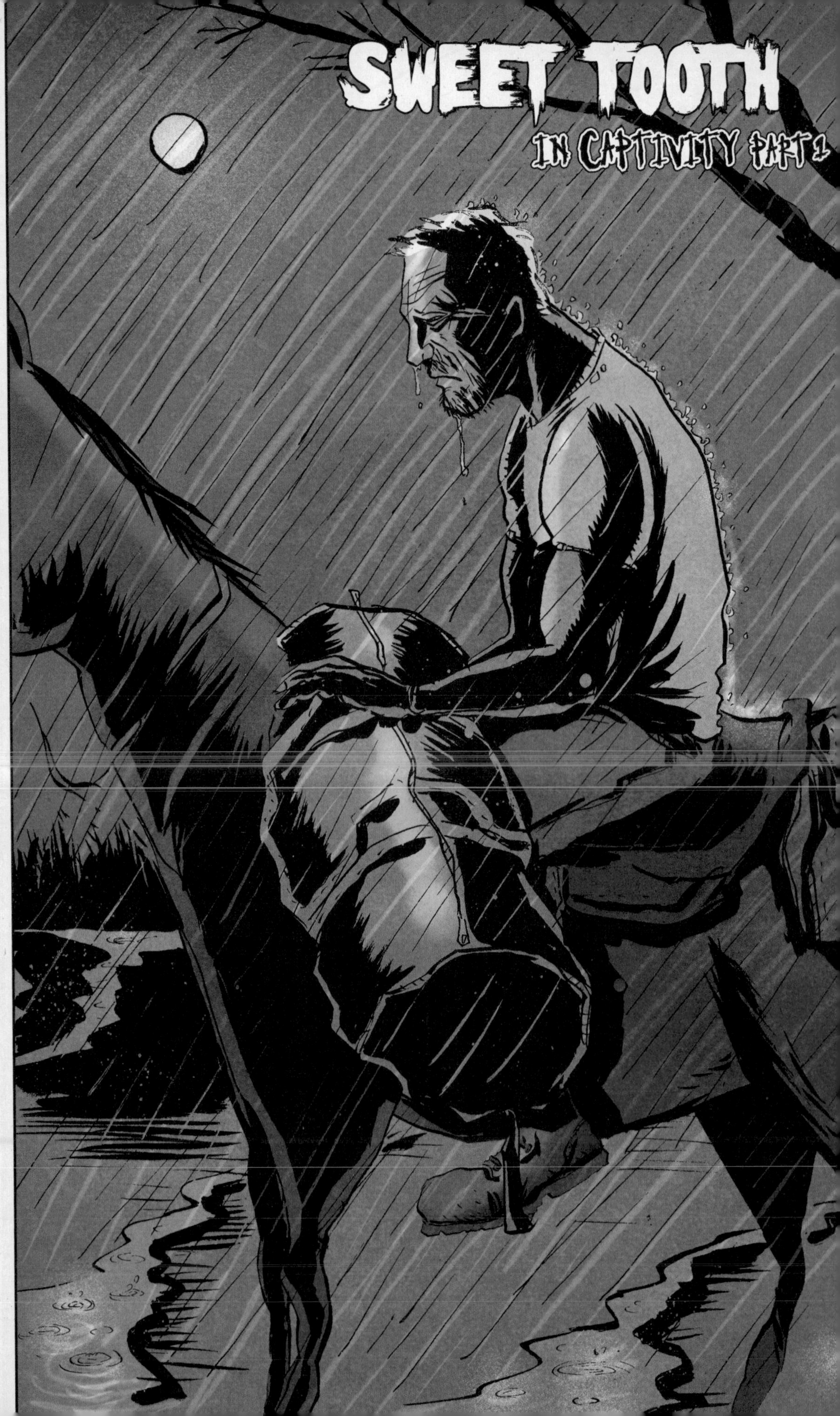
SWEET TOOTH
IN CAPTIVITY PART 1

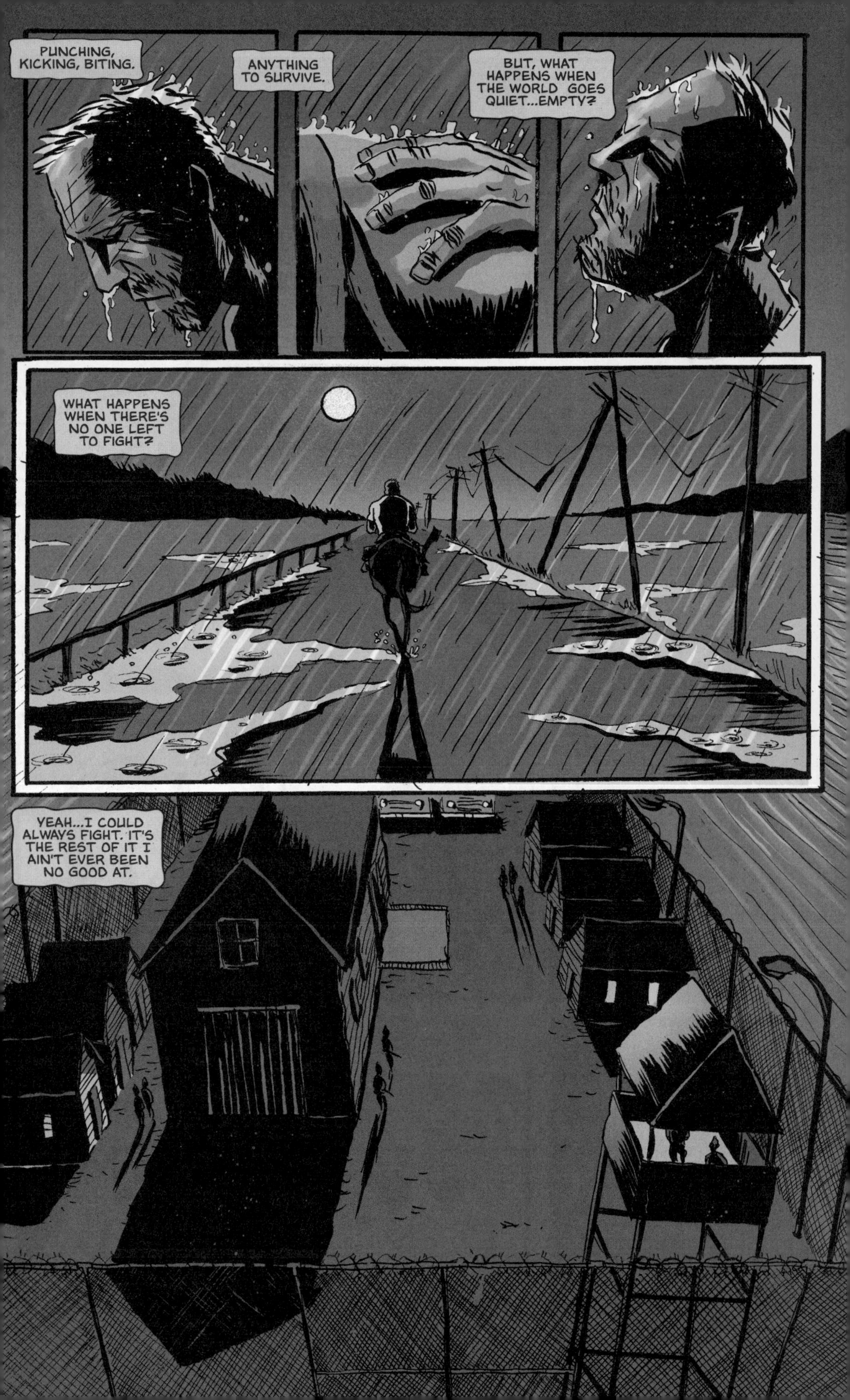
PUNCHING, KICKING, BITING.
ANYTHING TO SURVIVE.
BUT, WHAT HAPPENS WHEN THE WORLD GOES QUIET...EMPTY?
WHAT HAPPENS WHEN THERE'S NO ONE LEFT TO FIGHT?
YEAH...I COULD ALWAYS FIGHT. IT'S THE REST OF IT I AIN'T EVER BEEN NO GOOD AT.

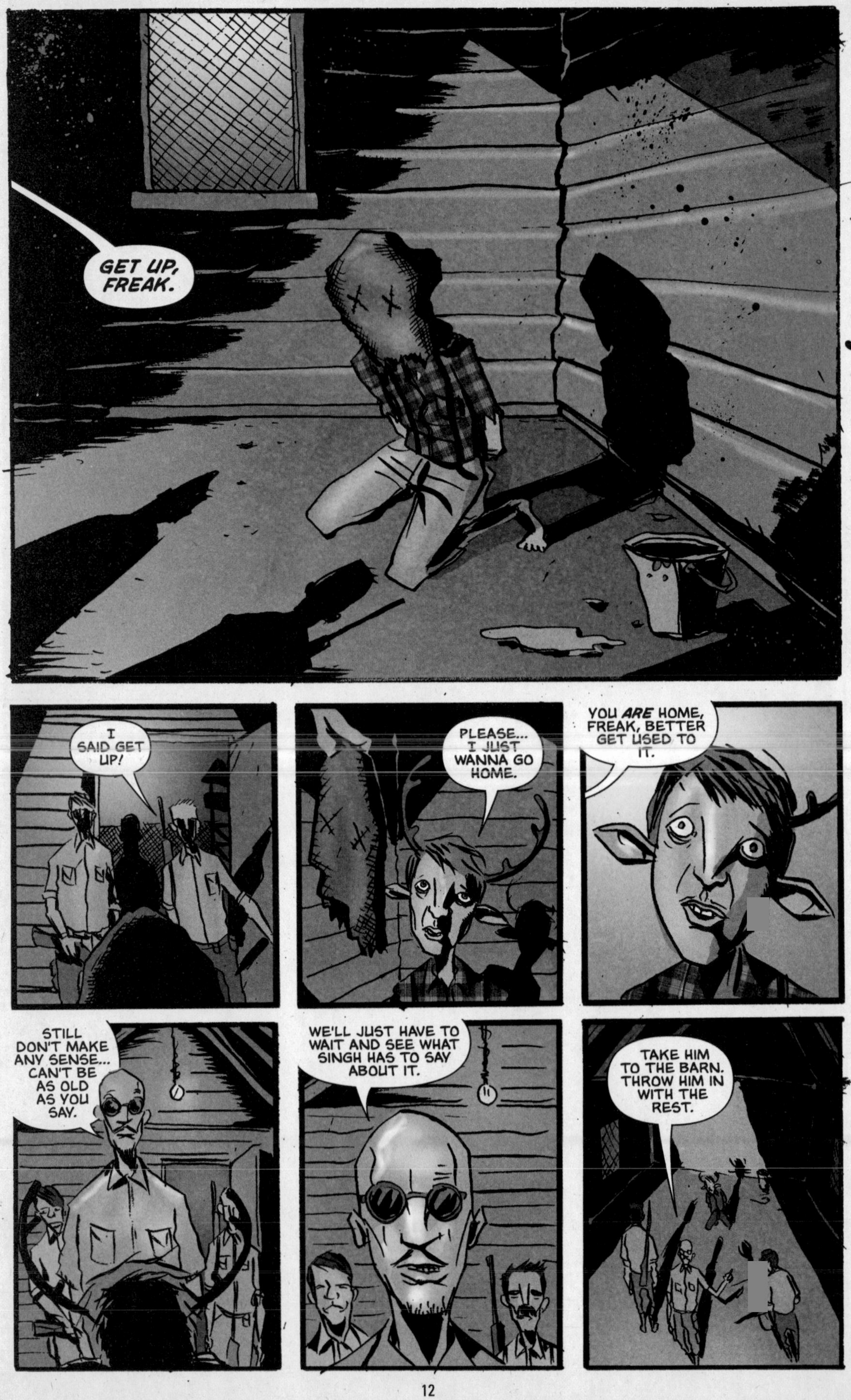
GET UP, FREAK.
I SAID GET UP!
PLEASE... I JUST WANNA GO HOME.
YOU *ARE* HOME, FREAK, BETTER GET USED TO IT.
STILL DON'T MAKE ANY SENSE... CAN'T BE AS OLD AS YOU SAY.
WE'LL JUST HAVE TO WAIT AND SEE WHAT SINGH HAS TO SAY ABOUT IT.
TAKE HIM TO THE BARN. THROW HIM IN WITH THE REST.

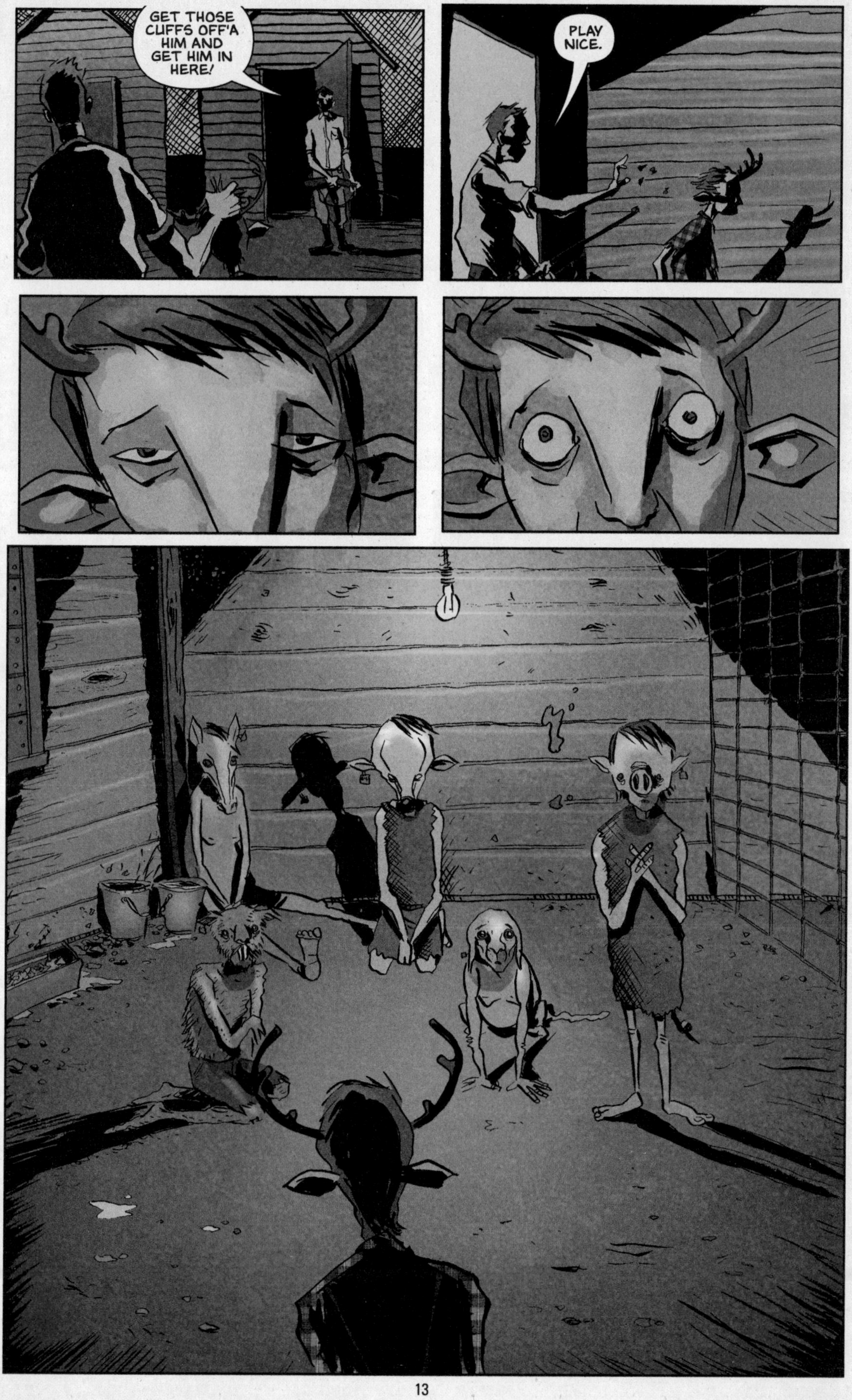
GET THOSE CUFFS OFF'A HIM AND GET HIM IN HERE!
PLAY NICE.

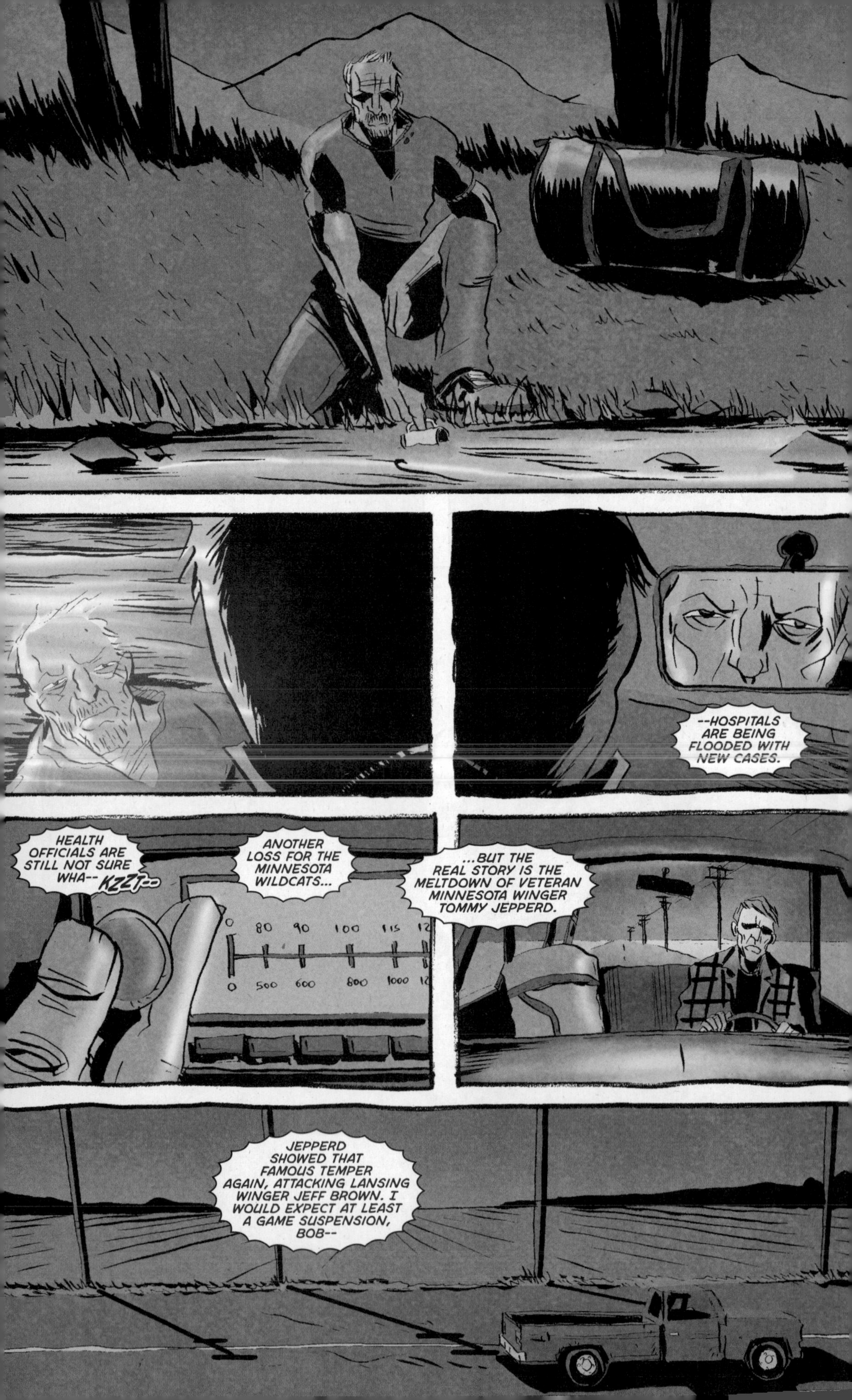
--HOSPITALS ARE BEING FLOODED WITH NEW CASES.
HEALTH OFFICIALS ARE STILL NOT SURE WHA-- KZZT--
ANOTHER LOSS FOR THE MINNESOTA WILDCATS...
...BUT THE REAL STORY IS THE MELTDOWN OF VETERAN MINNESOTA WINGER TOMMY JEPPERD.
JEPPERD SHOWED THAT FAMOUS TEMPER AGAIN, ATTACKING LANSING WINGER JEFF BROWN. I WOULD EXPECT AT LEAST A GAME SUSPENSION, BOB--

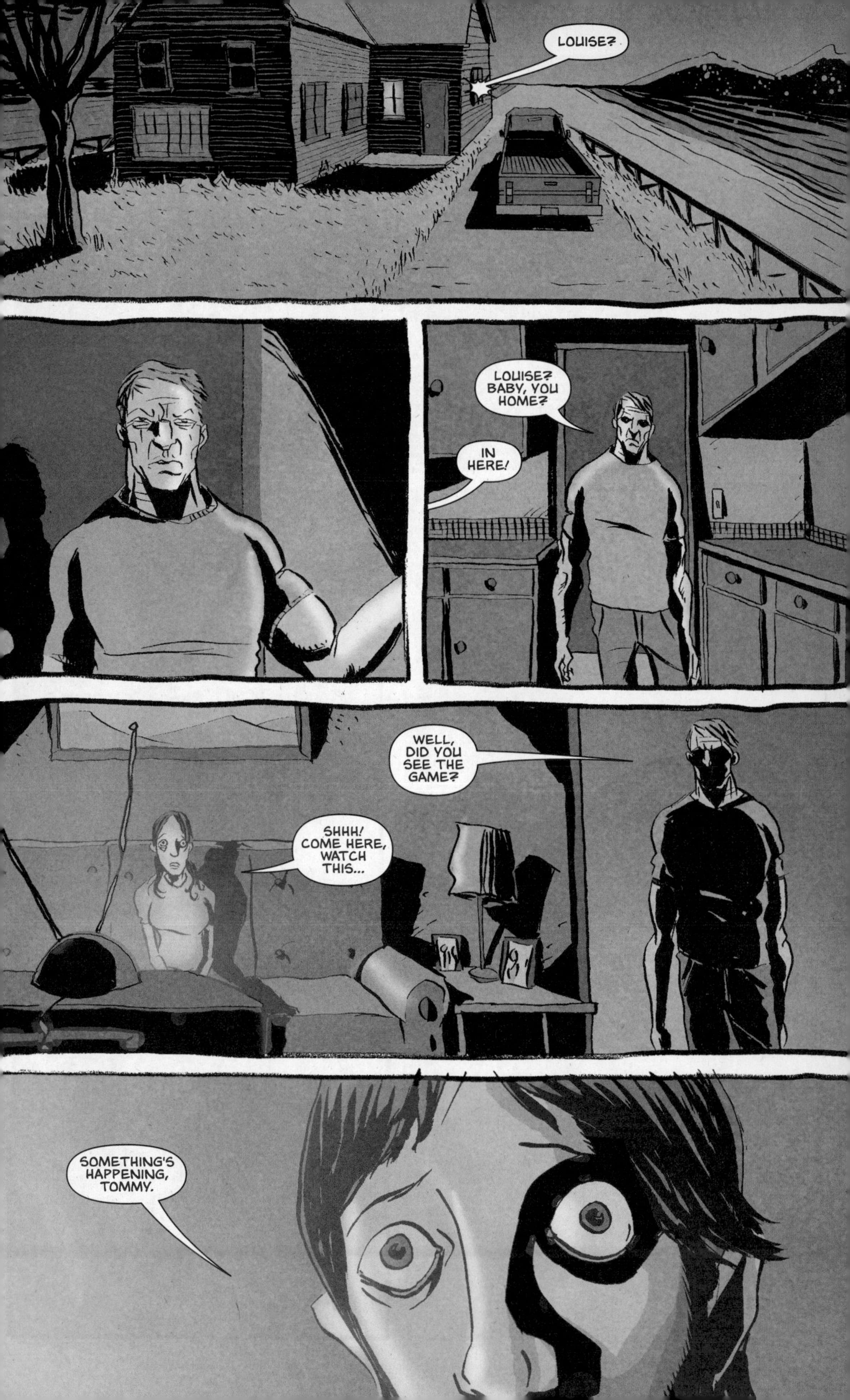
LOUISE?
LOUISE? BABY, YOU HOME?
IN HERE!
WELL, DID YOU SEE THE GAME?
SHHH! COME HERE, WATCH THIS...
SOMETHING'S HAPPENING, TOMMY.

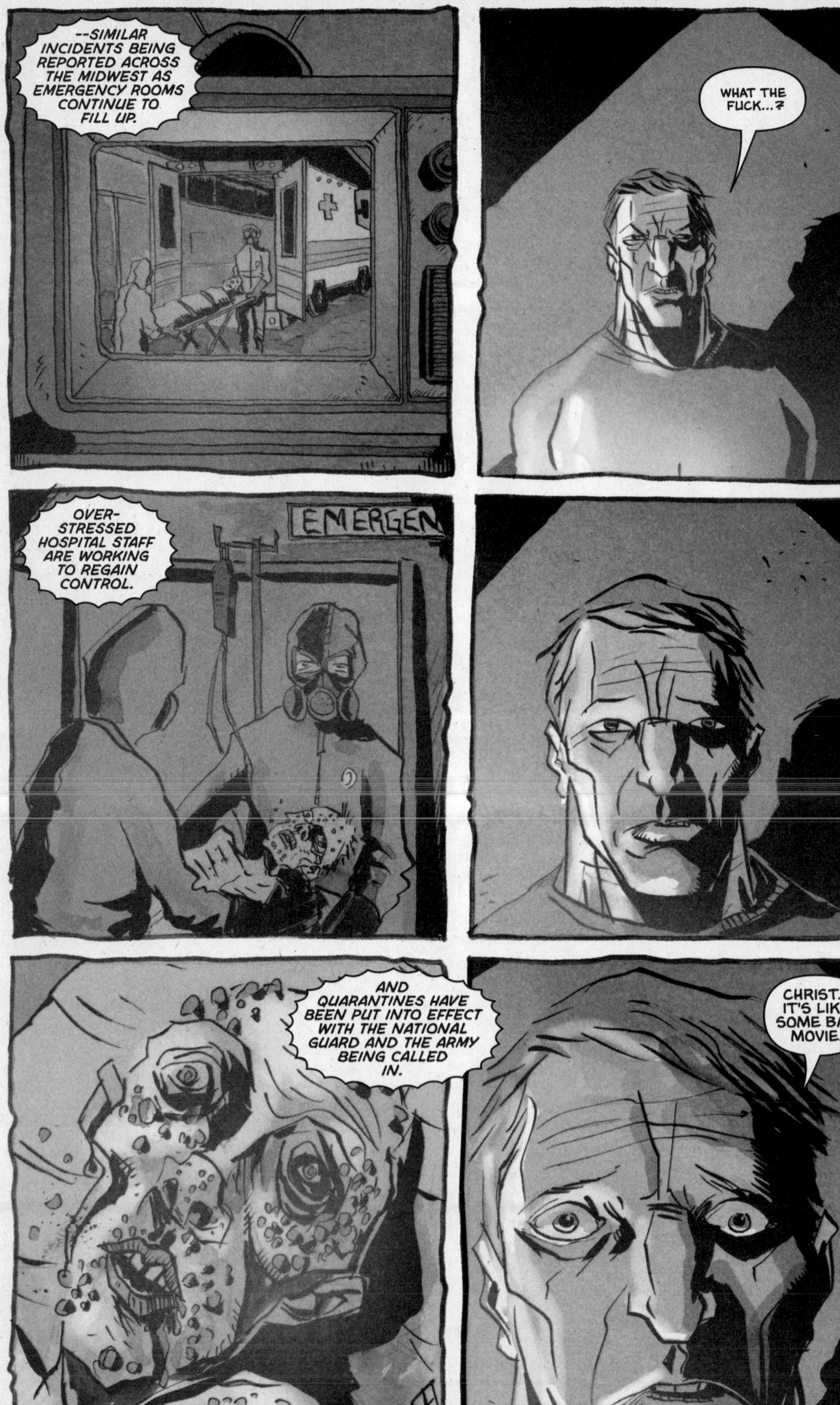
--SIMILAR INCIDENTS BEING REPORTED ACROSS THE MIDWEST AS EMERGENCY ROOMS CONTINUE TO FILL UP.
WHAT THE FUCK...?
EMERGEN
OVER-STRESSED HOSPITAL STAFF ARE WORKING TO REGAIN CONTROL.
AND QUARANTINES HAVE BEEN PUT INTO EFFECT WITH THE NATIONAL GUARD AND THE ARMY BEING CALLED IN.
CHRIST... IT'S LIKE SOME BAD MOVIE.

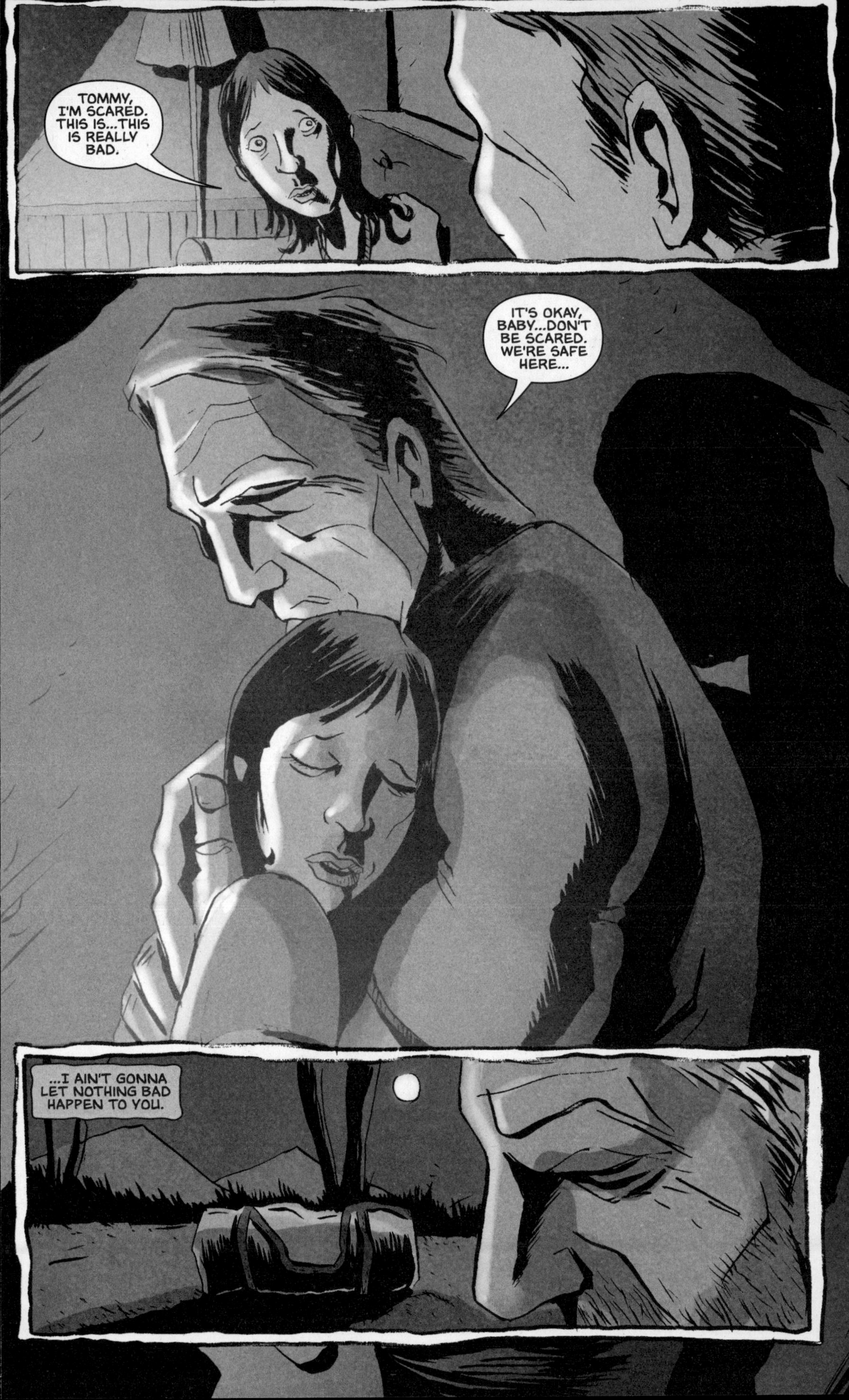
TOMMY, I'M SCARED. THIS IS...THIS IS REALLY BAD.
IT'S OKAY, BABY...DON'T BE SCARED. WE'RE SAFE HERE...
...I AIN'T GONNA LET NOTHING BAD HAPPEN TO YOU.

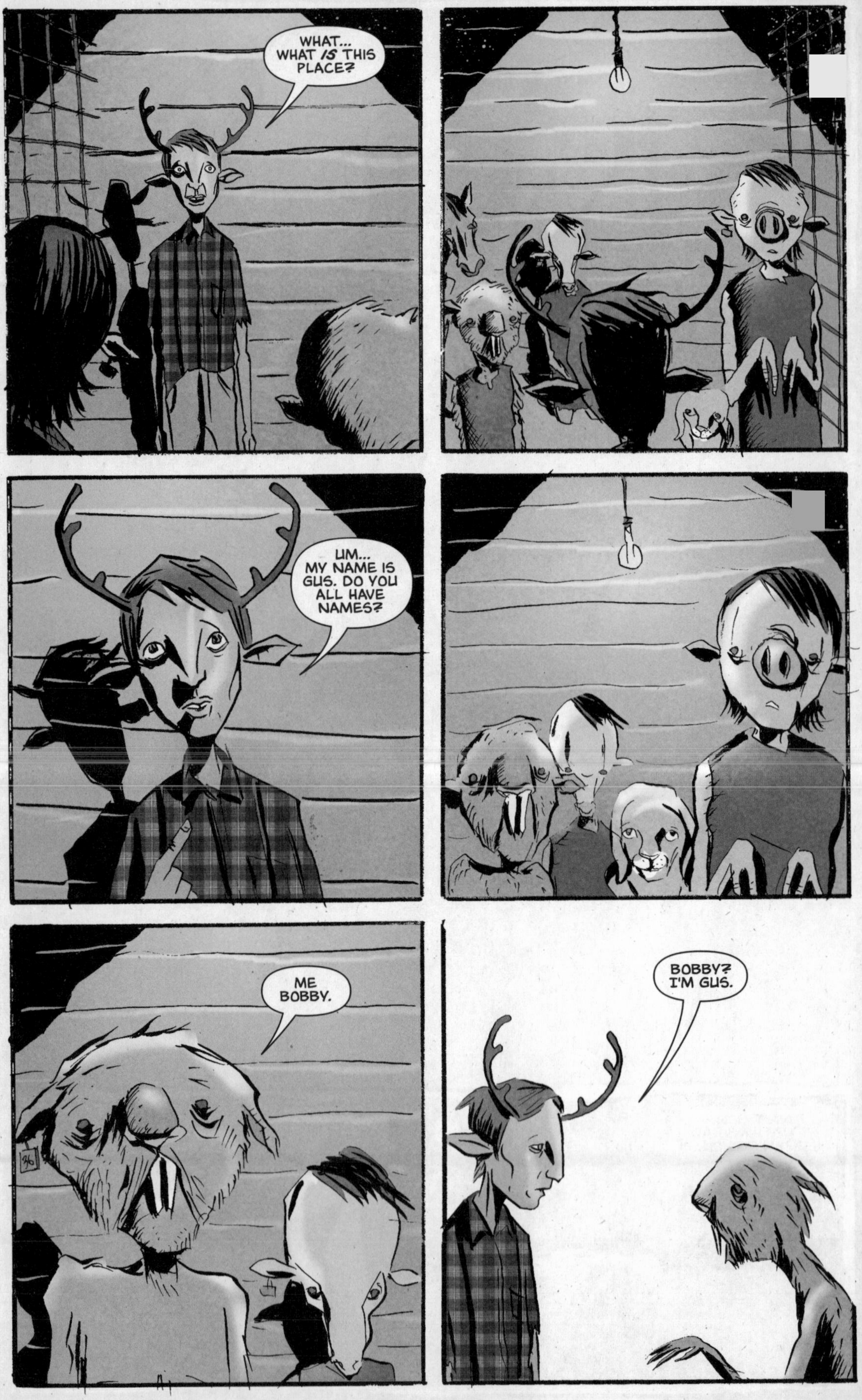
WHAT... WHAT IS THIS PLACE?
UM... MY NAME IS GUS. DO YOU ALL HAVE NAMES?
ME BOBBY.
BOBBY? I'M GUS.

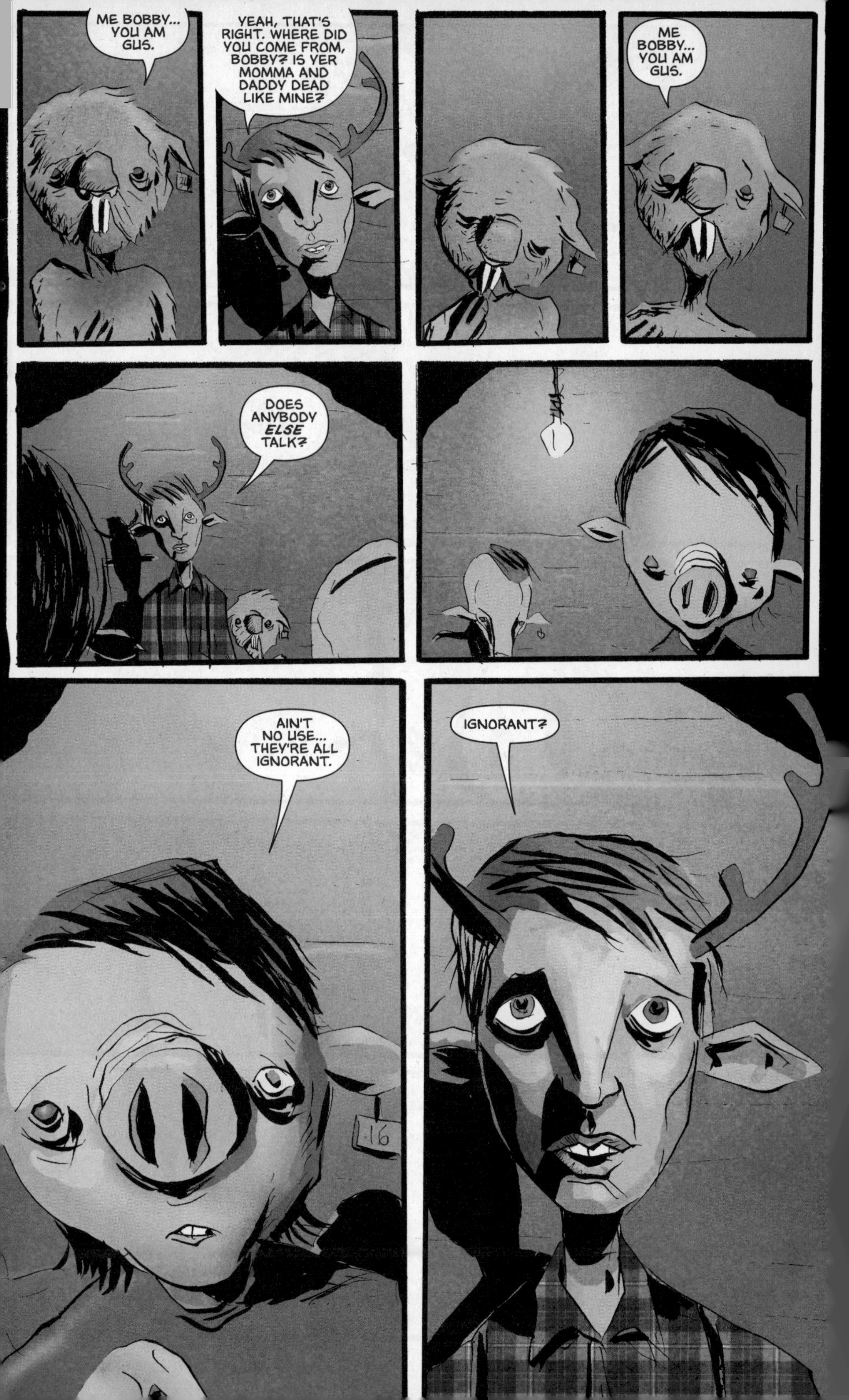
ME BOBBY... YOU AM GUS.
YEAH, THAT'S RIGHT. WHERE DID YOU COME FROM, BOBBY? IS YER MOMMA AND DADDY DEAD LIKE MINE?
ME BOBBY... YOU AM GUS.
DOES ANYBODY ELSE TALK?
AIN'T NO USE... THEY'RE ALL IGNORANT.
IGNORANT?

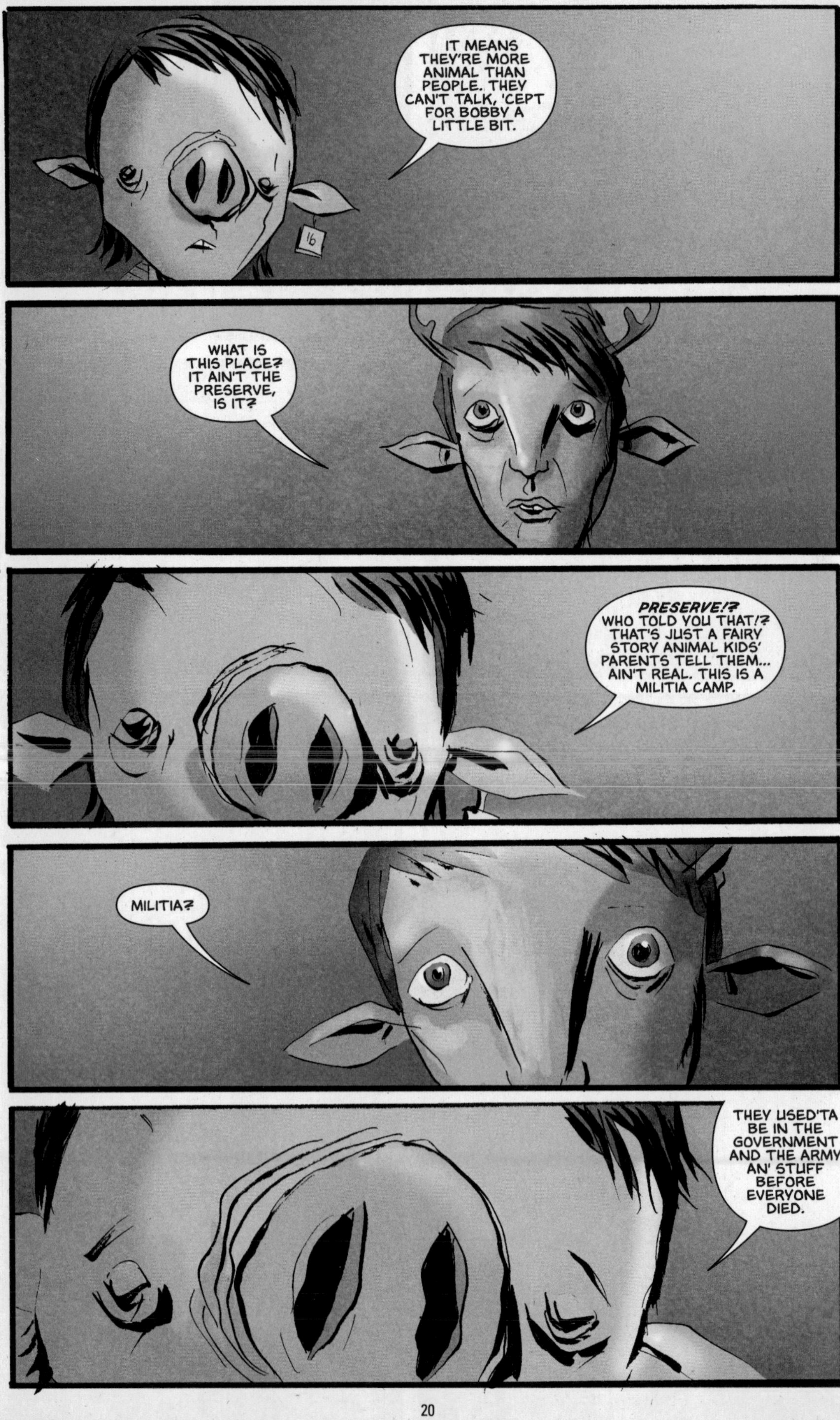

IT MEANS THEY'RE MORE ANIMAL THAN PEOPLE. THEY CAN'T TALK, 'CEPT FOR BOBBY A LITTLE BIT.
16
WHAT IS THIS PLACE? IT AIN'T THE PRESERVE, IS IT?
PRESERVE!? WHO TOLD YOU THAT!? THAT'S JUST A FAIRY STORY ANIMAL KIDS' PARENTS TELL THEM... AIN'T REAL. THIS IS A MILITIA CAMP.
MILITIA?
THEY USED'TA BE IN THE GOVERNMENT AND THE ARMY AN' STUFF BEFORE EVERYONE DIED.

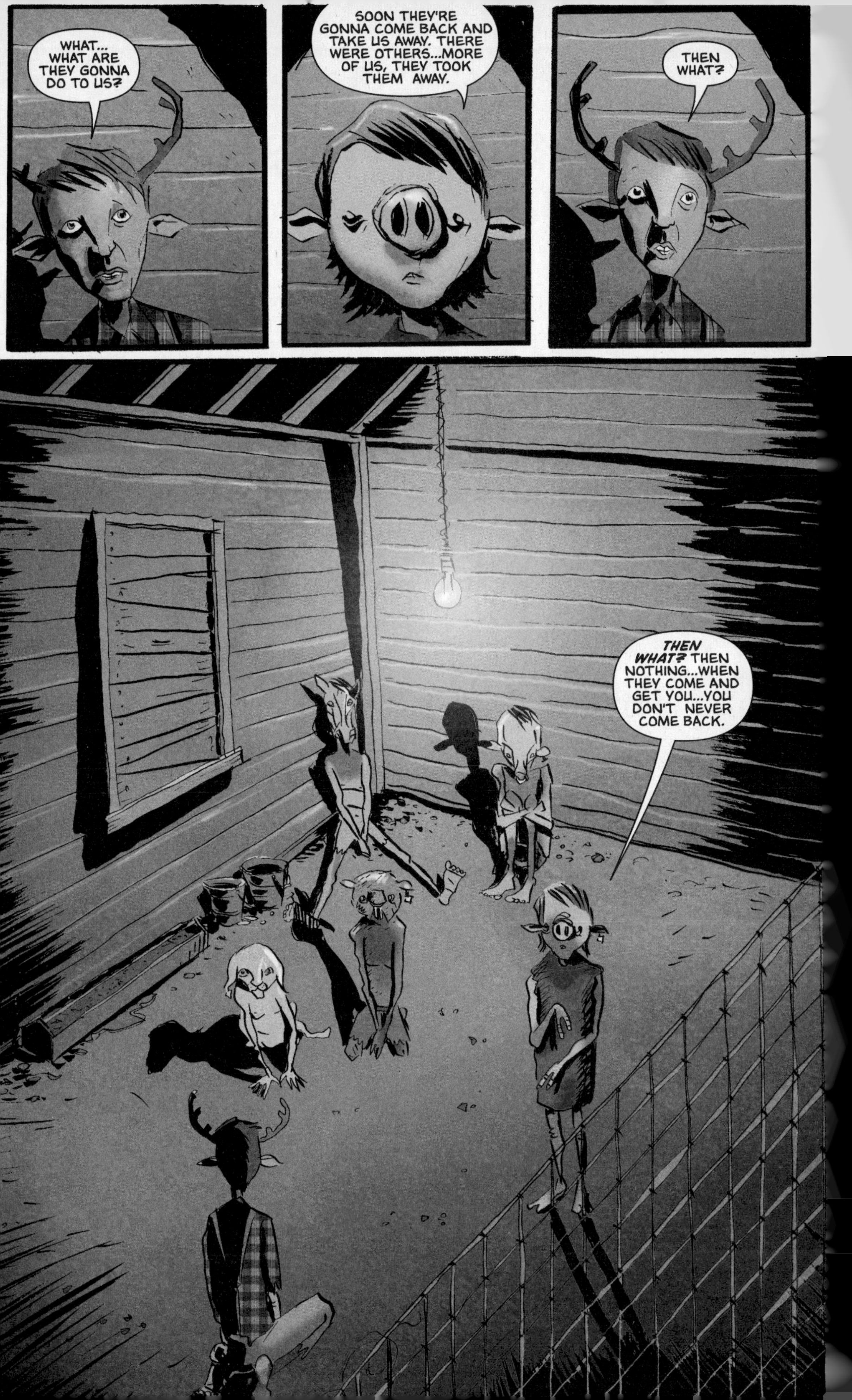
WHAT... WHAT ARE THEY GONNA DO TO US?
SOON THEY'RE GONNA COME BACK AND TAKE US AWAY. THERE WERE OTHERS...MORE OF US, THEY TOOK THEM AWAY.
THEN WHAT?
THEN WHAT? THEN NOTHING...WHEN THEY COME AND GET YOU...YOU DON'T NEVER COME BACK.

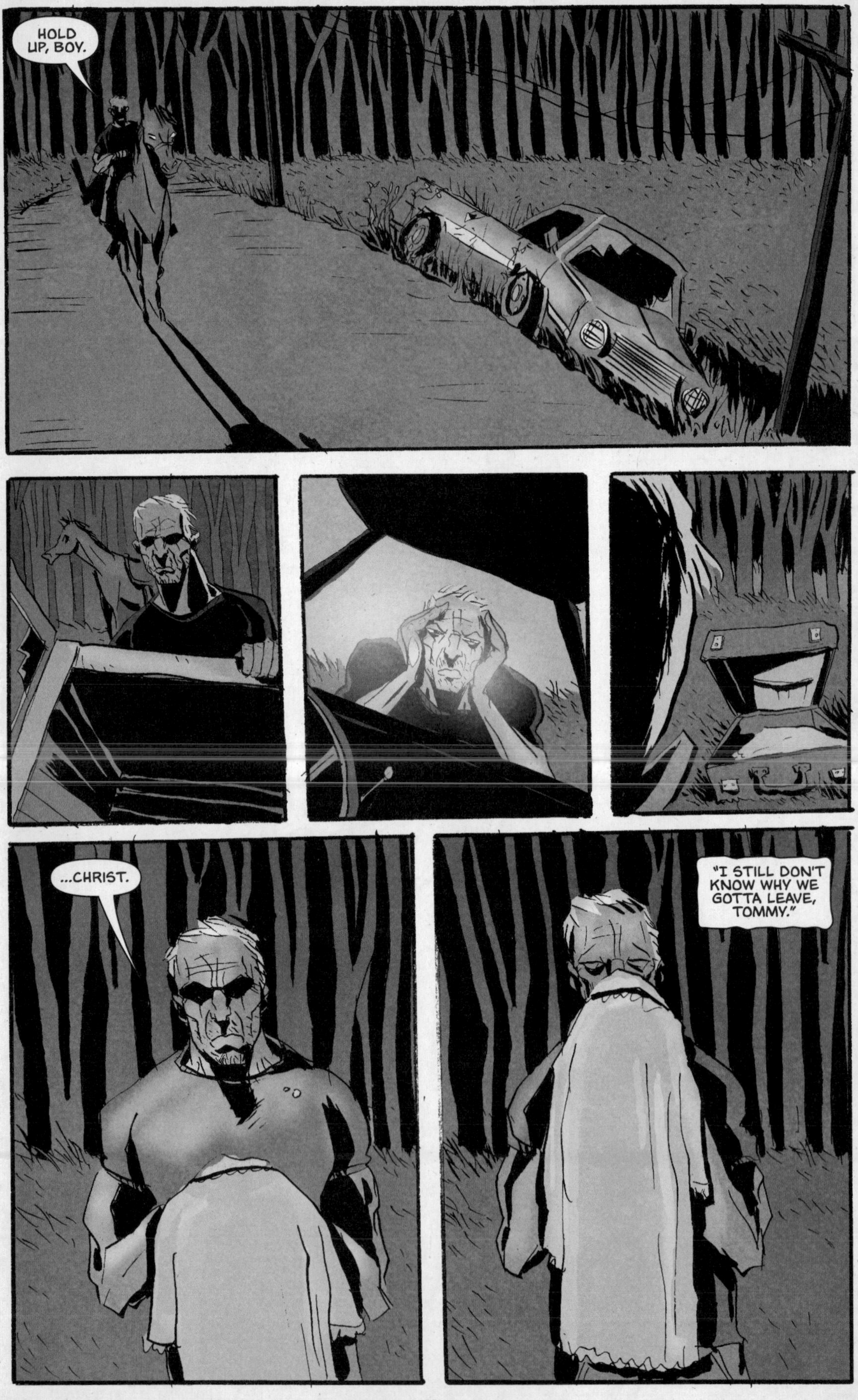
HOLD UP, BOY.
...CHRIST.
"I STILL DON'T KNOW WHY WE GOTTA LEAVE, TOMMY."

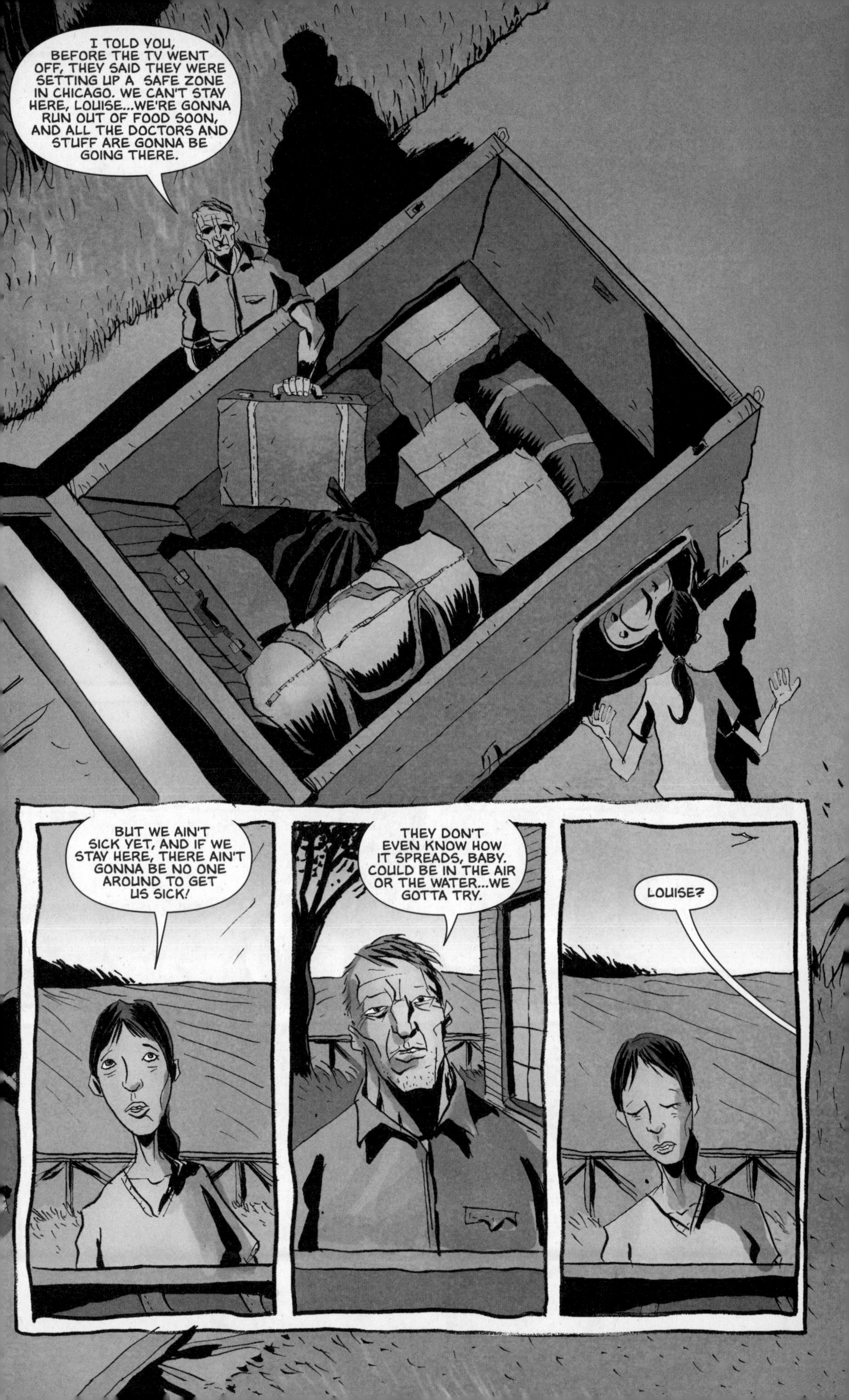
I TOLD YOU, BEFORE THE TV WENT OFF, THEY SAID THEY WERE SETTING UP A SAFE ZONE IN CHICAGO. WE CAN'T STAY HERE, LOUISE...WE'RE GONNA RUN OUT OF FOOD SOON, AND ALL THE DOCTORS AND STUFF ARE GONNA BE GOING THERE.
BUT WE AIN'T SICK YET, AND IF WE STAY HERE, THERE AIN'T GONNA BE NO ONE AROUND TO GET US SICK!
THEY DON'T EVEN KNOW HOW IT SPREADS, BABY. COULD BE IN THE AIR OR THE WATER...WE GOTTA TRY.
LOUISE?

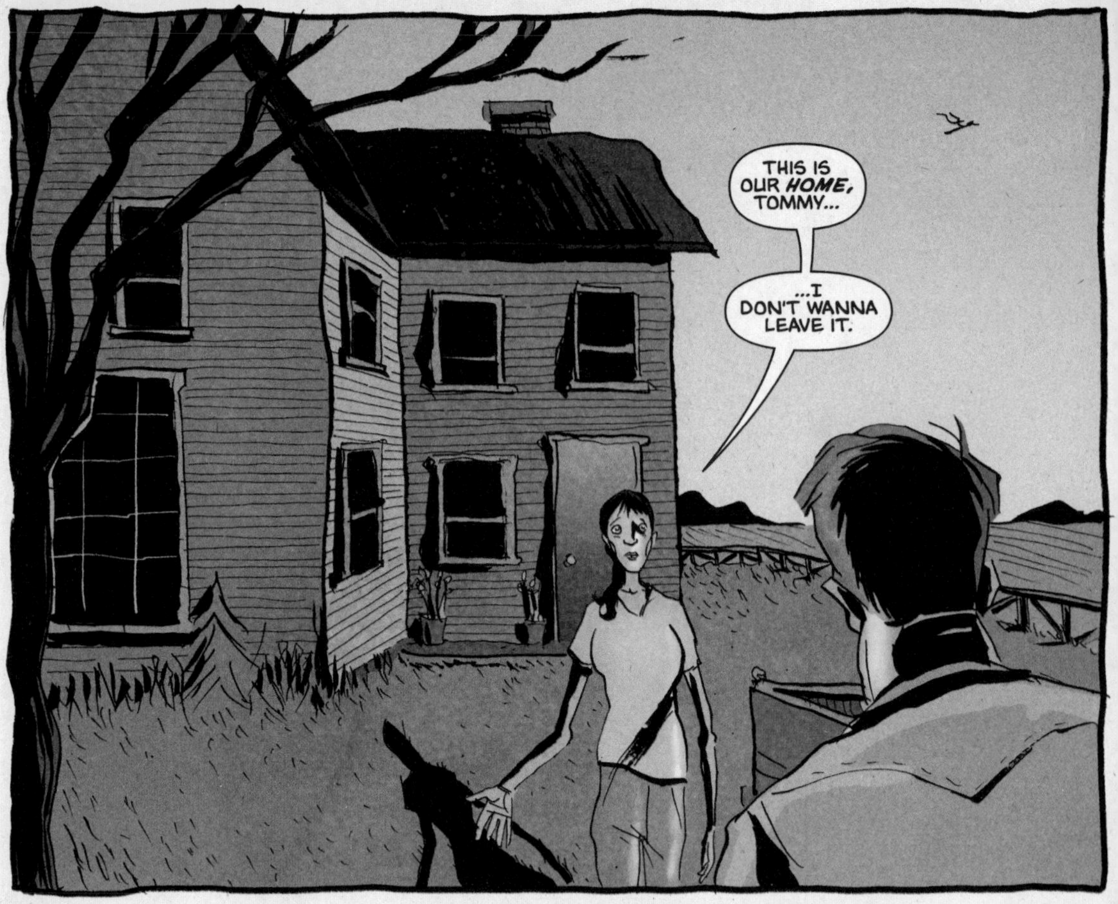
THIS IS OUR HOME, TOMMY...
...I DON'T WANNA LEAVE IT.

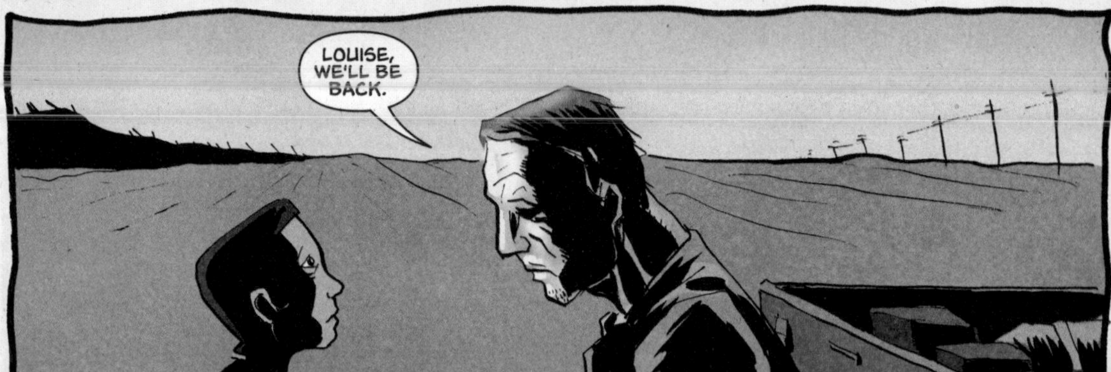
LOUISE, WE'LL BE BACK.

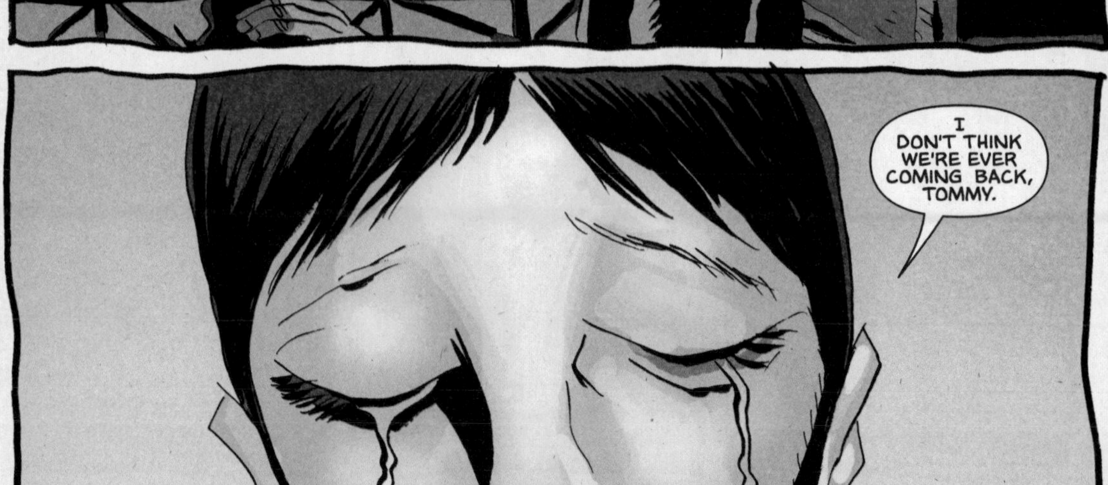
I DON'T THINK WE'RE EVER COMING BACK, TOMMY.

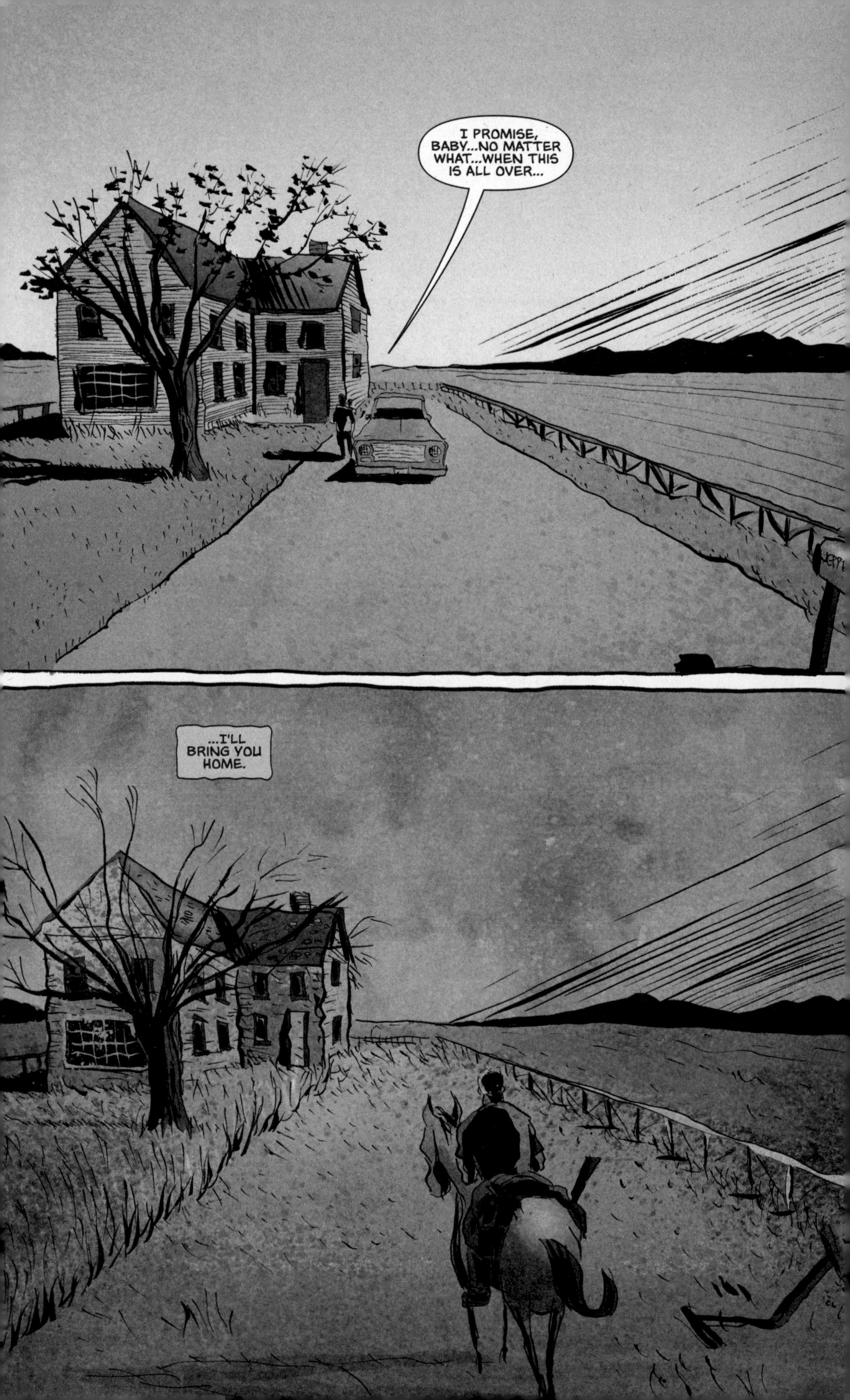
I PROMISE, BABY...NO MATTER WHAT...WHEN THIS IS ALL OVER...
...I'LL BRING YOU HOME.

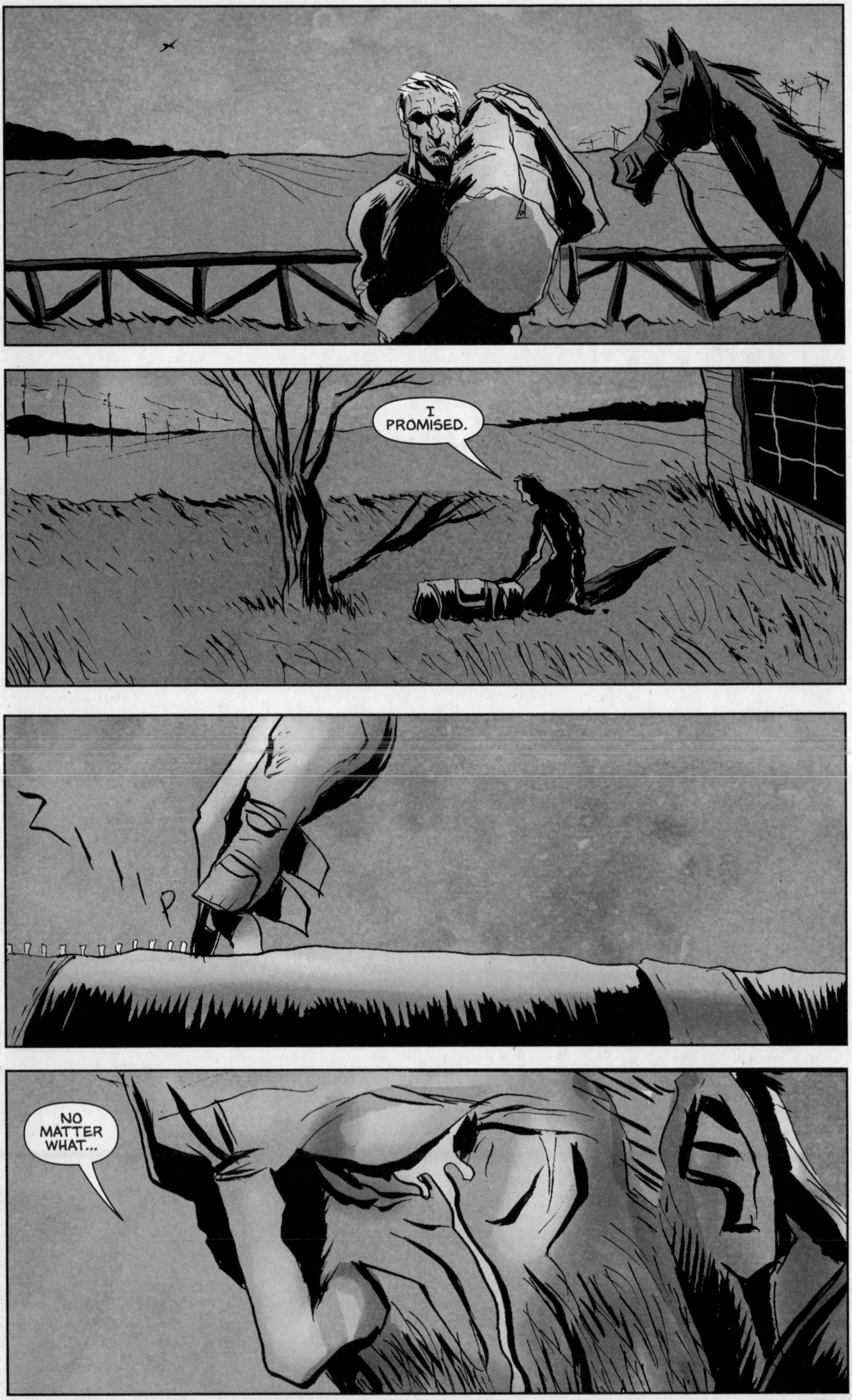
I PROMISED.
ZIIIP
NO MATTER WHAT...

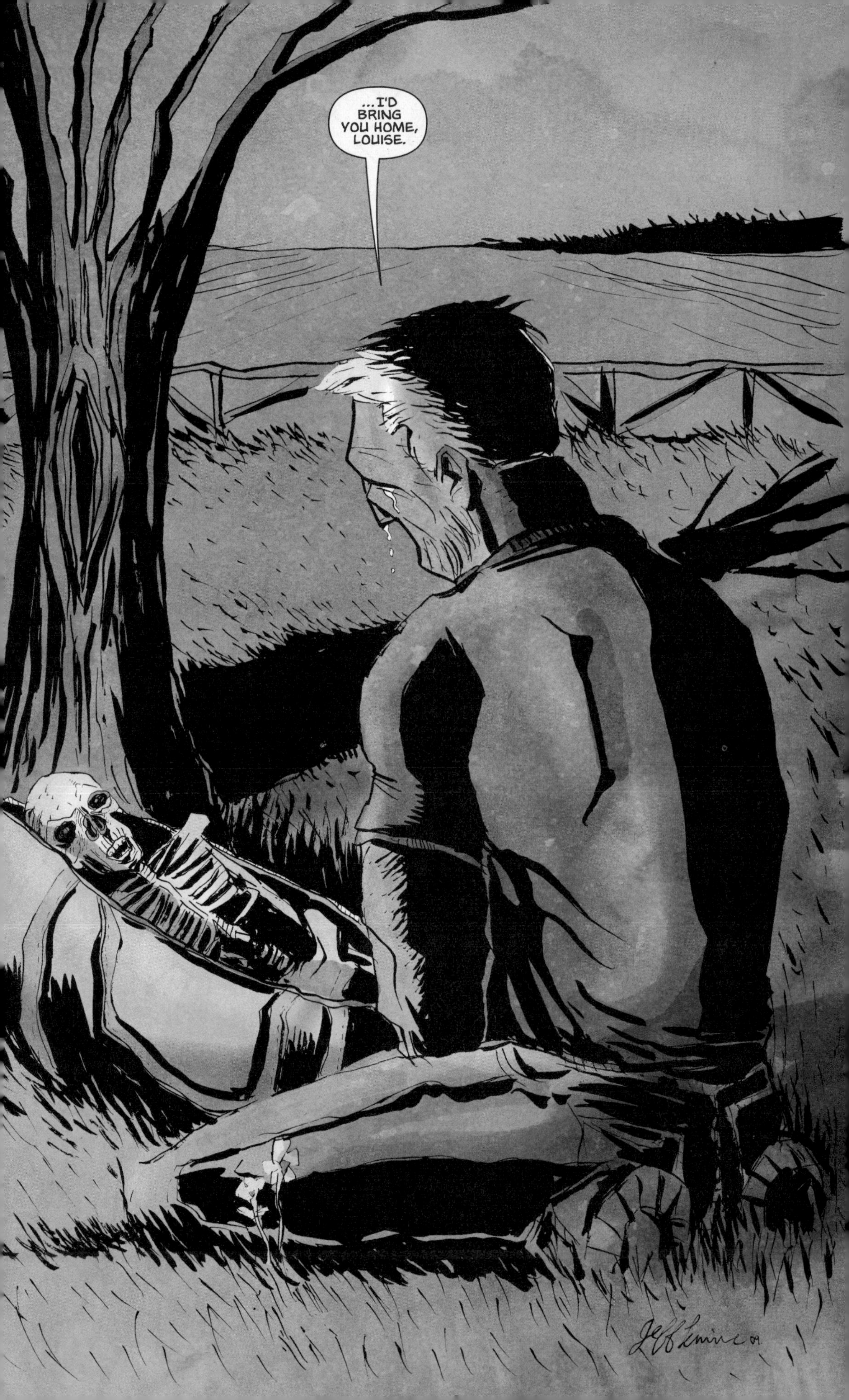
...I'D BRING YOU HOME, LOUISE.

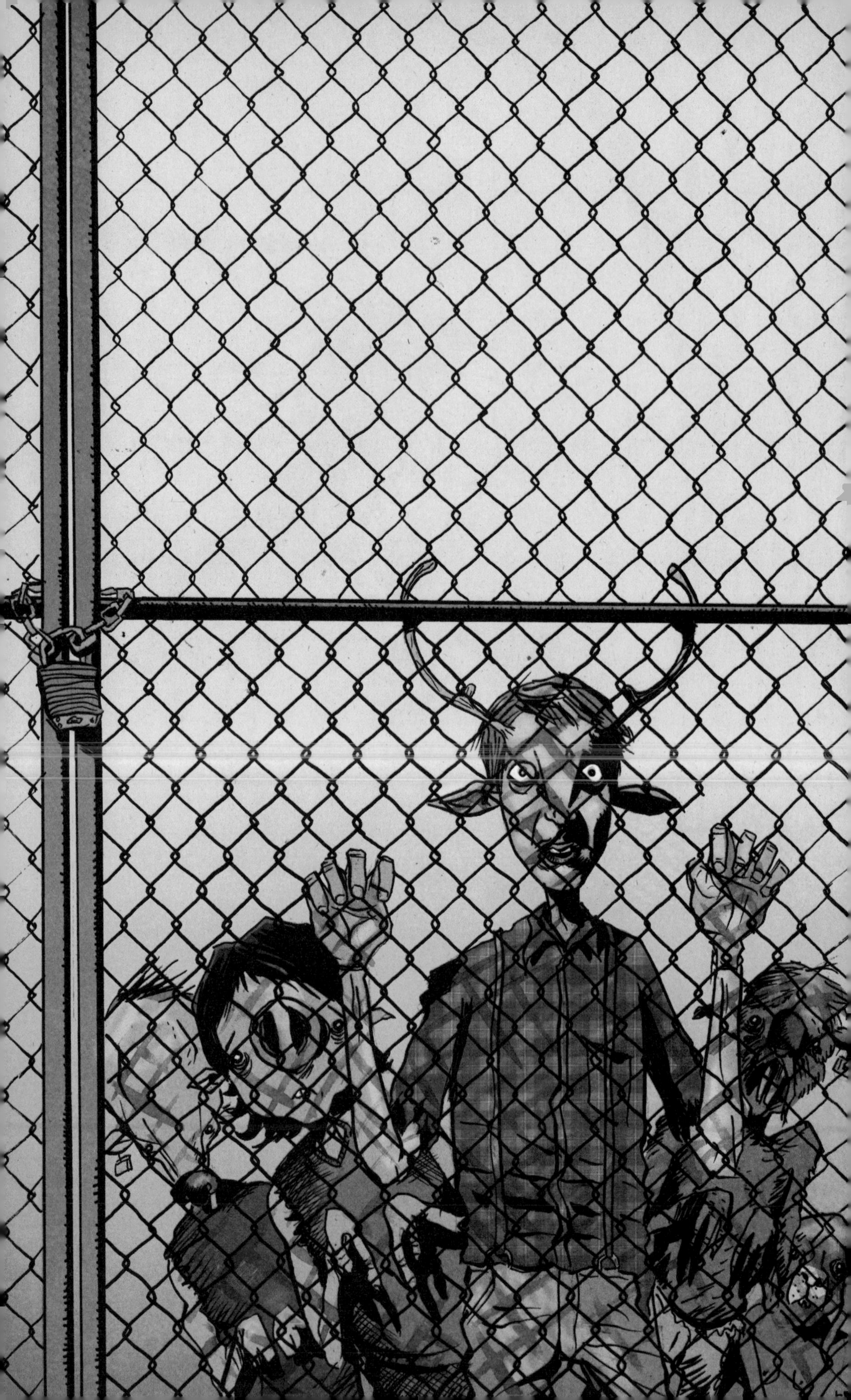

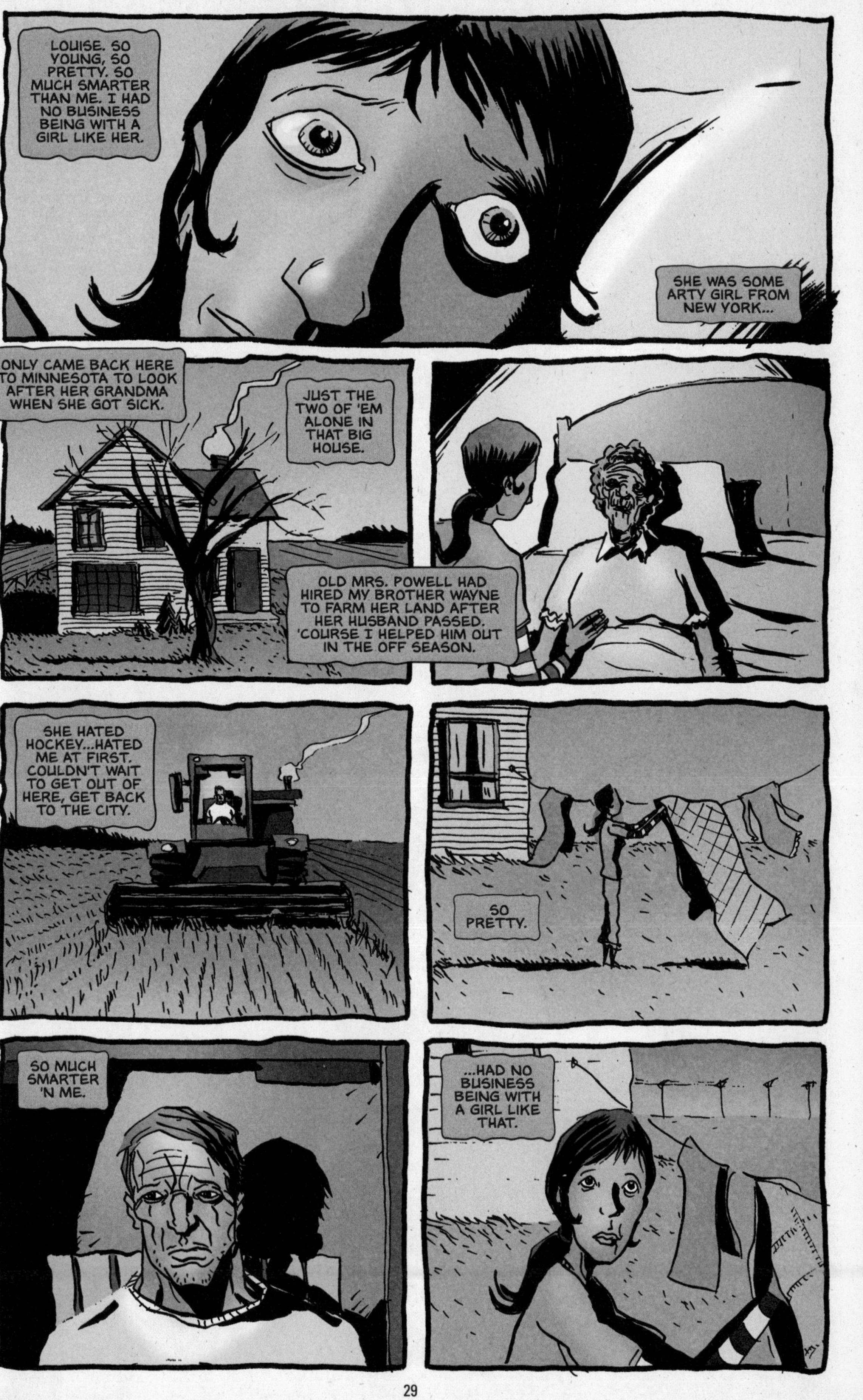
LOUISE. SO YOUNG, SO PRETTY. SO MUCH SMARTER THAN ME. I HAD NO BUSINESS BEING WITH A GIRL LIKE HER.
SHE WAS SOME ARTY GIRL FROM NEW YORK...
ONLY CAME BACK HERE TO MINNESOTA TO LOOK AFTER HER GRANDMA WHEN SHE GOT SICK.
JUST THE TWO OF 'EM ALONE IN THAT BIG HOUSE.
OLD MRS. POWELL HAD HIRED MY BROTHER WAYNE TO FARM HER LAND AFTER HER HUSBAND PASSED. 'COURSE I HELPED HIM OUT IN THE OFF SEASON.
SHE HATED HOCKEY...HATED ME AT FIRST. COULDN'T WAIT TO GET OUT OF HERE, GET BACK TO THE CITY.
SO PRETTY.
SO MUCH SMARTER 'N ME.
...HAD NO BUSINESS BEING WITH A GIRL LIKE THAT.

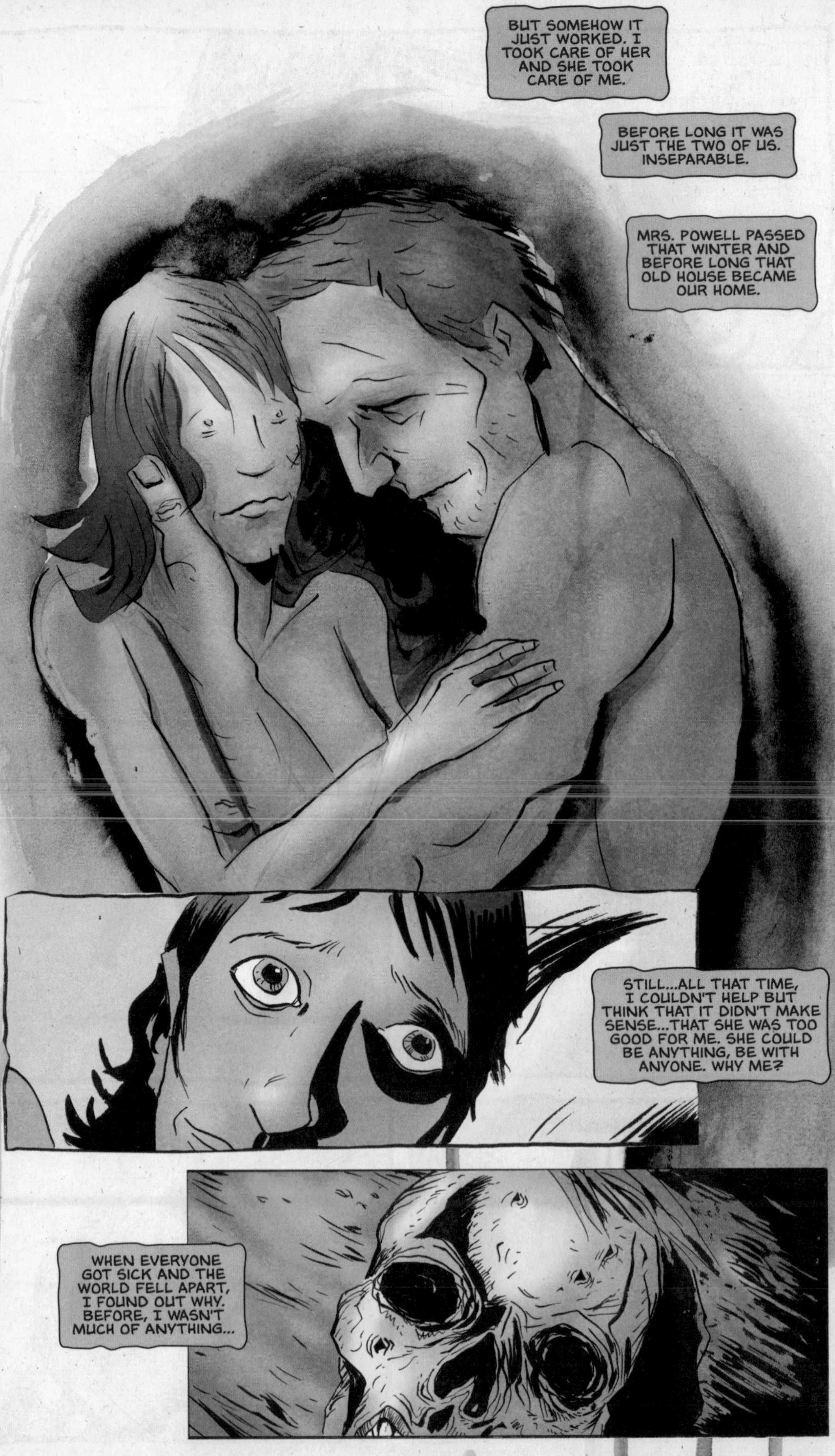
BUT SOMEHOW IT JUST WORKED. I TOOK CARE OF HER AND SHE TOOK CARE OF ME.
BEFORE LONG IT WAS JUST THE TWO OF US. INSEPARABLE.
MRS. POWELL PASSED THAT WINTER AND BEFORE LONG THAT OLD HOUSE BECAME OUR HOME.
STILL...ALL THAT TIME, I COULDN'T HELP BUT THINK THAT IT DIDN'T MAKE SENSE...THAT SHE WAS TOO GOOD FOR ME. SHE COULD BE ANYTHING, BE WITH ANYONE. WHY ME?
WHEN EVERYONE GOT SICK AND THE WORLD FELL APART, I FOUND OUT WHY. BEFORE, I WASN'T MUCH OF ANYTHING...

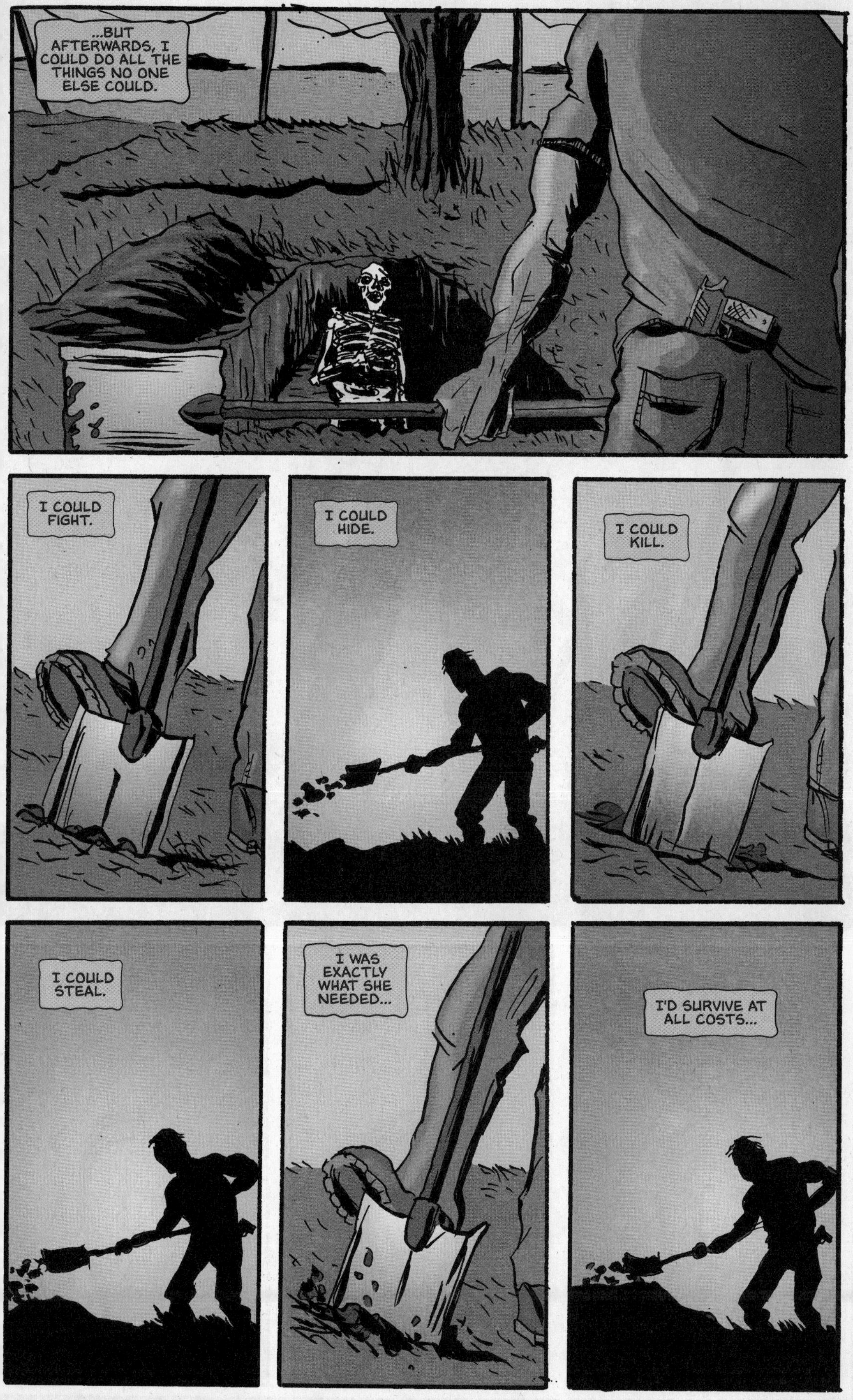

...BUT AFTERWARDS, I COULD DO ALL THE THINGS NO ONE ELSE COULD.
I COULD FIGHT.
I COULD HIDE.
I COULD KILL.
I COULD STEAL.
I WAS EXACTLY WHAT SHE NEEDED...
I'D SURVIVE AT ALL COSTS...

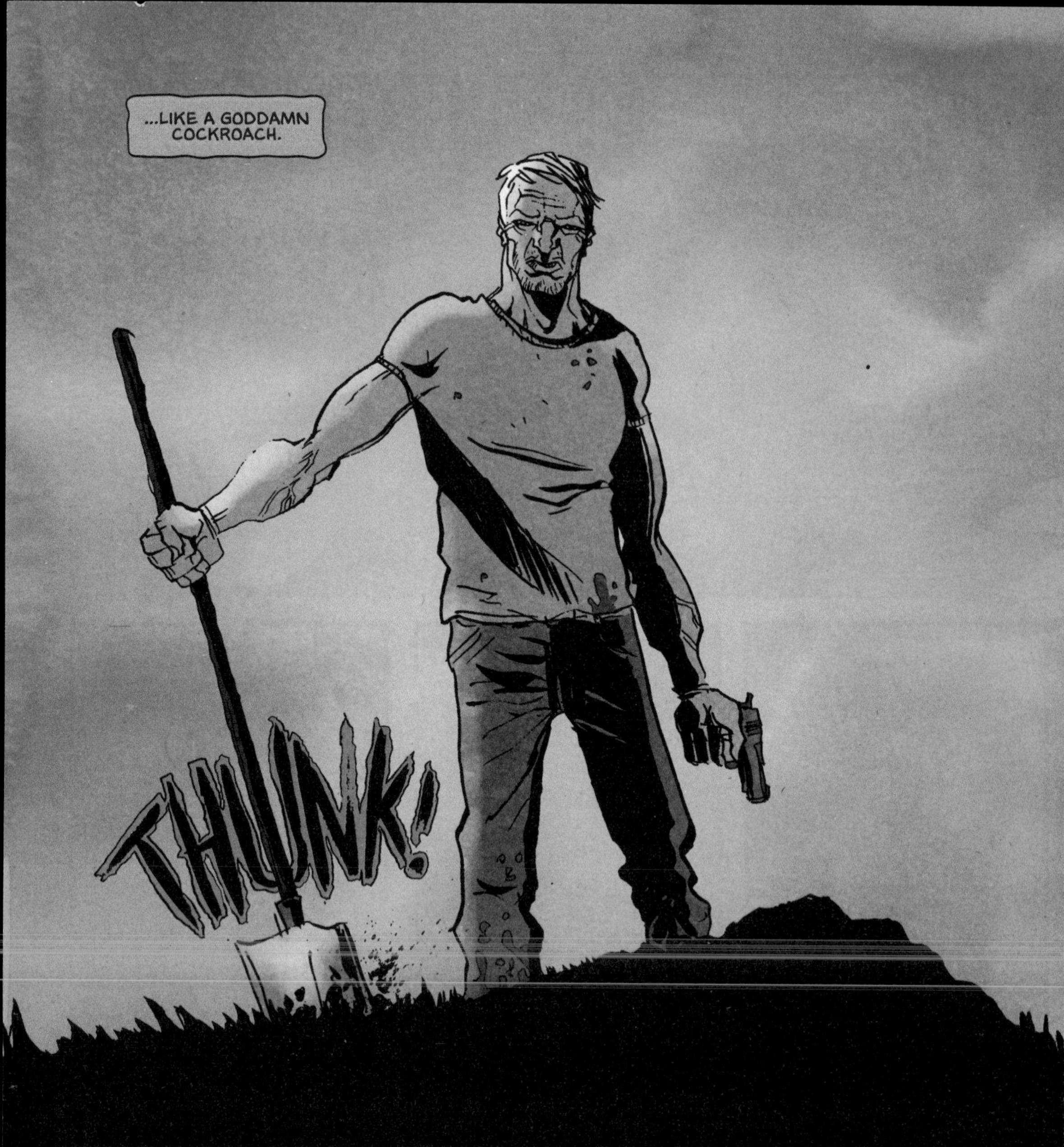
...LIKE A GODDAMN COCKROACH.
THUNK!

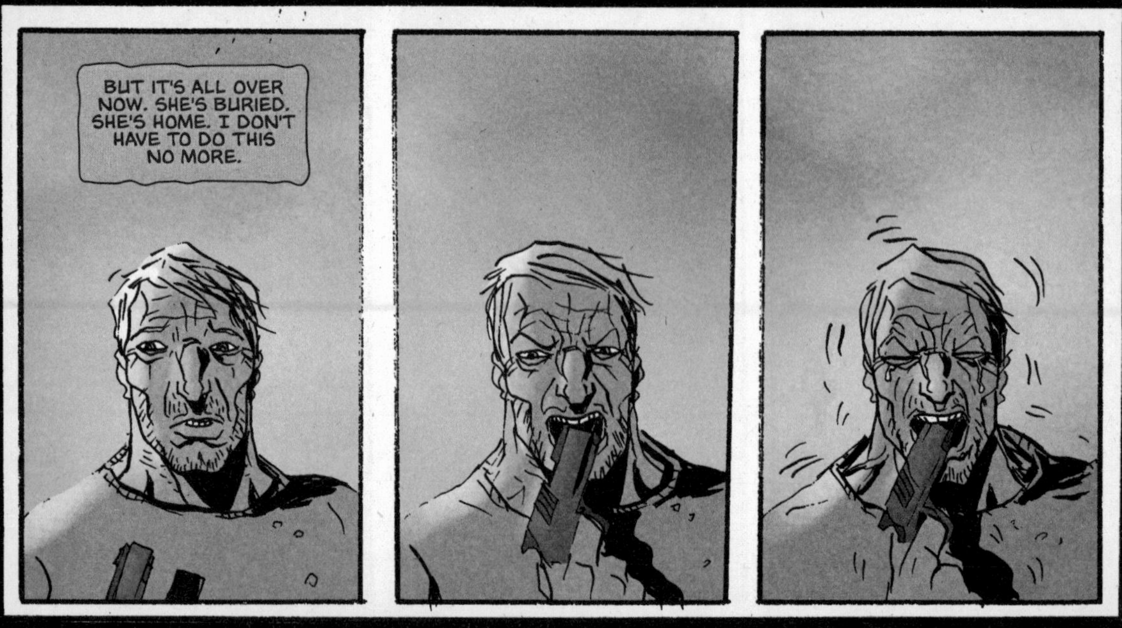
BUT IT'S ALL OVER NOW. SHE'S BURIED. SHE'S HOME. I DON'T HAVE TO DO THIS NO MORE.

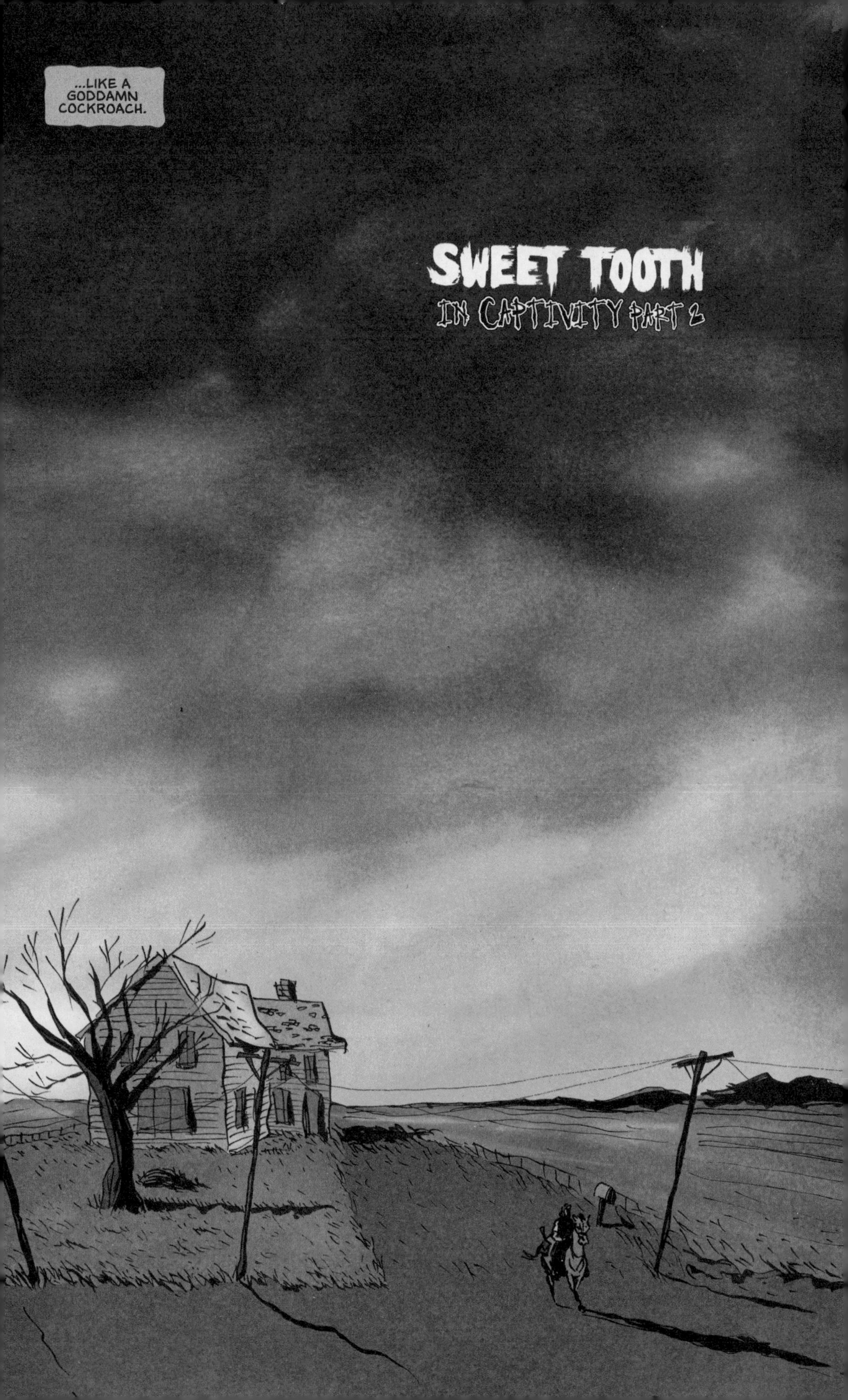
...LIKE A GODDAMN COCKROACH.
SWEET TOOTH
IN CAPTIVITY PART 2

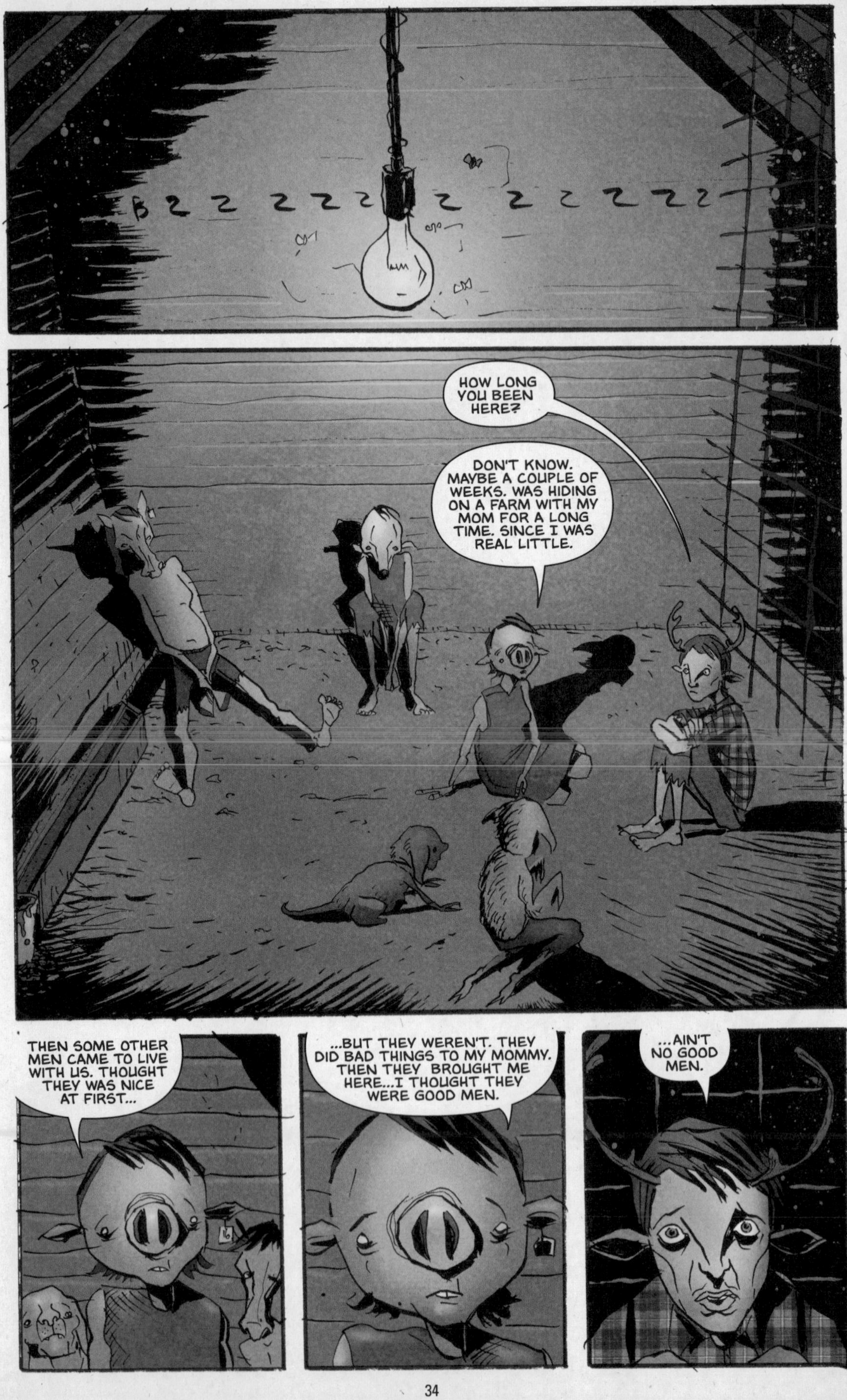
BZZZZZZZZZZZZZ
HOW LONG YOU BEEN HERE?
DON'T KNOW. MAYBE A COUPLE OF WEEKS. WAS HIDING ON A FARM WITH MY MOM FOR A LONG TIME. SINCE I WAS REAL LITTLE.
THEN SOME OTHER MEN CAME TO LIVE WITH US. THOUGHT THEY WAS NICE AT FIRST...
...BUT THEY WEREN'T. THEY DID BAD THINGS TO MY MOMMY. THEN THEY BROUGHT ME HERE...I THOUGHT THEY WERE GOOD MEN.
...AIN'T NO GOOD MEN.

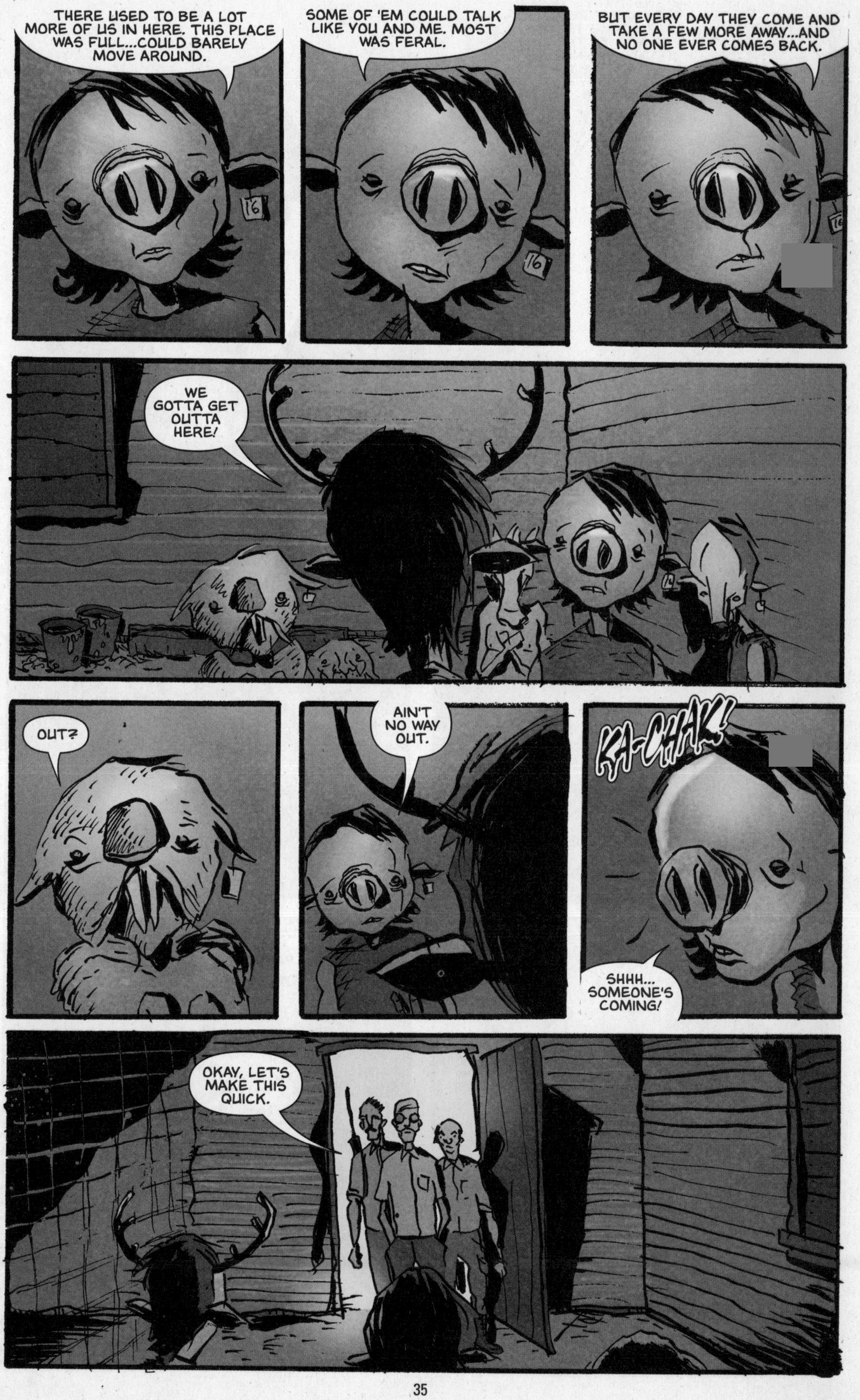
THERE USED TO BE A LOT MORE OF US IN HERE. THIS PLACE WAS FULL...COULD BARELY MOVE AROUND.
SOME OF 'EM COULD TALK LIKE YOU AND ME. MOST WAS FERAL.
BUT EVERY DAY THEY COME AND TAKE A FEW MORE AWAY...AND NO ONE EVER COMES BACK.
WE GOTTA GET OUTTA HERE!
OUT?
AIN'T NO WAY OUT.
KA-CHAK!
SHHH... SOMEONE'S COMING!
OKAY, LET'S MAKE THIS QUICK.

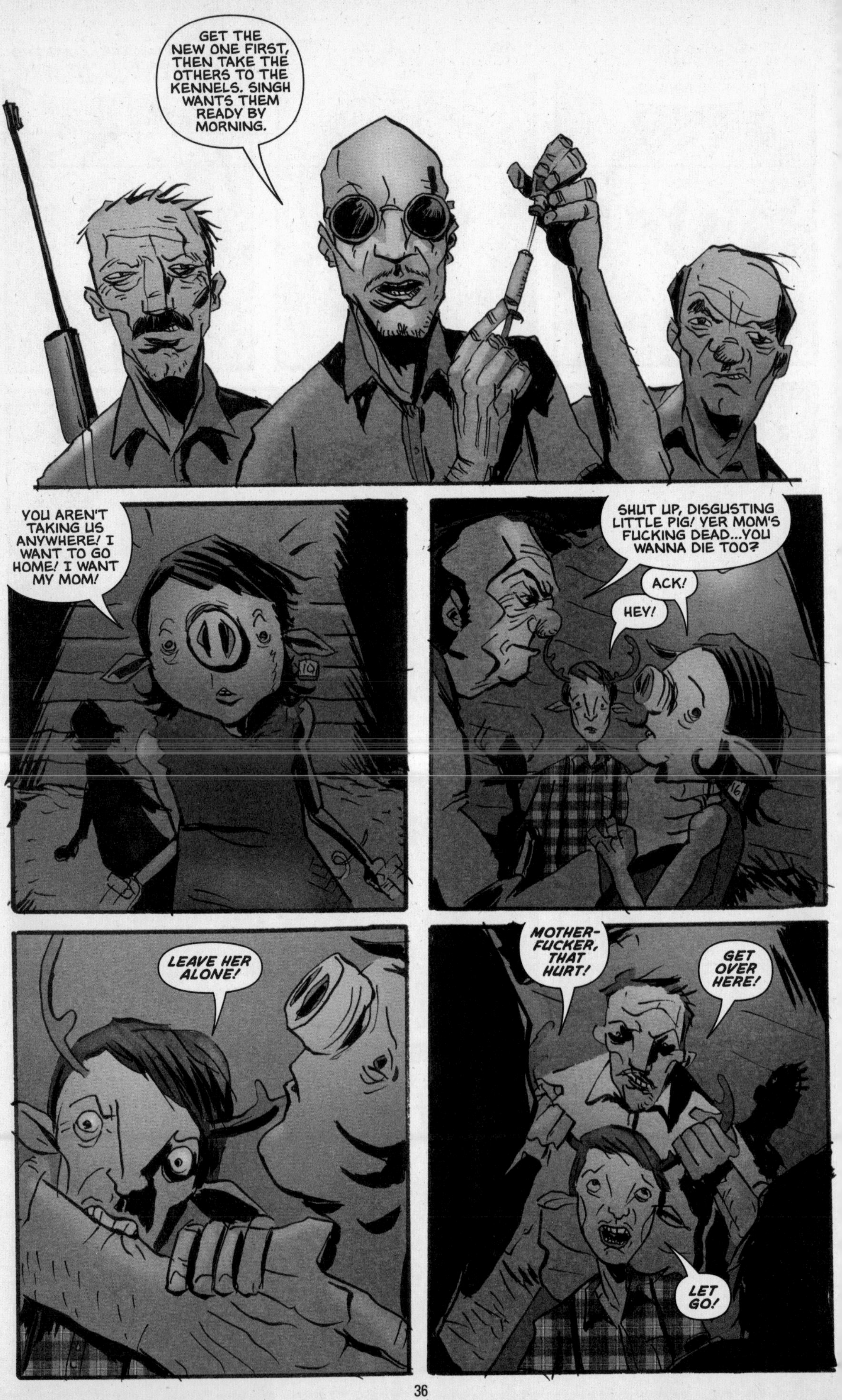
GET THE NEW ONE FIRST, THEN TAKE THE OTHERS TO THE KENNELS. SINGH WANTS THEM READY BY MORNING.
YOU AREN'T TAKING US ANYWHERE! I WANT TO GO HOME! I WANT MY MOM!
SHUT UP, DISGUSTING LITTLE PIG! YER MOM'S FUCKING DEAD...YOU WANNA DIE TOO?
ACK!
HEY!
LEAVE HER ALONE!
MOTHER-FUCKER, THAT HURT!
GET OVER HERE!
LET GO!

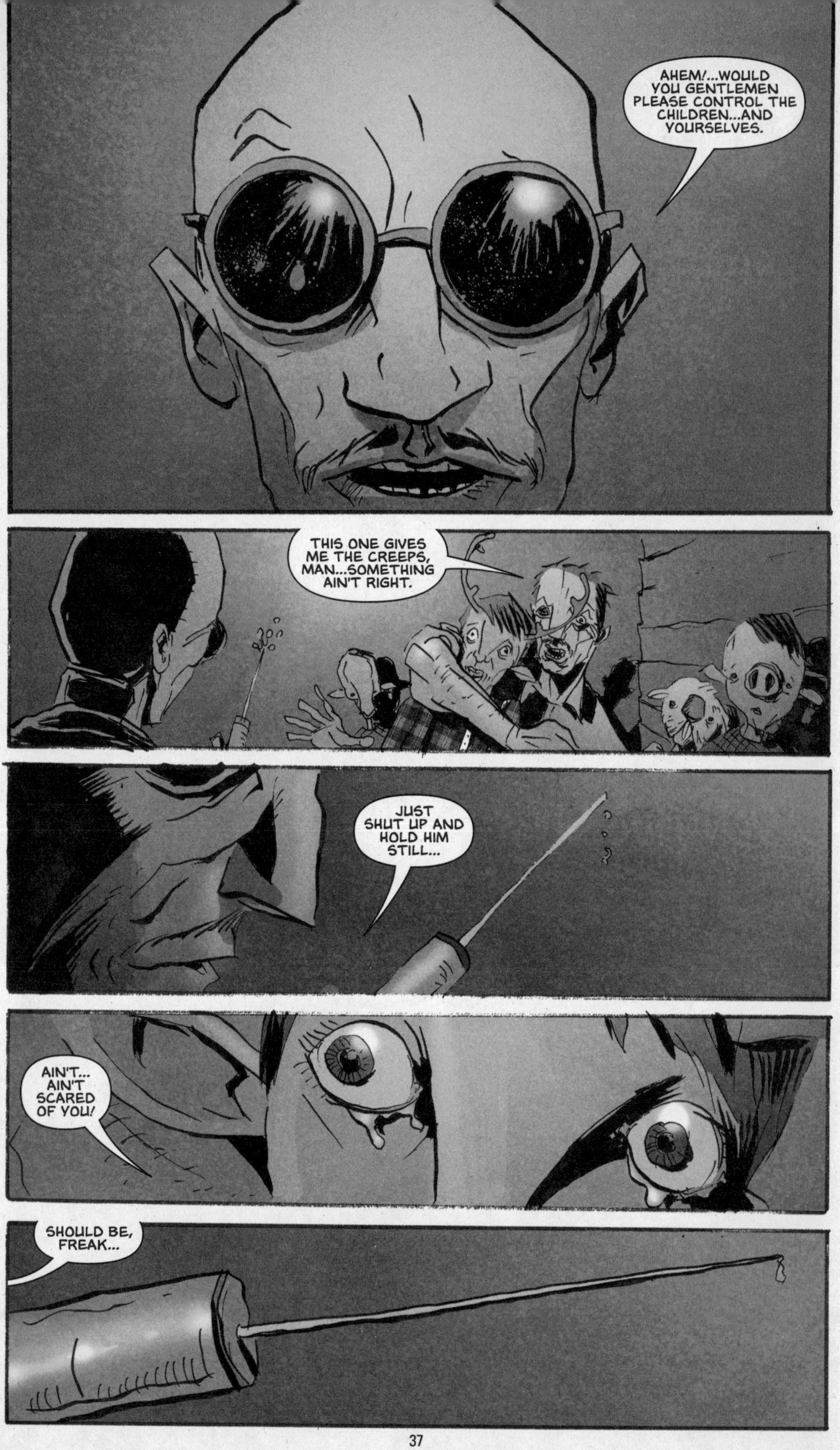
AHEM!...WOULD YOU GENTLEMEN PLEASE CONTROL THE CHILDREN...AND YOURSELVES.
THIS ONE GIVES ME THE CREEPS, MAN...SOMETHING AIN'T RIGHT.
JUST SHUT UP AND HOLD HIM STILL...
AIN'T... AIN'T SCARED OF YOU!
SHOULD BE, FREAK...

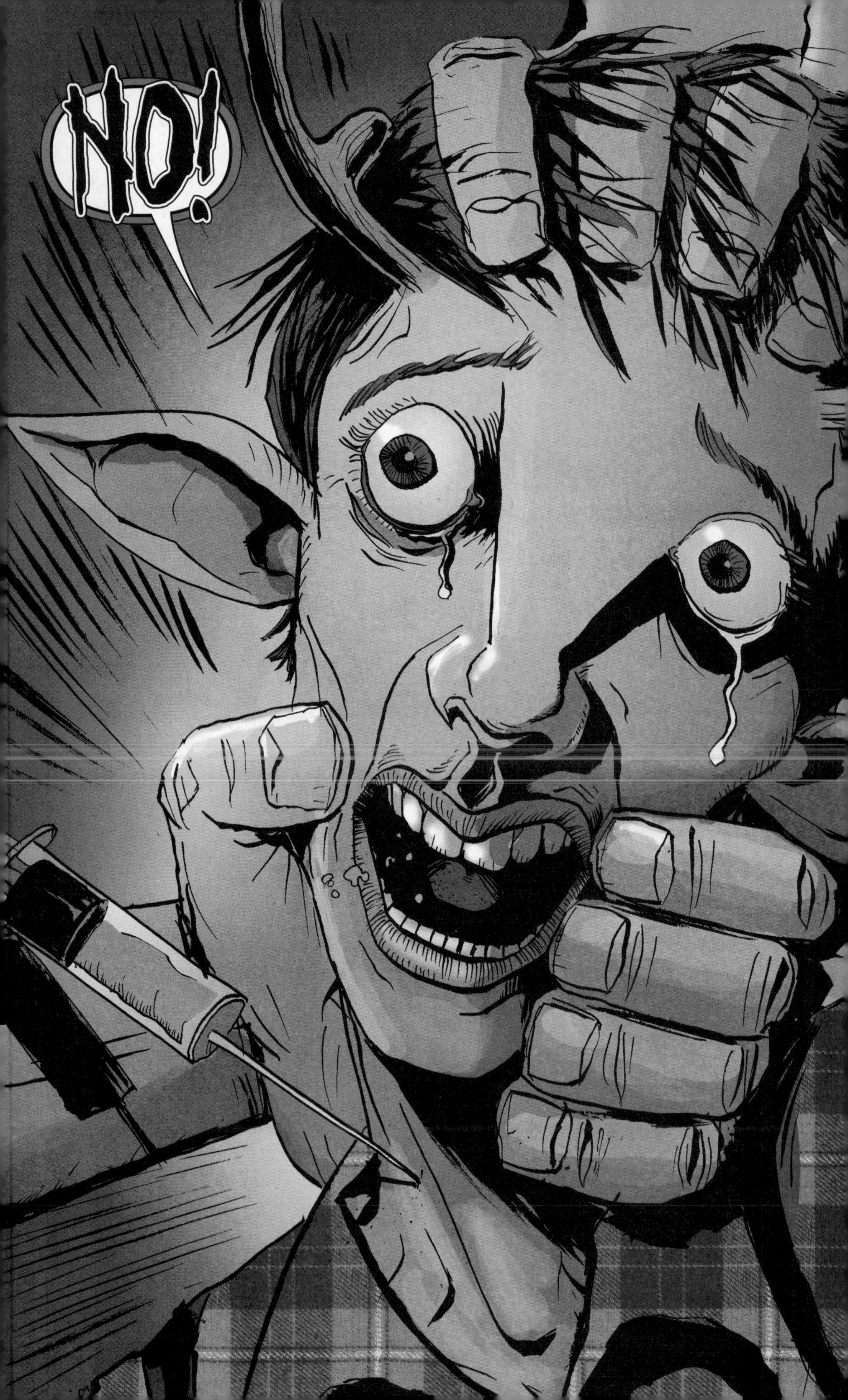
NO!

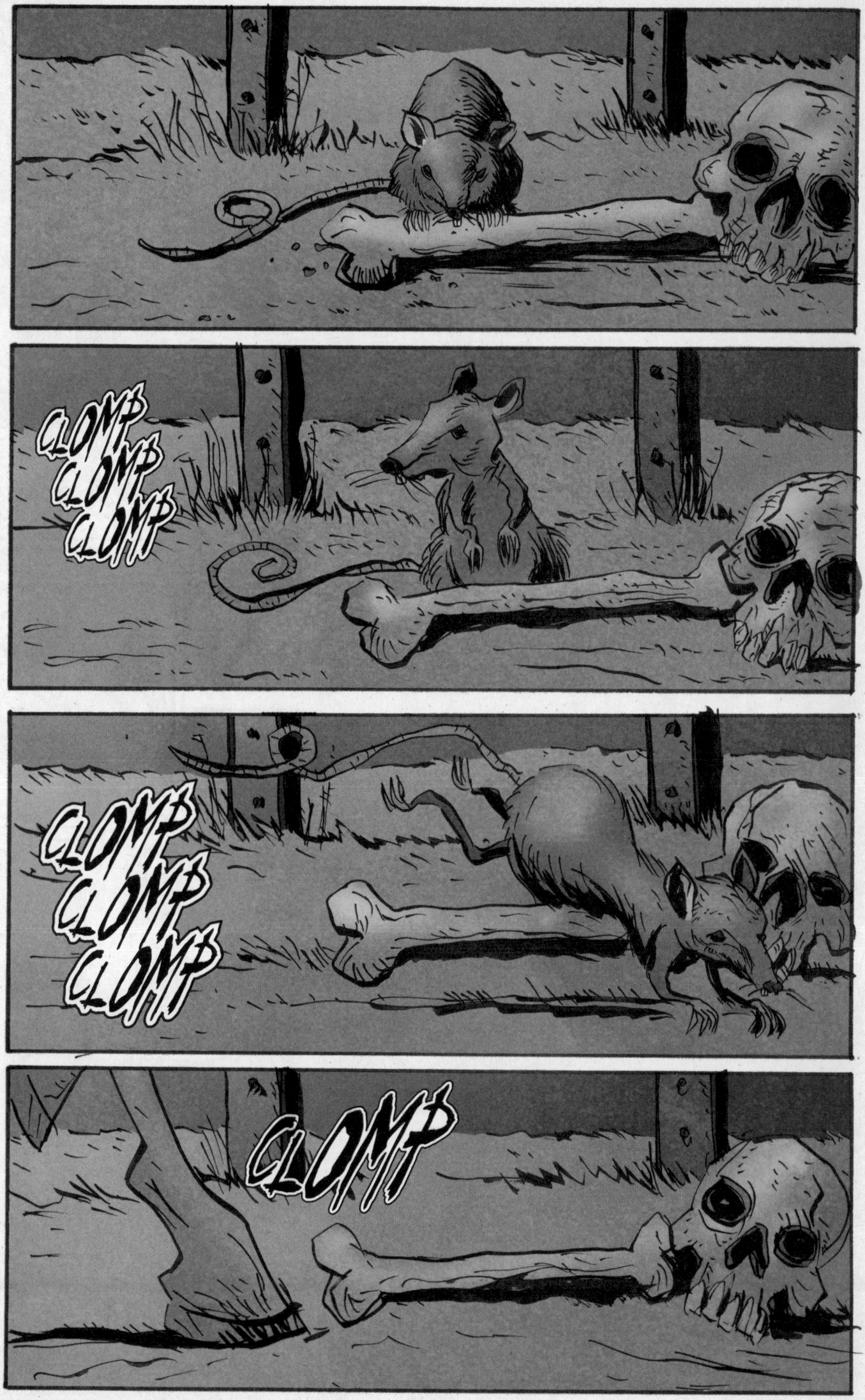
CLOMP
CLOMP
CLOMP
CLOMP
CLOMP
CLOMP
CLOMP

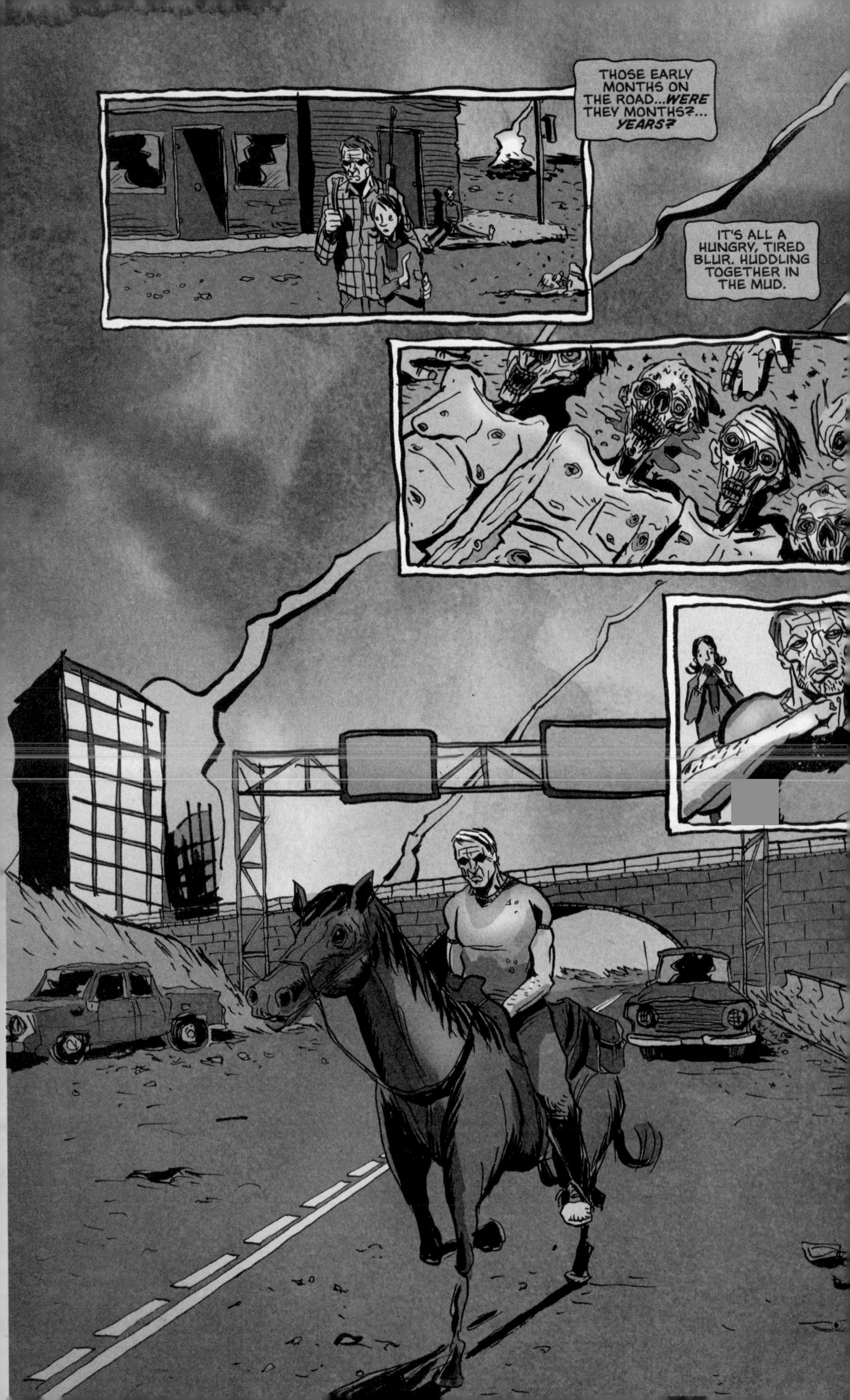
THOSE EARLY MONTHS ON THE ROAD...WERE THEY MONTHS?...YEARS?
IT'S ALL A HUNGRY, TIRED BLUR. HUDDLING TOGETHER IN THE MUD.

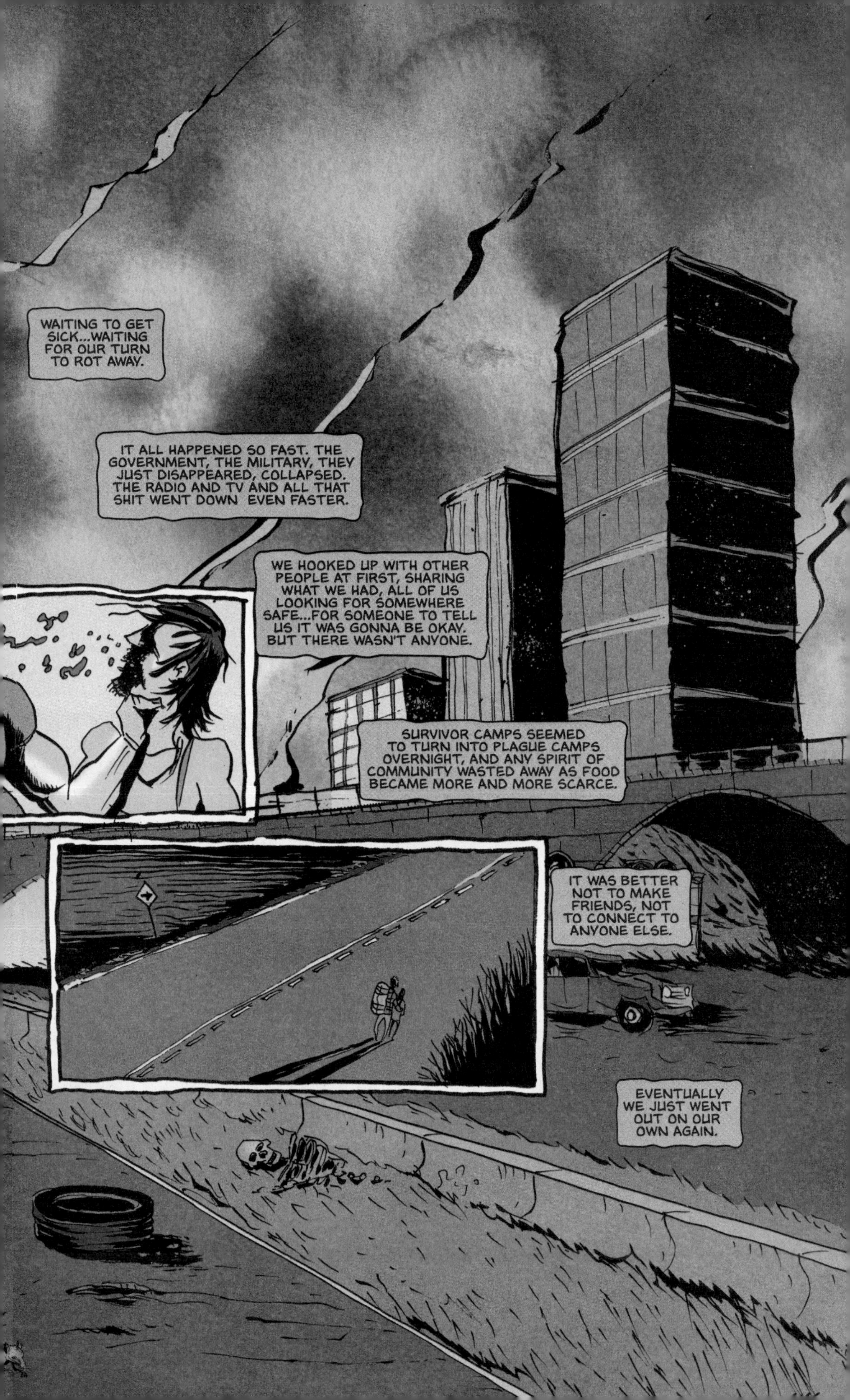
WAITING TO GET SICK...WAITING FOR OUR TURN TO ROT AWAY.
IT ALL HAPPENED SO FAST. THE GOVERNMENT, THE MILITARY, THEY JUST DISAPPEARED, COLLAPSED. THE RADIO AND TV AND ALL THAT SHIT WENT DOWN EVEN FASTER.
WE HOOKED UP WITH OTHER PEOPLE AT FIRST, SHARING WHAT WE HAD, ALL OF US LOOKING FOR SOMEWHERE SAFE...FOR SOMEONE TO TELL US IT WAS GONNA BE OKAY. BUT THERE WASN'T ANYONE.
SURVIVOR CAMPS SEEMED TO TURN INTO PLAGUE CAMPS OVERNIGHT, AND ANY SPIRIT OF COMMUNITY WASTED AWAY AS FOOD BECAME MORE AND MORE SCARCE.
IT WAS BETTER NOT TO MAKE FRIENDS, NOT TO CONNECT TO ANYONE ELSE.
EVENTUALLY WE JUST WENT OUT ON OUR OWN AGAIN.

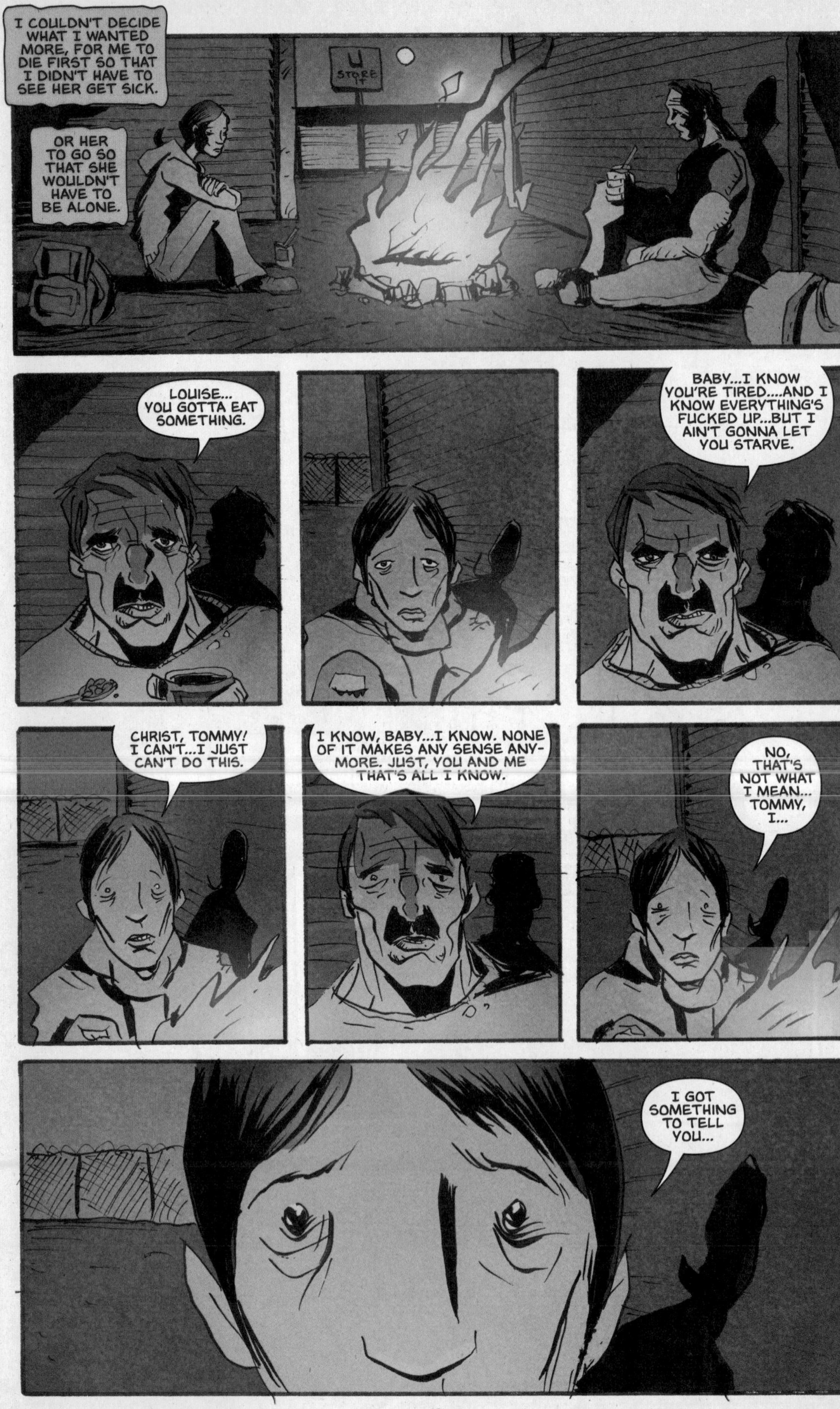
I COULDN'T DECIDE WHAT I WANTED MORE, FOR ME TO DIE FIRST SO THAT I DIDN'T HAVE TO SEE HER GET SICK.
OR HER TO GO SO THAT SHE WOULDN'T HAVE TO BE ALONE.
U STORE IT
LOUISE... YOU GOTTA EAT SOMETHING.
BABY...I KNOW YOU'RE TIRED....AND I KNOW EVERYTHING'S FUCKED UP...BUT I AIN'T GONNA LET YOU STARVE.
CHRIST, TOMMY! I CAN'T...I JUST CAN'T DO THIS.
I KNOW, BABY...I KNOW. NONE OF IT MAKES ANY SENSE ANY-MORE. JUST, YOU AND ME THAT'S ALL I KNOW.
NO, THAT'S NOT WHAT I MEAN... TOMMY, I...
I GOT SOMETHING TO TELL YOU...

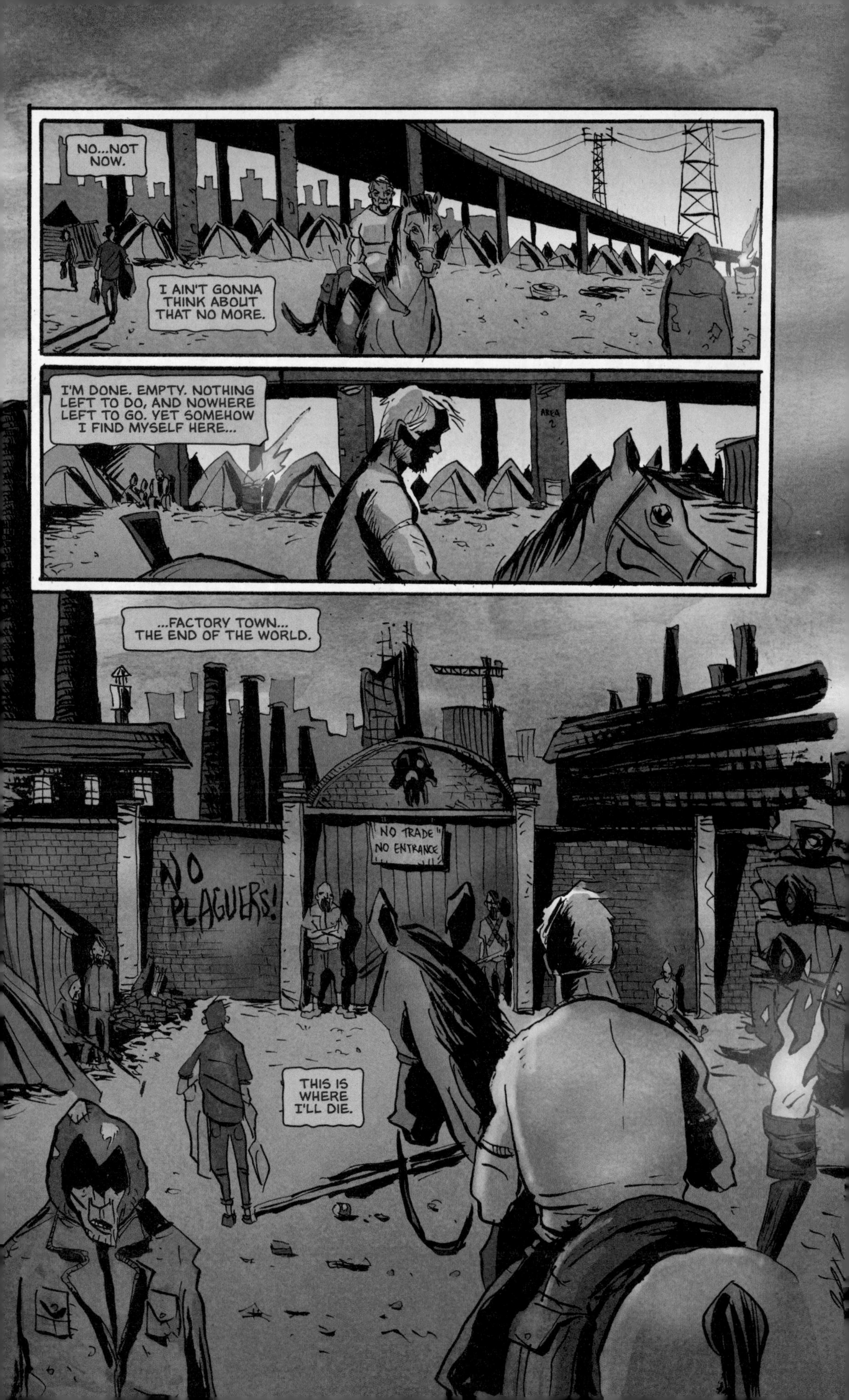
NO...NOT NOW.
I AIN'T GONNA THINK ABOUT THAT NO MORE.
I'M DONE. EMPTY. NOTHING LEFT TO DO, AND NOWHERE LEFT TO GO. YET SOMEHOW I FIND MYSELF HERE...
AREA 2
...FACTORY TOWN... THE END OF THE WORLD.
NO TRADE NO ENTRANCE
NO PLAGUERS!
THIS IS WHERE I'LL DIE.

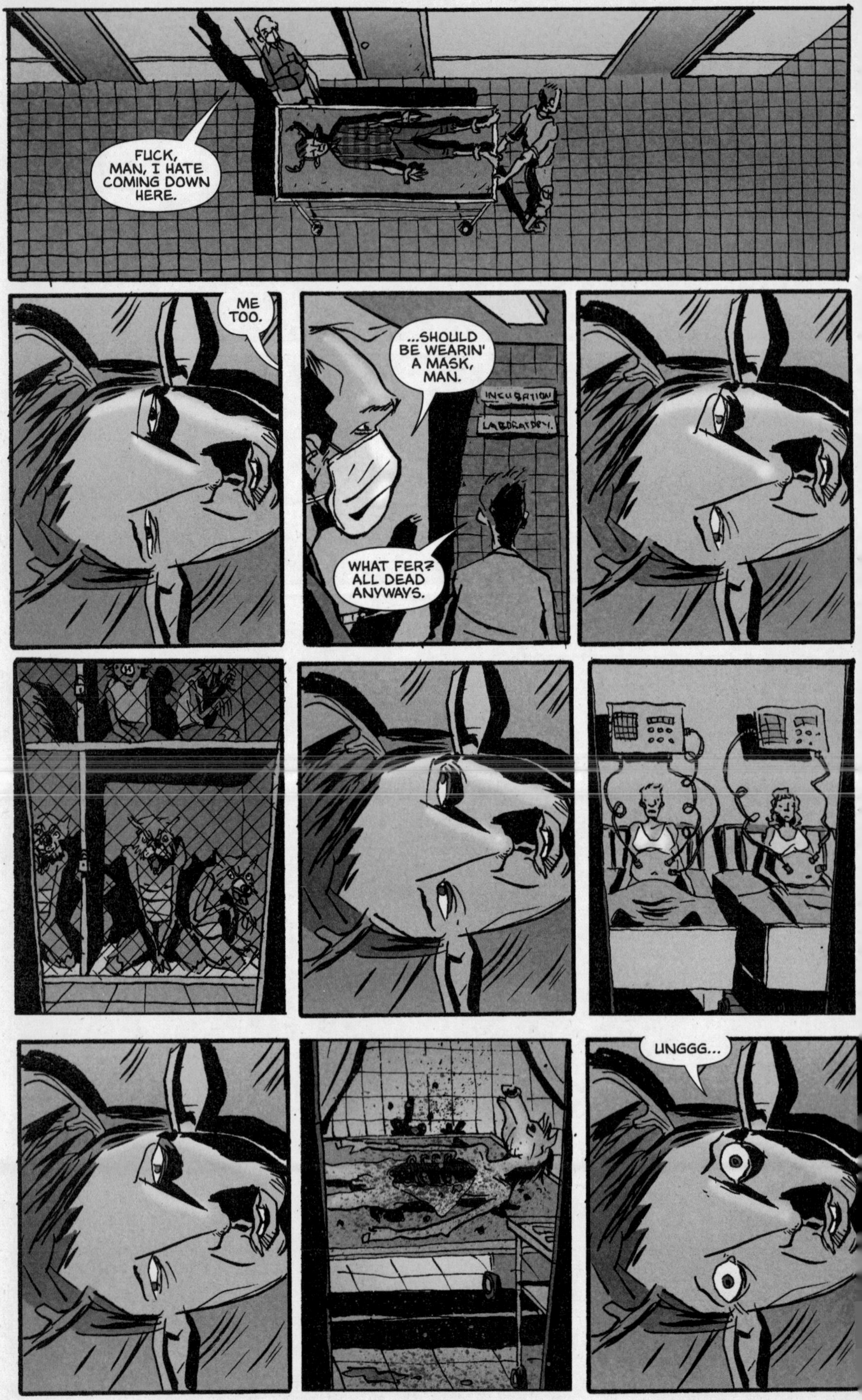
FUCK, MAN, I HATE COMING DOWN HERE.
ME TOO.
...SHOULD BE WEARIN' A MASK, MAN.
INCUBATION
LABORATORY
WHAT FER? ALL DEAD ANYWAYS.
UNGGG...

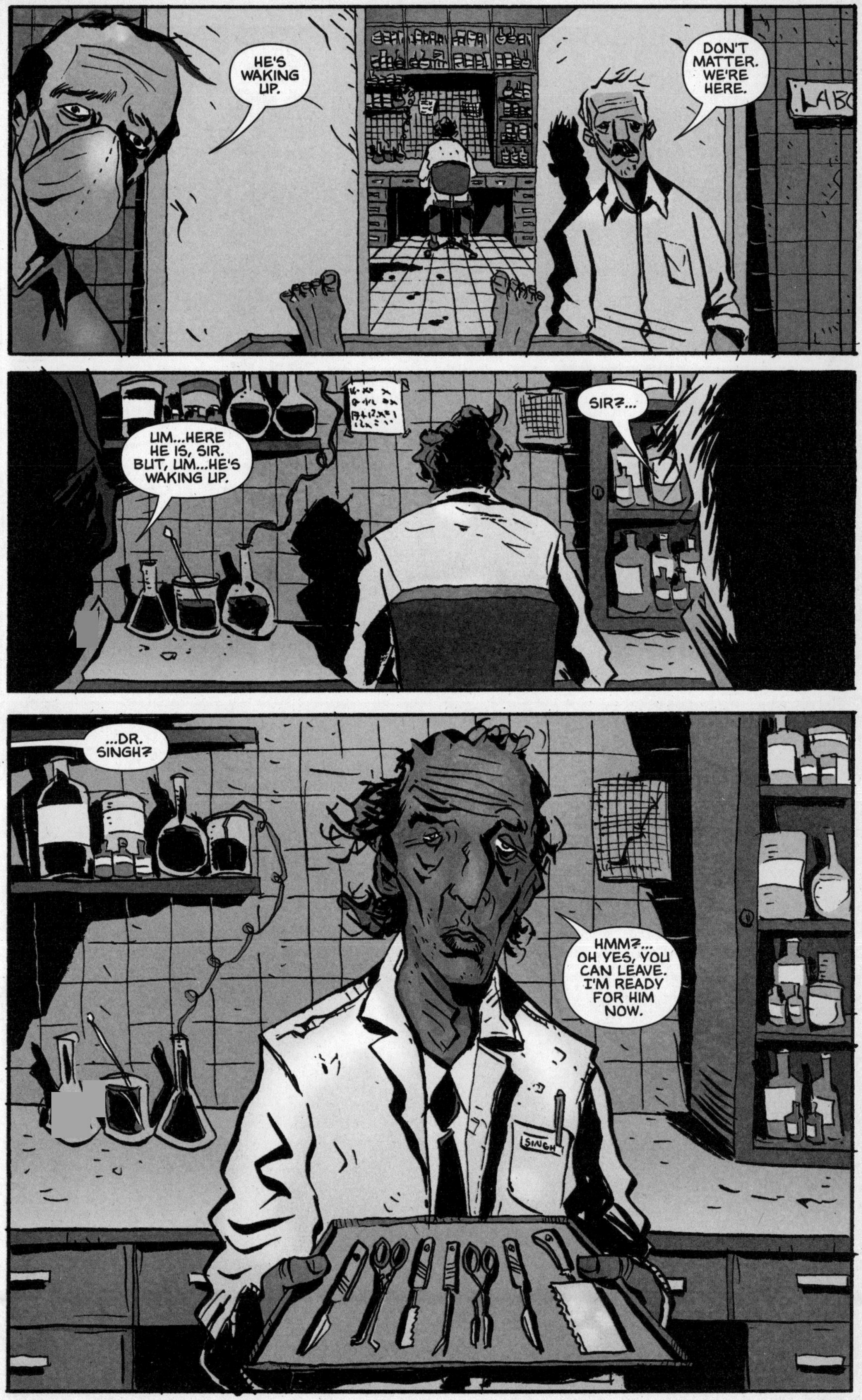
HE'S WAKING UP.
DON'T MATTER. WE'RE HERE.
LABO
UM...HERE HE IS, SIR. BUT, UM...HE'S WAKING UP.
SIR?...
...DR. SINGH?
HMM?... OH YES, YOU CAN LEAVE. I'M READY FOR HIM NOW.
SINGH

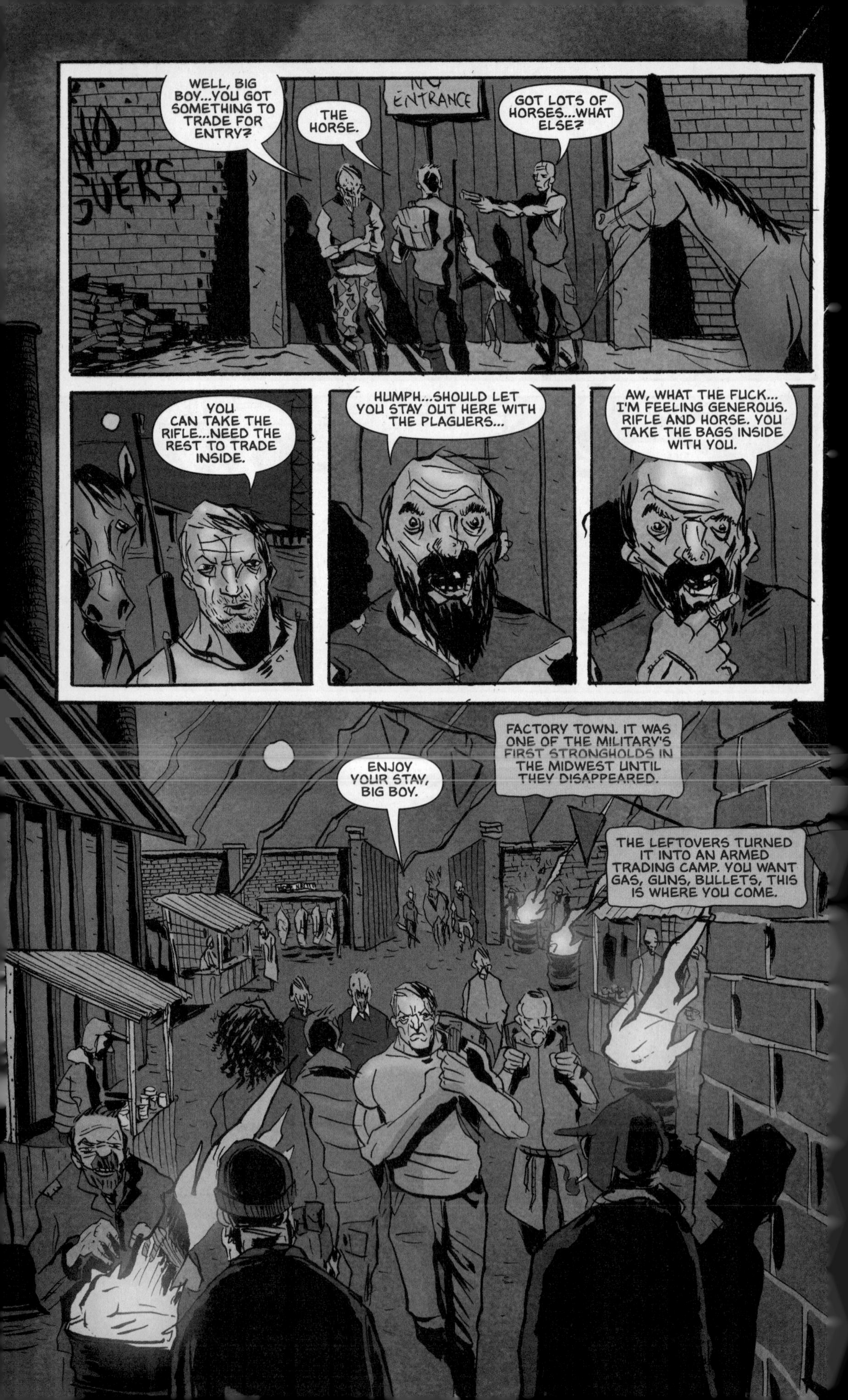
WELL, BIG BOY...YOU GOT SOMETHING TO TRADE FOR ENTRY?
ENTRANCE
THE HORSE.
GOT LOTS OF HORSES...WHAT ELSE?
YOU CAN TAKE THE RIFLE...NEED THE REST TO TRADE INSIDE.
HUMPH...SHOULD LET YOU STAY OUT HERE WITH THE PLAGUERS...
AW, WHAT THE FUCK... I'M FEELING GENEROUS. RIFLE AND HORSE. YOU TAKE THE BAGS INSIDE WITH YOU.
ENJOY YOUR STAY, BIG BOY.
FACTORY TOWN. IT WAS ONE OF THE MILITARY'S FIRST STRONGHOLDS IN THE MIDWEST UNTIL THEY DISAPPEARED.
THE LEFTOVERS TURNED IT INTO AN ARMED TRADING CAMP. YOU WANT GAS, GUNS, BULLETS, THIS IS WHERE YOU COME.

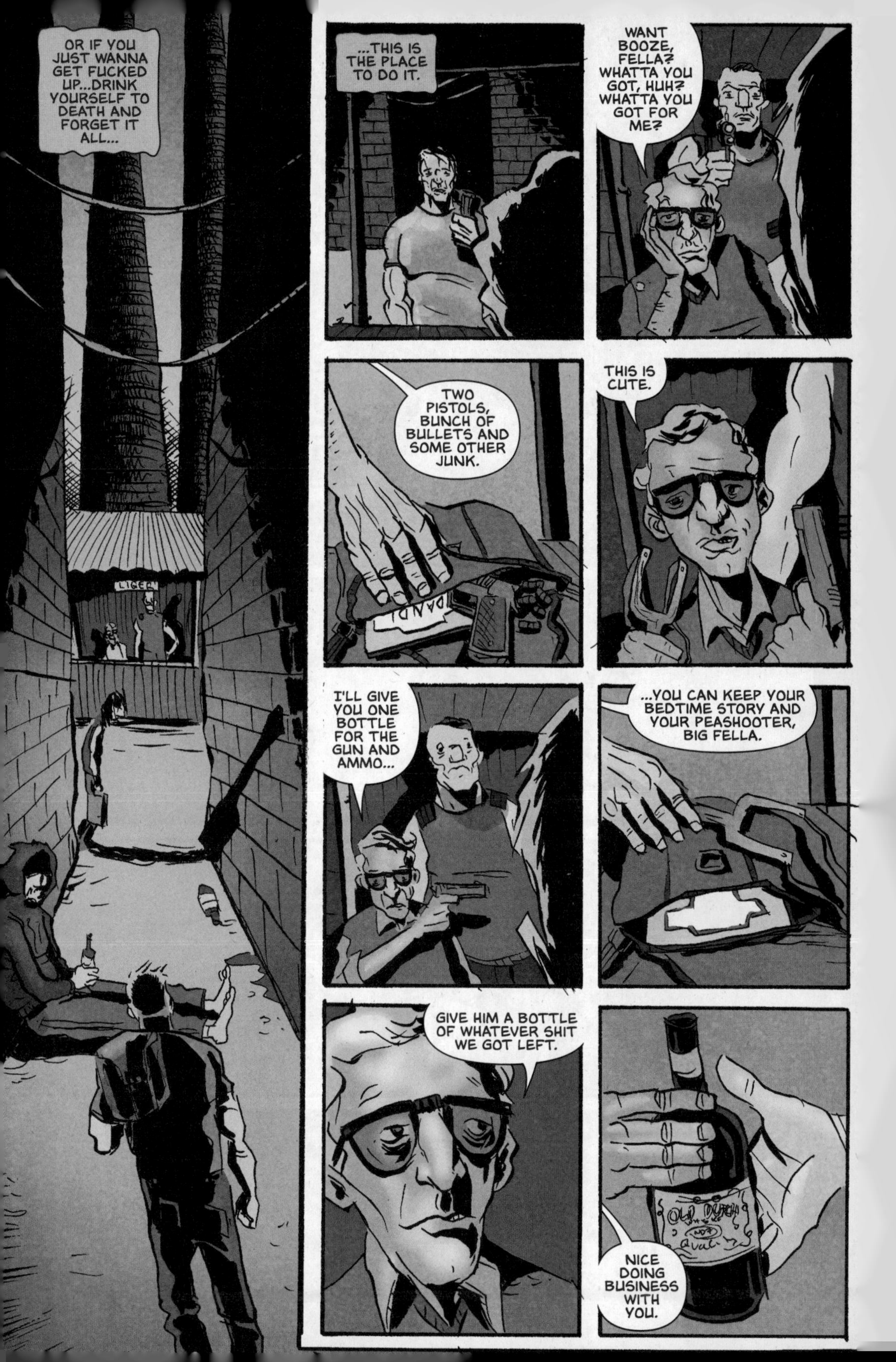
OR IF YOU JUST WANNA GET FUCKED UP...DRINK YOURSELF TO DEATH AND FORGET IT ALL...
LIGER
...THIS IS THE PLACE TO DO IT.
WANT BOOZE, FELLA? WHATTA YOU GOT, HUH? WHATTA YOU GOT FOR ME?
TWO PISTOLS, BUNCH OF BULLETS AND SOME OTHER JUNK.
THIS IS CUTE.
I'LL GIVE YOU ONE BOTTLE FOR THE GUN AND AMMO...
...YOU CAN KEEP YOUR BEDTIME STORY AND YOUR PEASHOOTER, BIG FELLA.
GIVE HIM A BOTTLE OF WHATEVER SHIT WE GOT LEFT.
OLD DUTCH
NICE DOING BUSINESS WITH YOU.

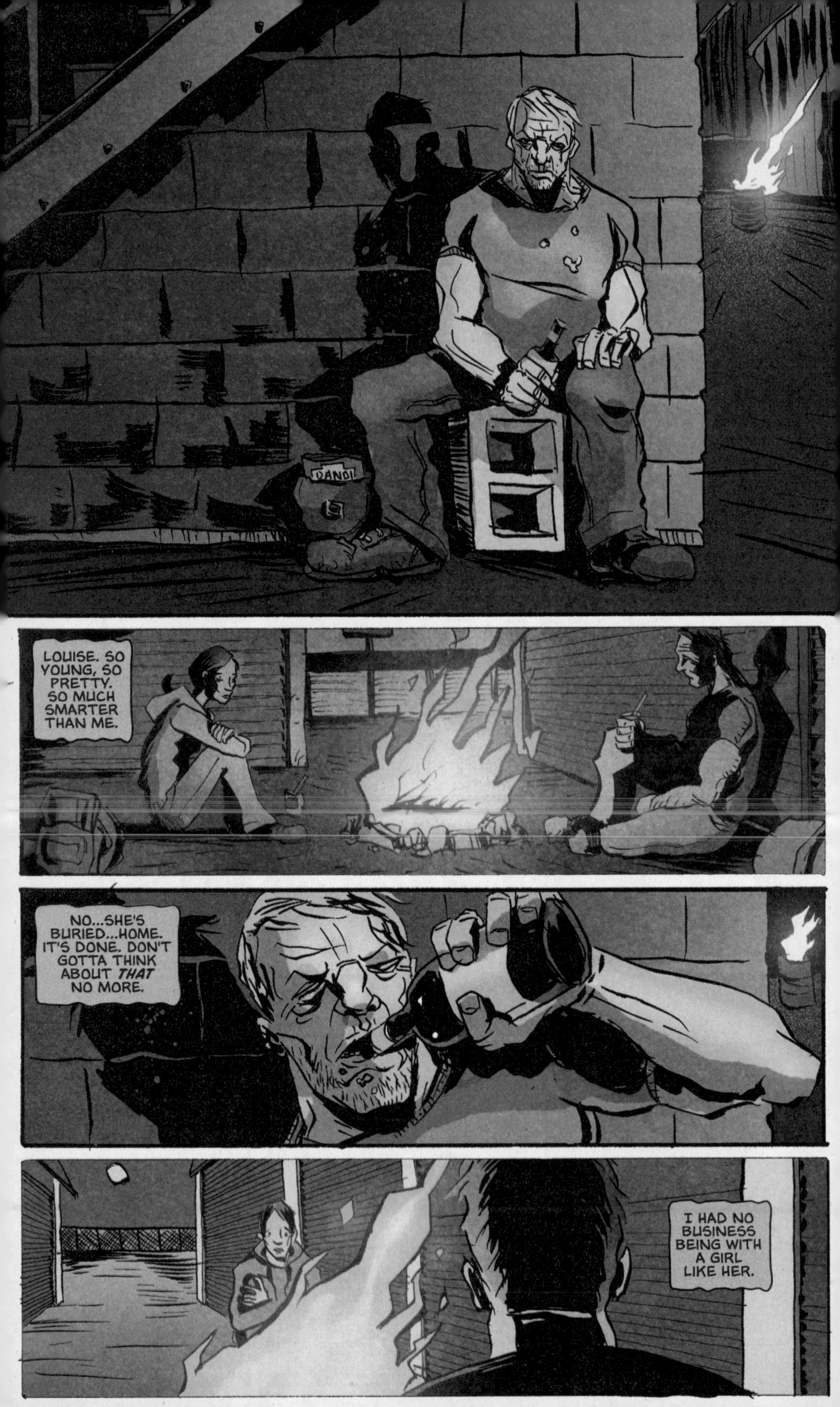
LOUISE. SO YOUNG, SO PRETTY. SO MUCH SMARTER THAN ME.
NO...SHE'S BURIED...HOME. IT'S DONE. DON'T GOTTA THINK ABOUT *THAT* NO MORE.
I HAD NO BUSINESS BEING WITH A GIRL LIKE HER.

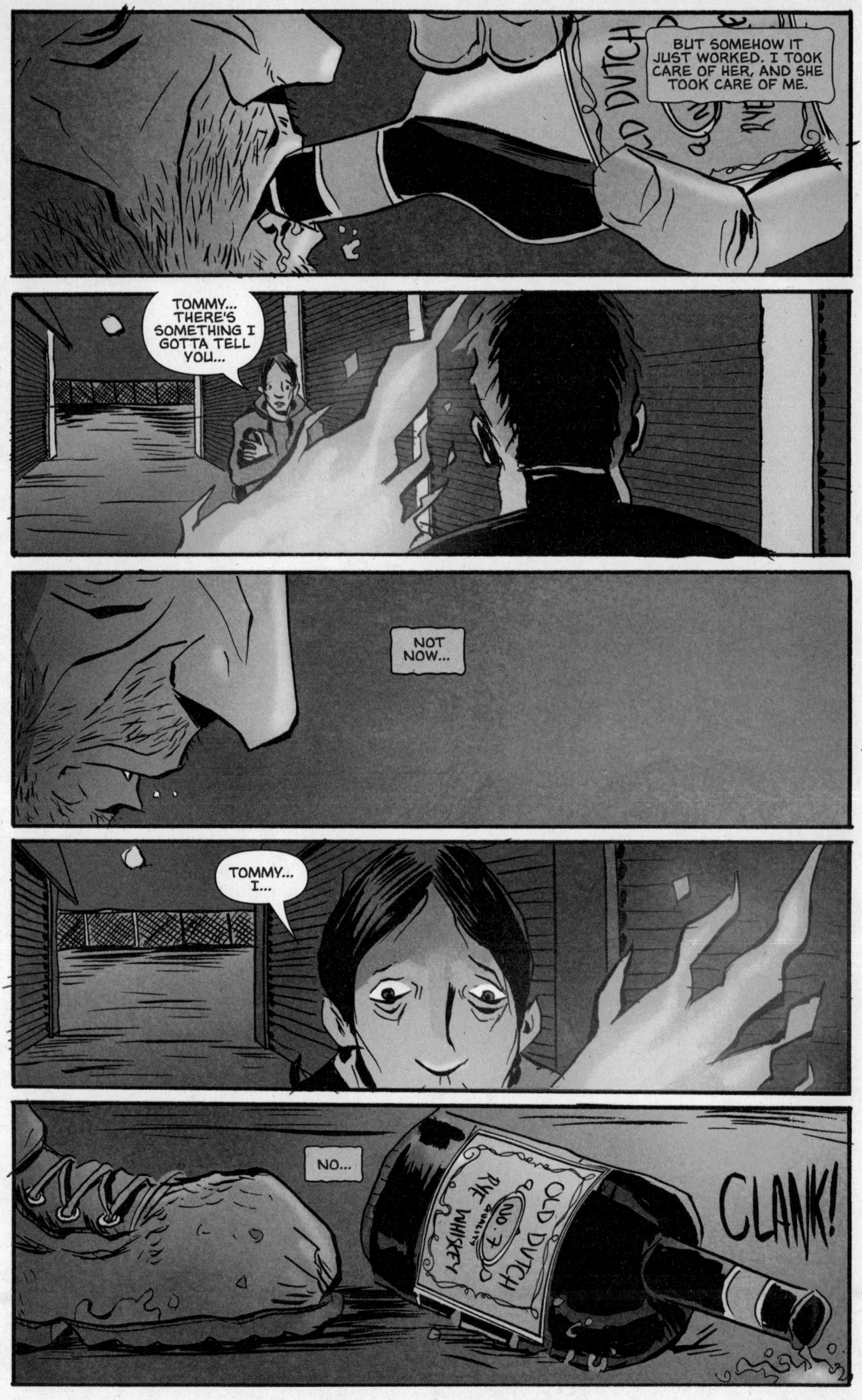
BUT SOMEHOW IT JUST WORKED. I TOOK CARE OF HER, AND SHE TOOK CARE OF ME.
OLD DUTCH
RYE
TOMMY... THERE'S SOMETHING I GOTTA TELL YOU...
NOT NOW...
TOMMY... I...
NO...
OLD DUTCH
NO. 7
QUALITY
RYE WHISKEY
CLANK!

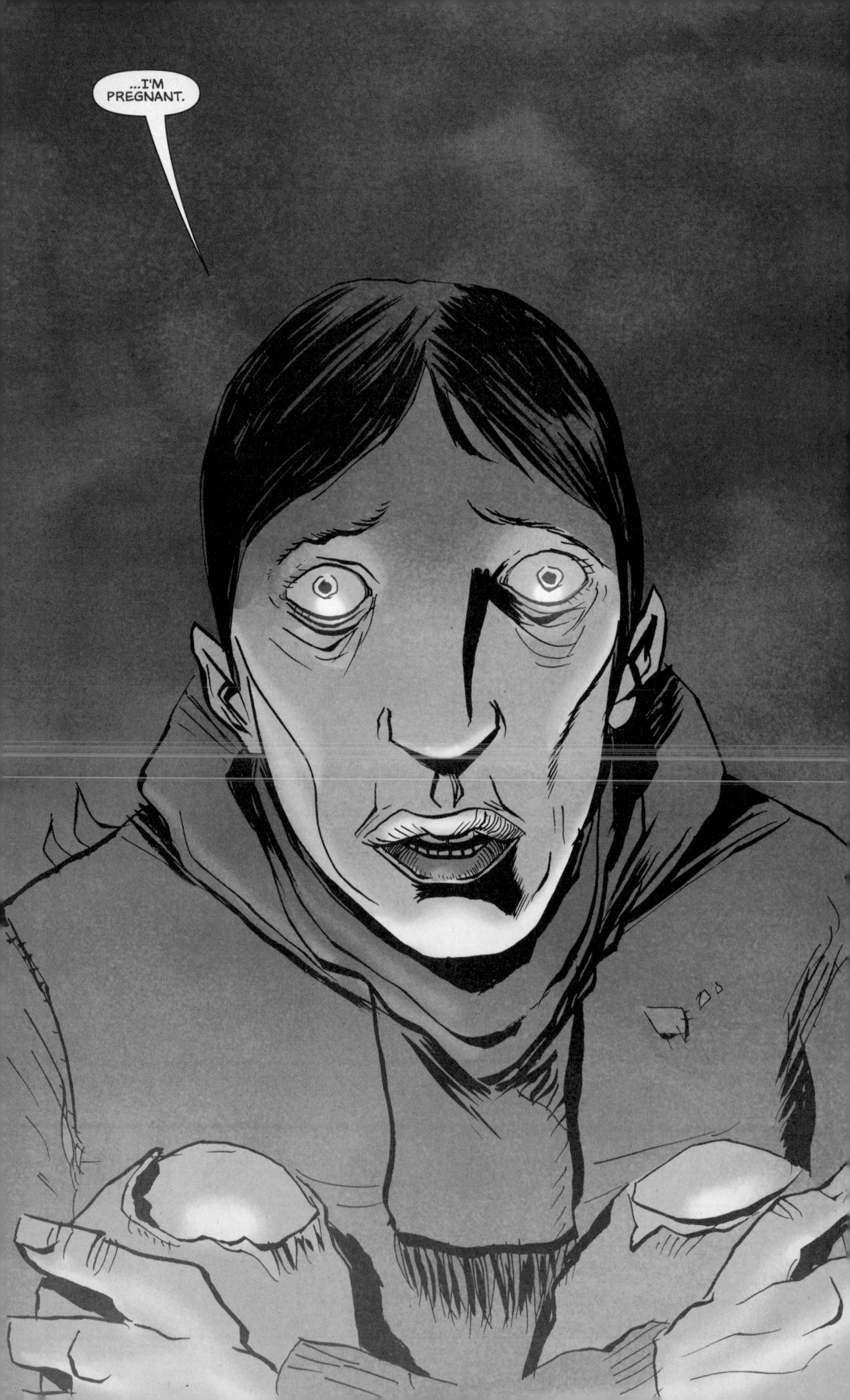
...I'M PREGNANT.

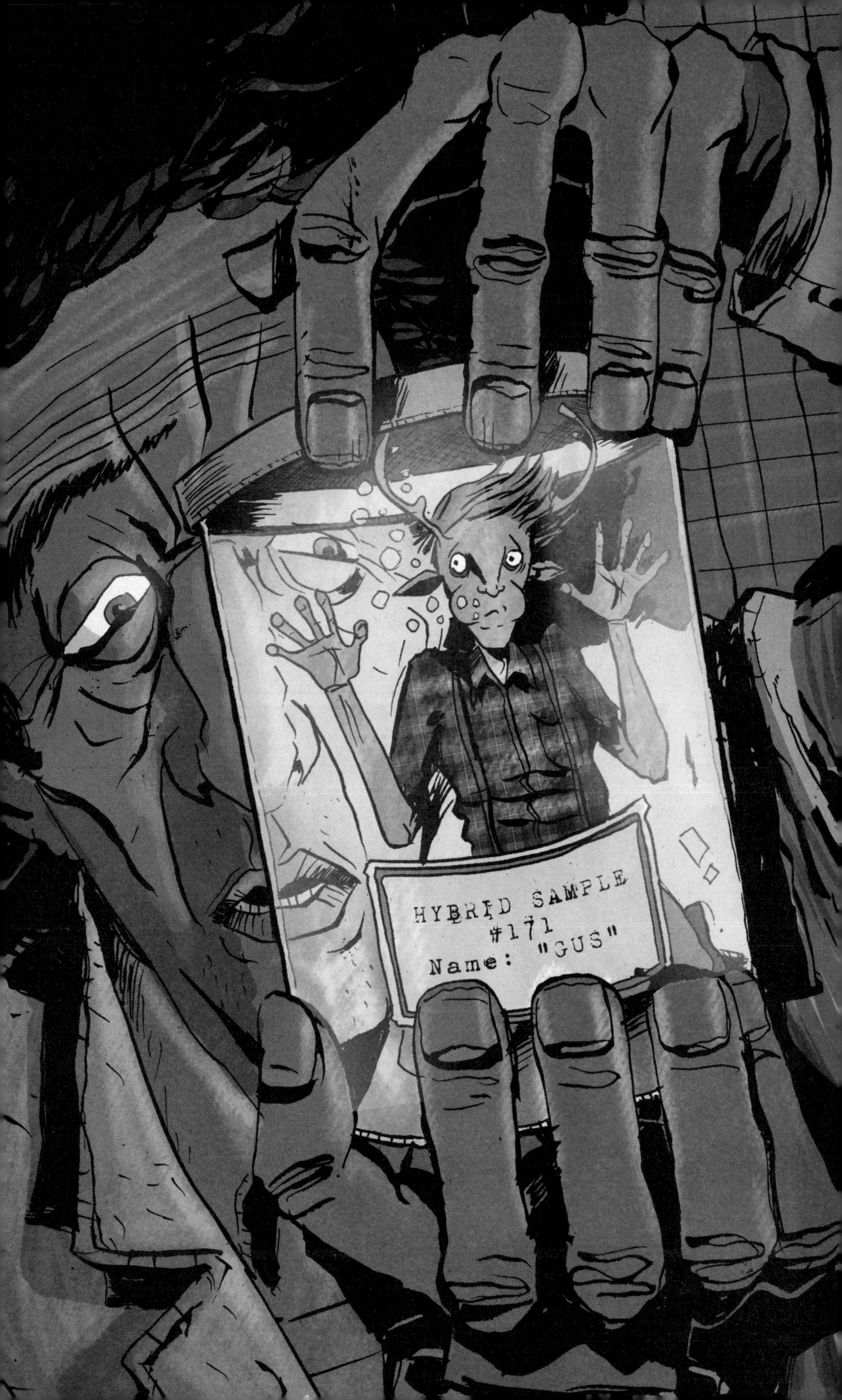
HYBRID SAMPLE
#171
Name: "GUS"

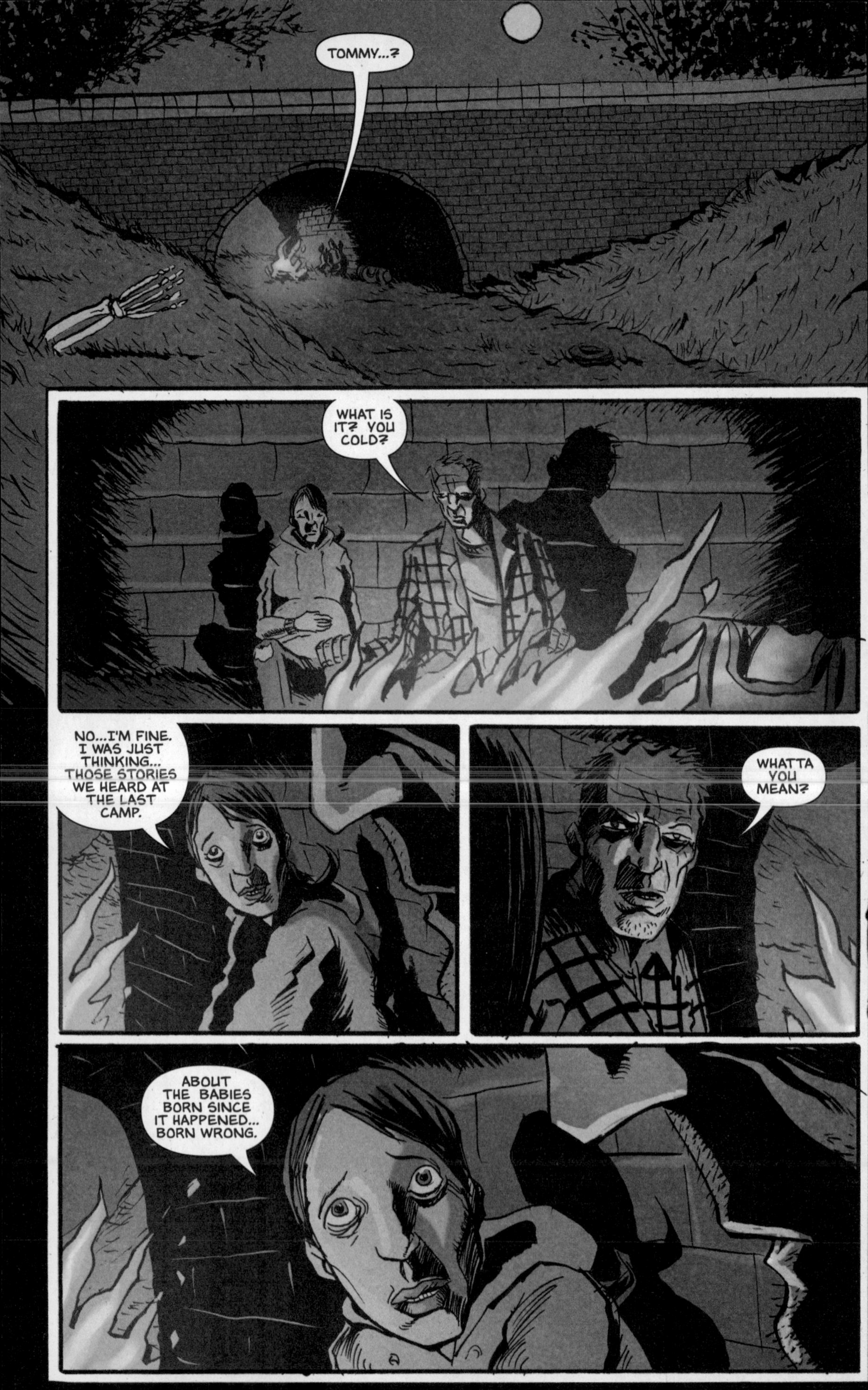
TOMMY...?
WHAT IS IT? YOU COLD?
NO...I'M FINE. I WAS JUST THINKING... THOSE STORIES WE HEARD AT THE LAST CAMP.
WHATTA YOU MEAN?
ABOUT THE BABIES BORN SINCE IT HAPPENED... BORN WRONG.

LOUISE, YOU DON'T REALLY BELIEVE THAT NONSENSE, DO YA?

NO...I DON'T KNOW. I KNOW IT'S SILLY, BUT THEY SAID THEY SAW A LITTLE GIRL BORN WITH A TAIL AND FUR ALL OVER HER.

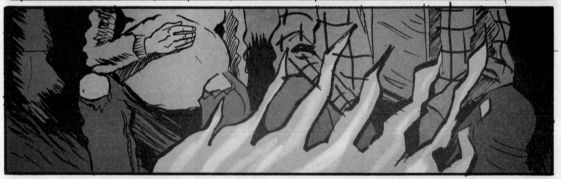

HA HA HA!

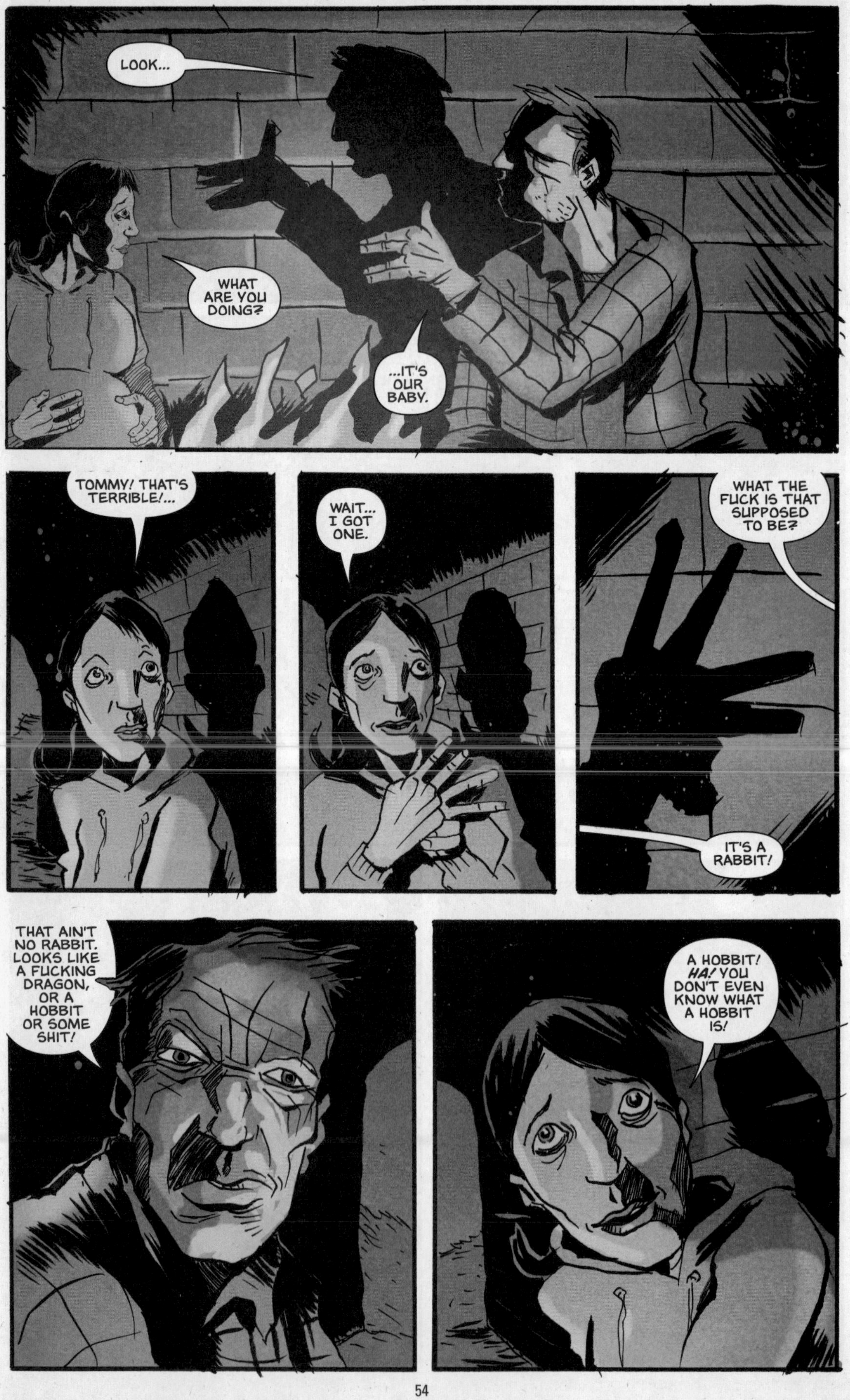
LOOK...
WHAT ARE YOU DOING?
...IT'S OUR BABY.
TOMMY! THAT'S TERRIBLE!...
WAIT... I GOT ONE.
WHAT THE FUCK IS THAT SUPPOSED TO BE?
IT'S A RABBIT!
THAT AIN'T NO RABBIT. LOOKS LIKE A FUCKING DRAGON, OR A HOBBIT OR SOME SHIT!
A HOBBIT! HA! YOU DON'T EVEN KNOW WHAT A HOBBIT IS!

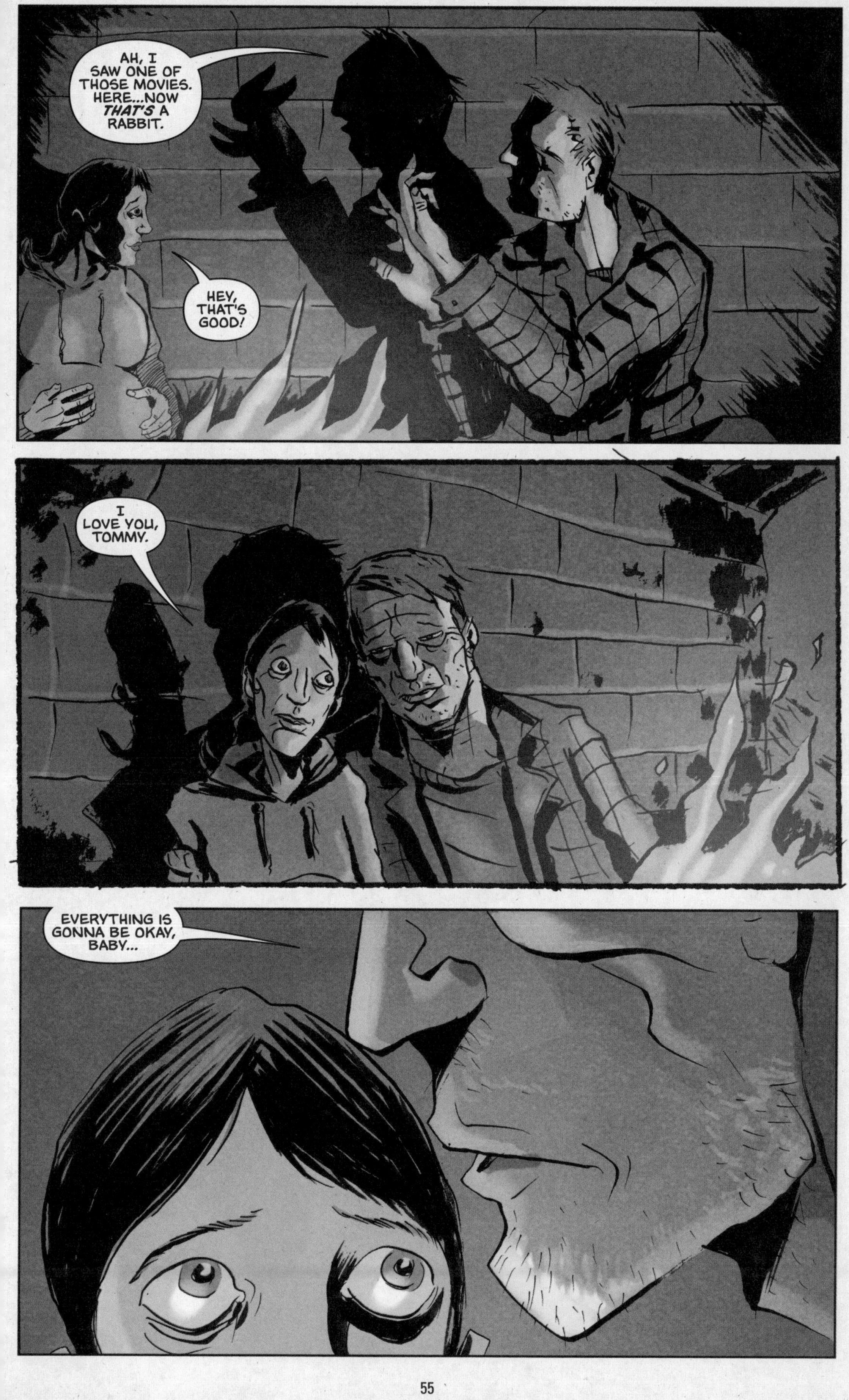
AH, I SAW ONE OF THOSE MOVIES. HERE...NOW *THAT'S* A RABBIT.
HEY, THAT'S GOOD!
I LOVE YOU, TOMMY.
EVERYTHING IS GONNA BE OKAY, BABY...

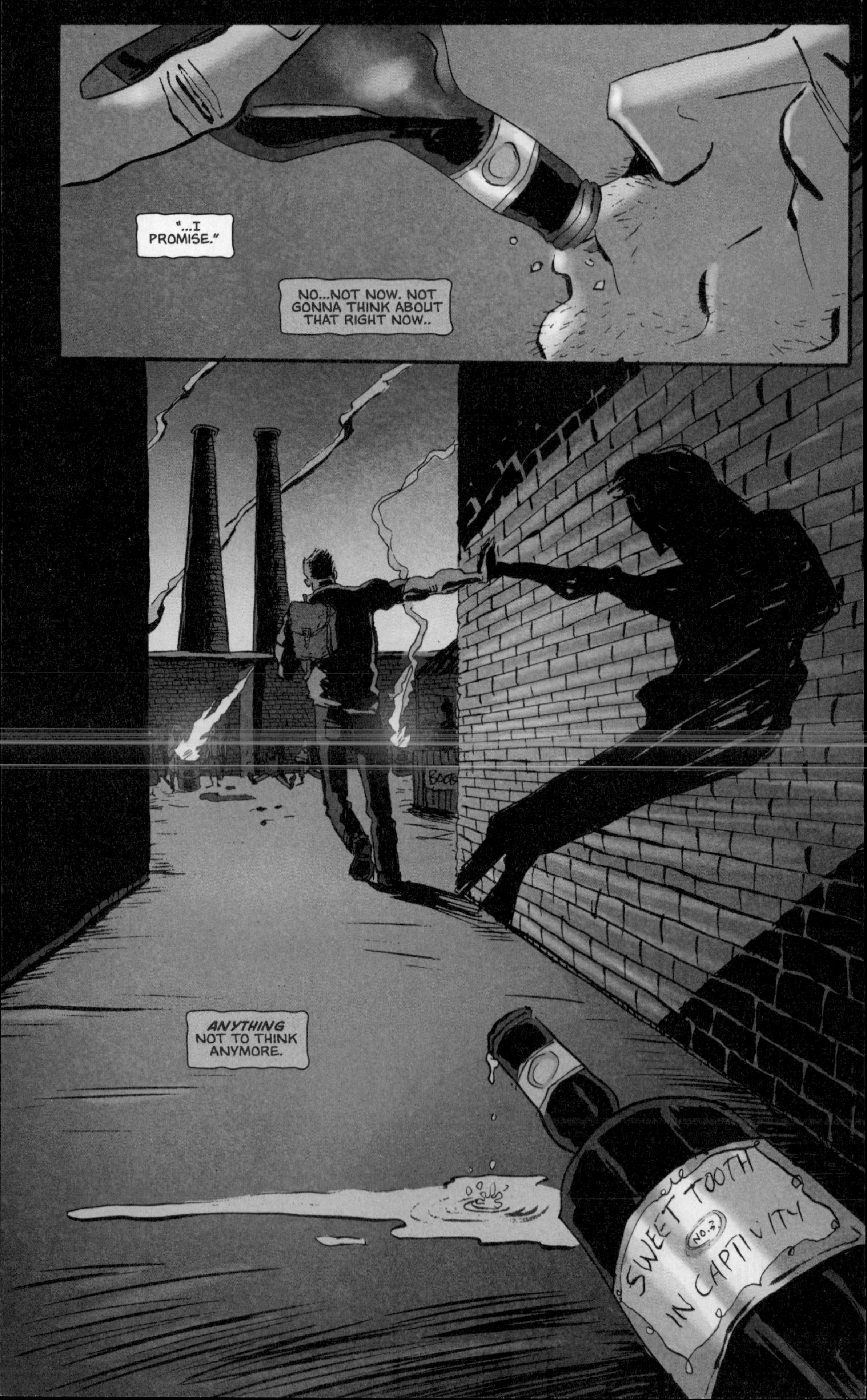
"...I PROMISE."
NO...NOT NOW. NOT GONNA THINK ABOUT THAT RIGHT NOW..
ANYTHING NOT TO THINK ANYMORE.
SWEET TOOTH
NO.3
IN CAPTIVITY

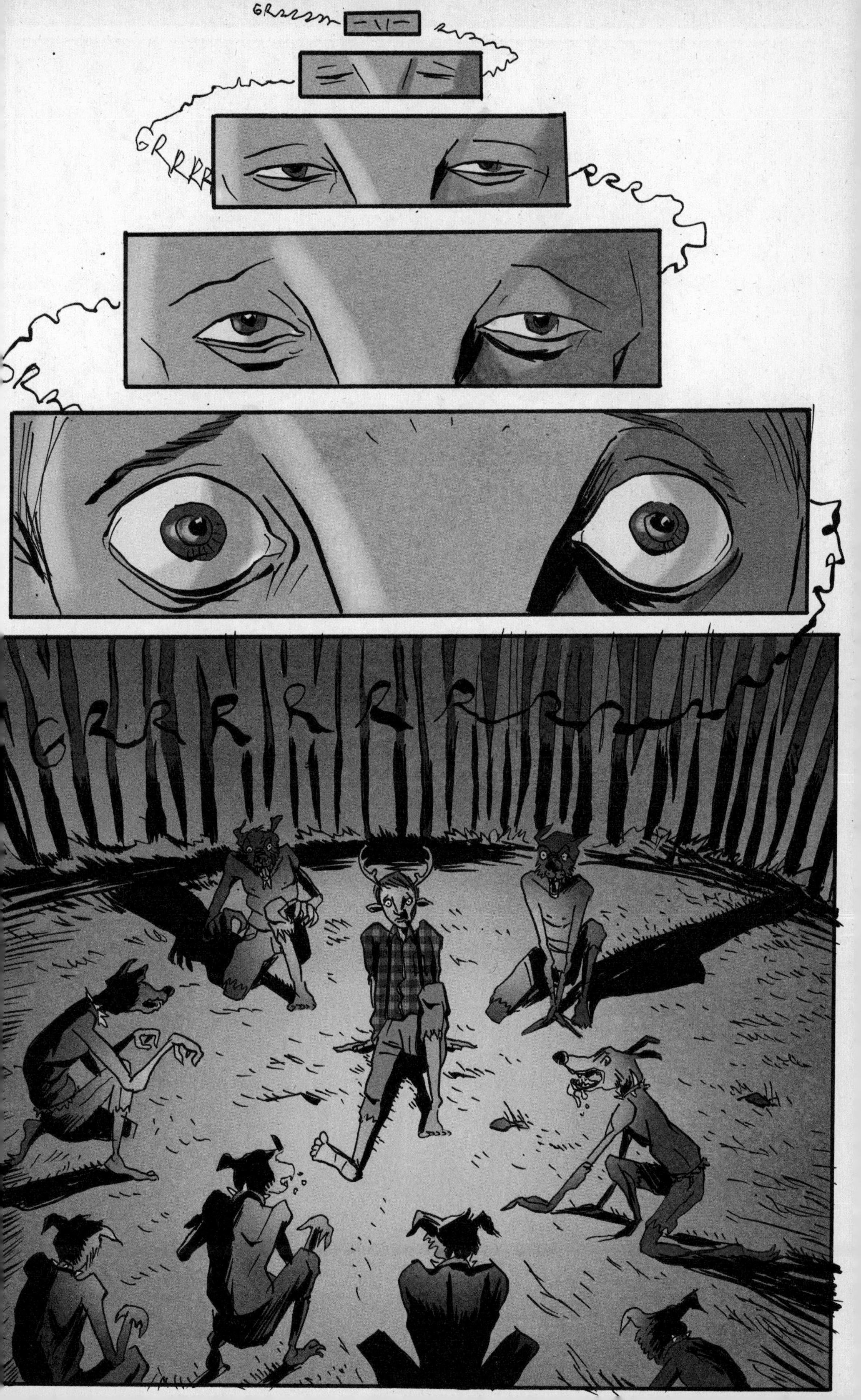
GRRRRR
GRRRRRR

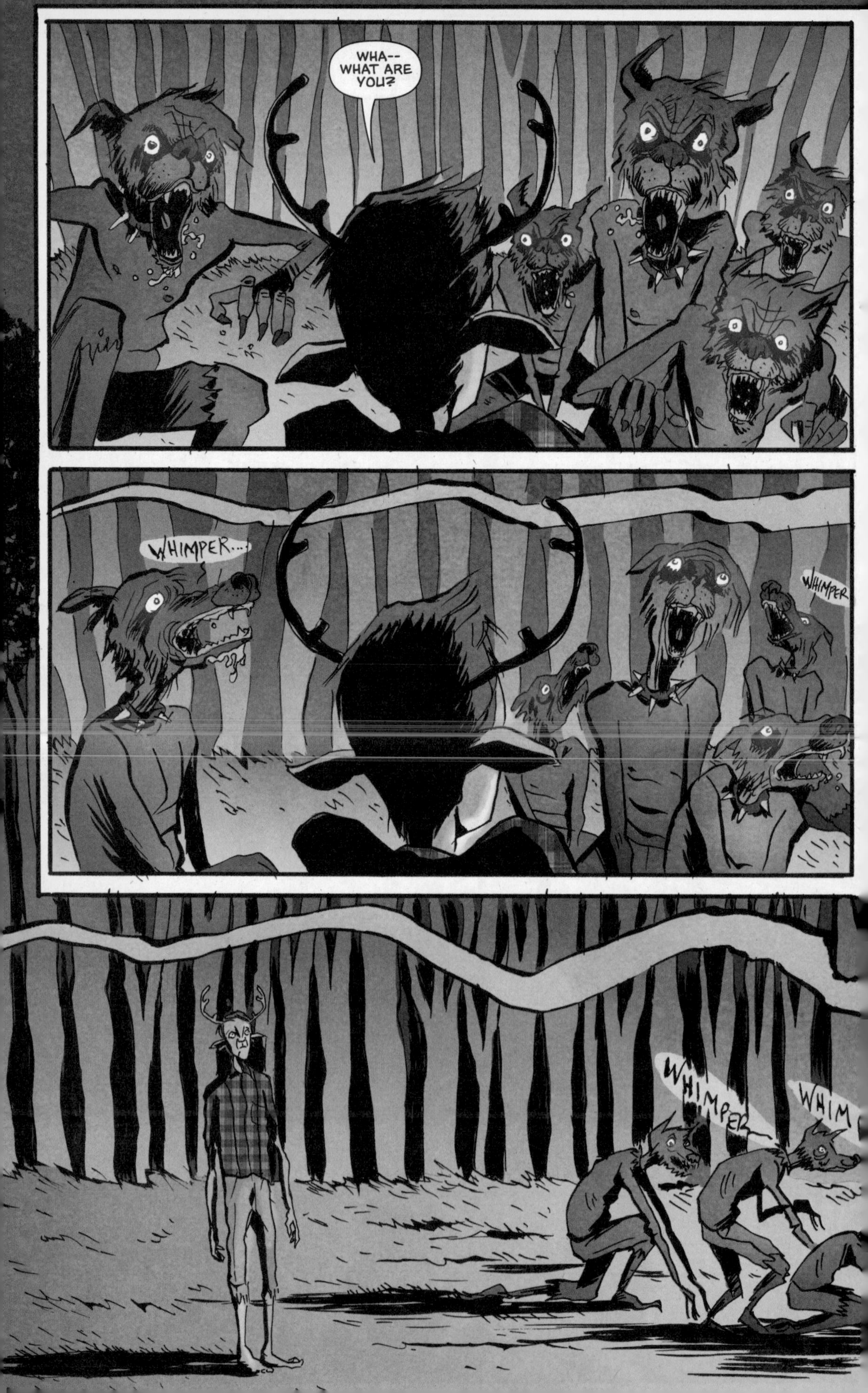
WHA--
WHAT ARE
YOU?
WHIMPER...
WHIMPER
WHIMPER
WHIM

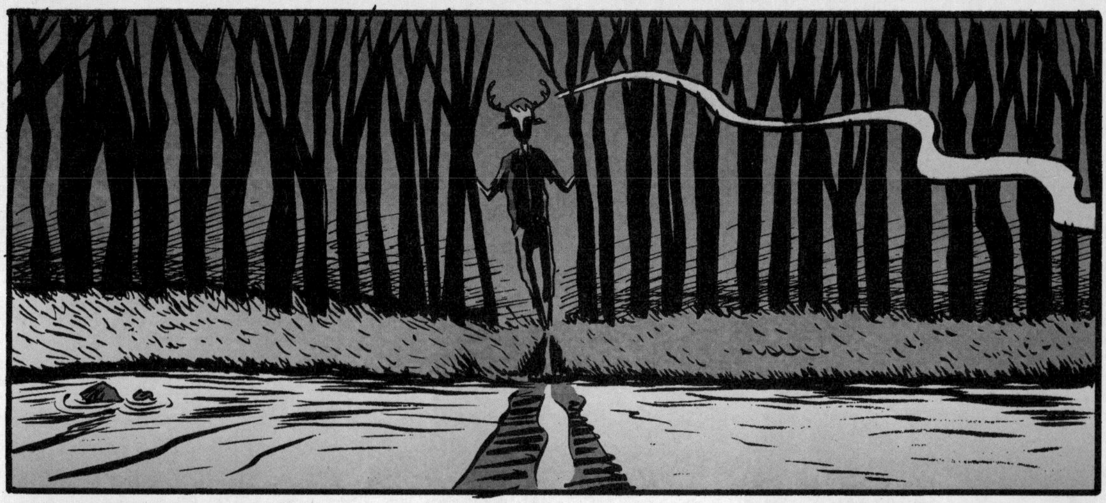

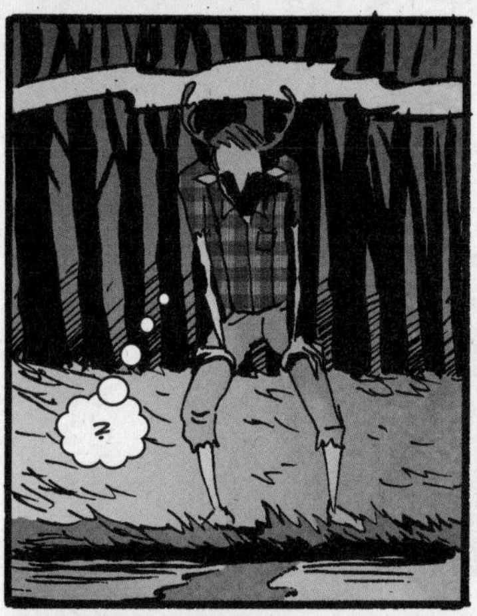

?

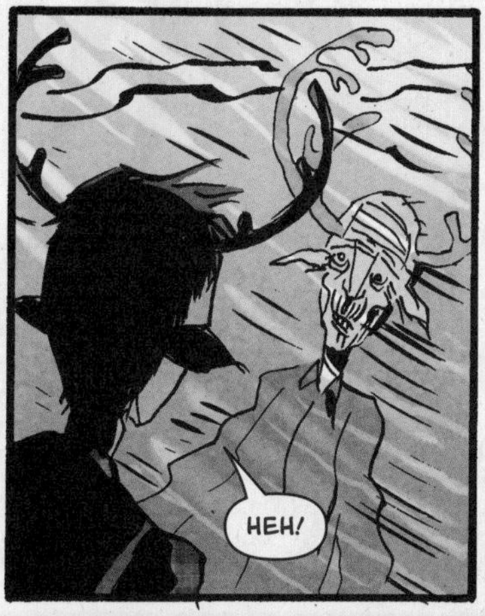

HEH!

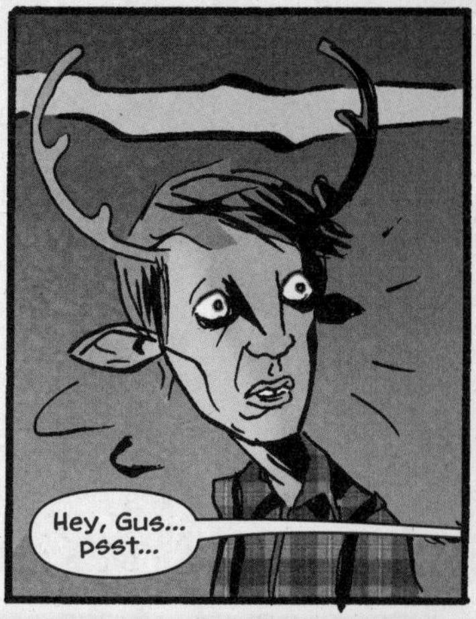

Hey, Gus... psst...

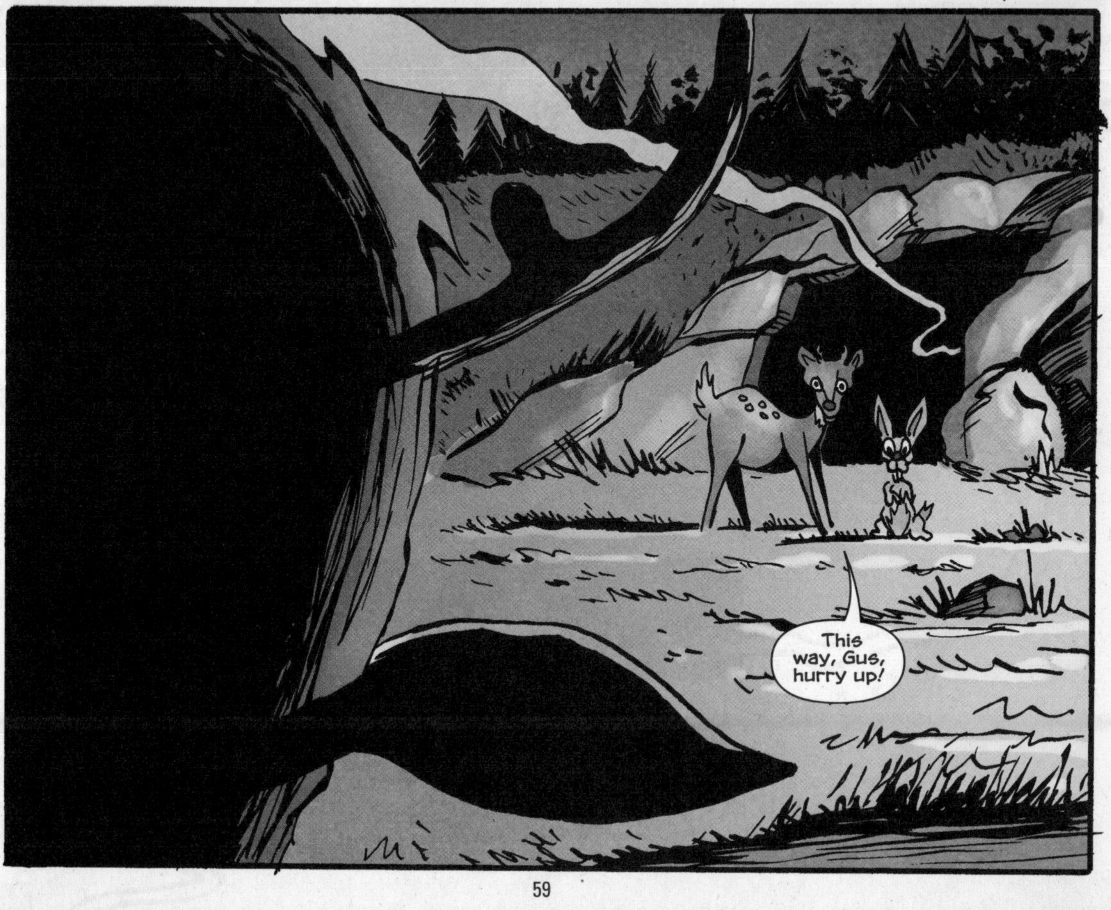

This way, Gus, hurry up!

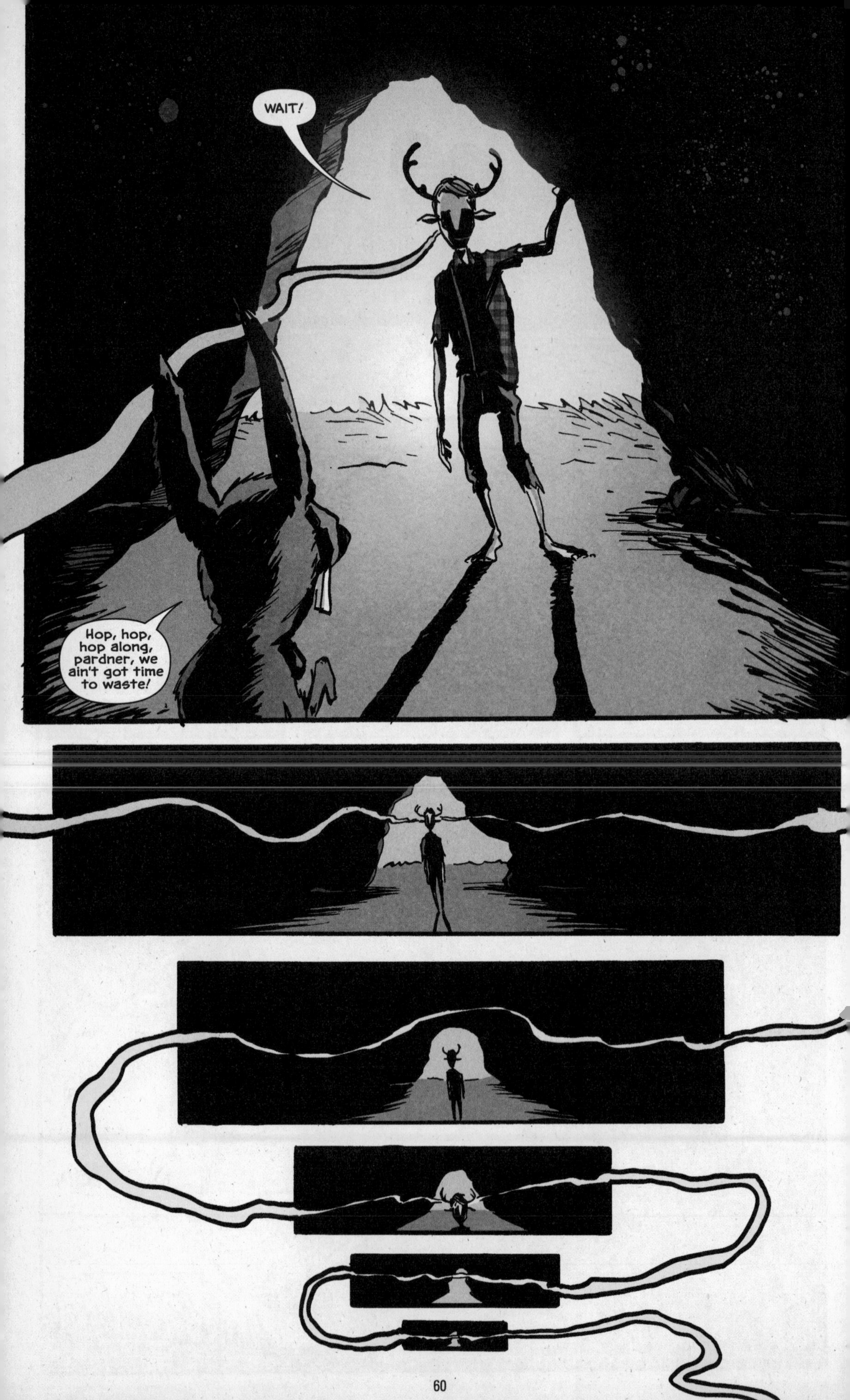
WAIT!
Hop, hop, hop along, pardner, we ain't got time to waste!

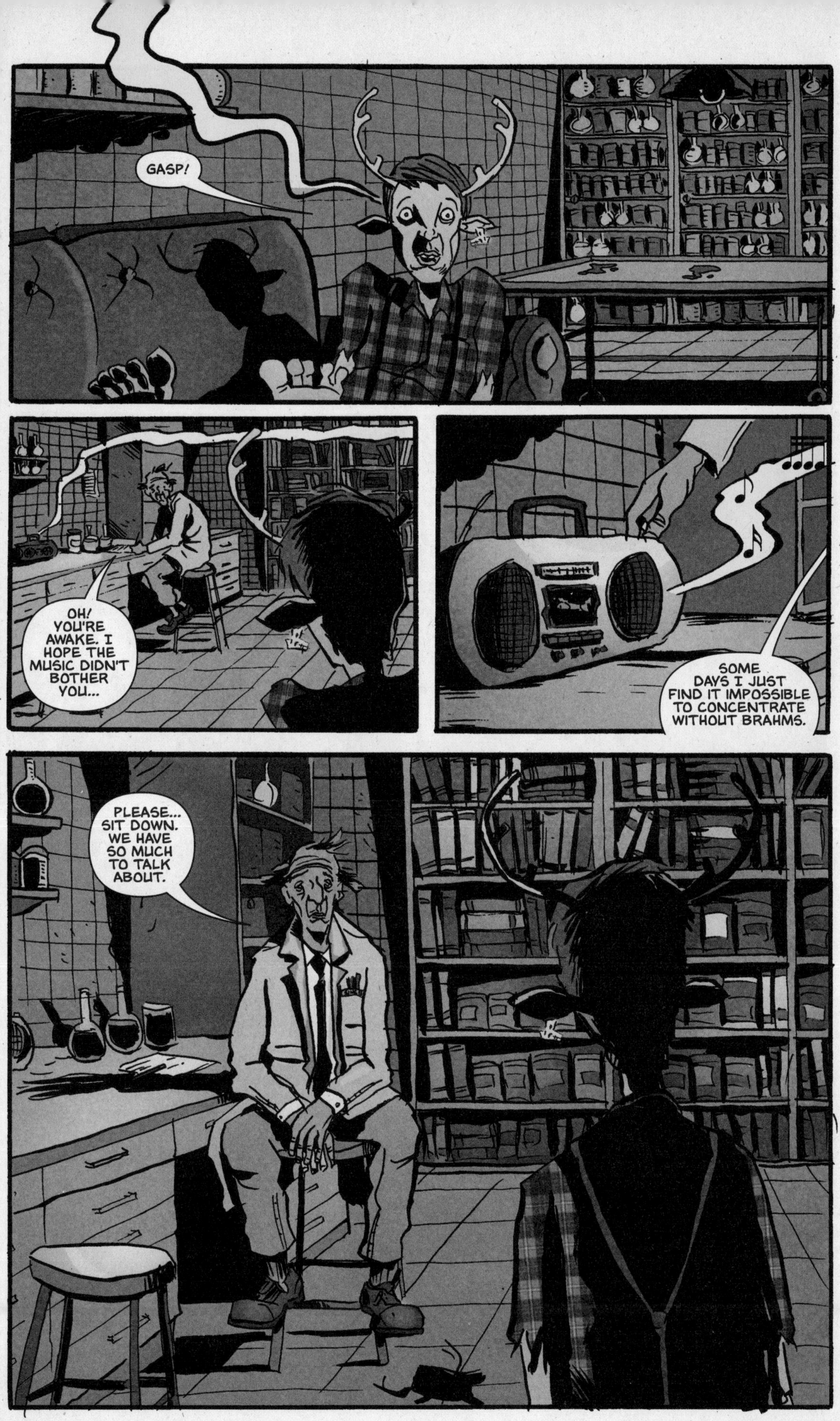
GASP!
OH! YOU'RE AWAKE. I HOPE THE MUSIC DIDN'T BOTHER YOU...
SOME DAYS I JUST FIND IT IMPOSSIBLE TO CONCENTRATE WITHOUT BRAHMS.
PLEASE... SIT DOWN. WE HAVE SO MUCH TO TALK ABOUT.

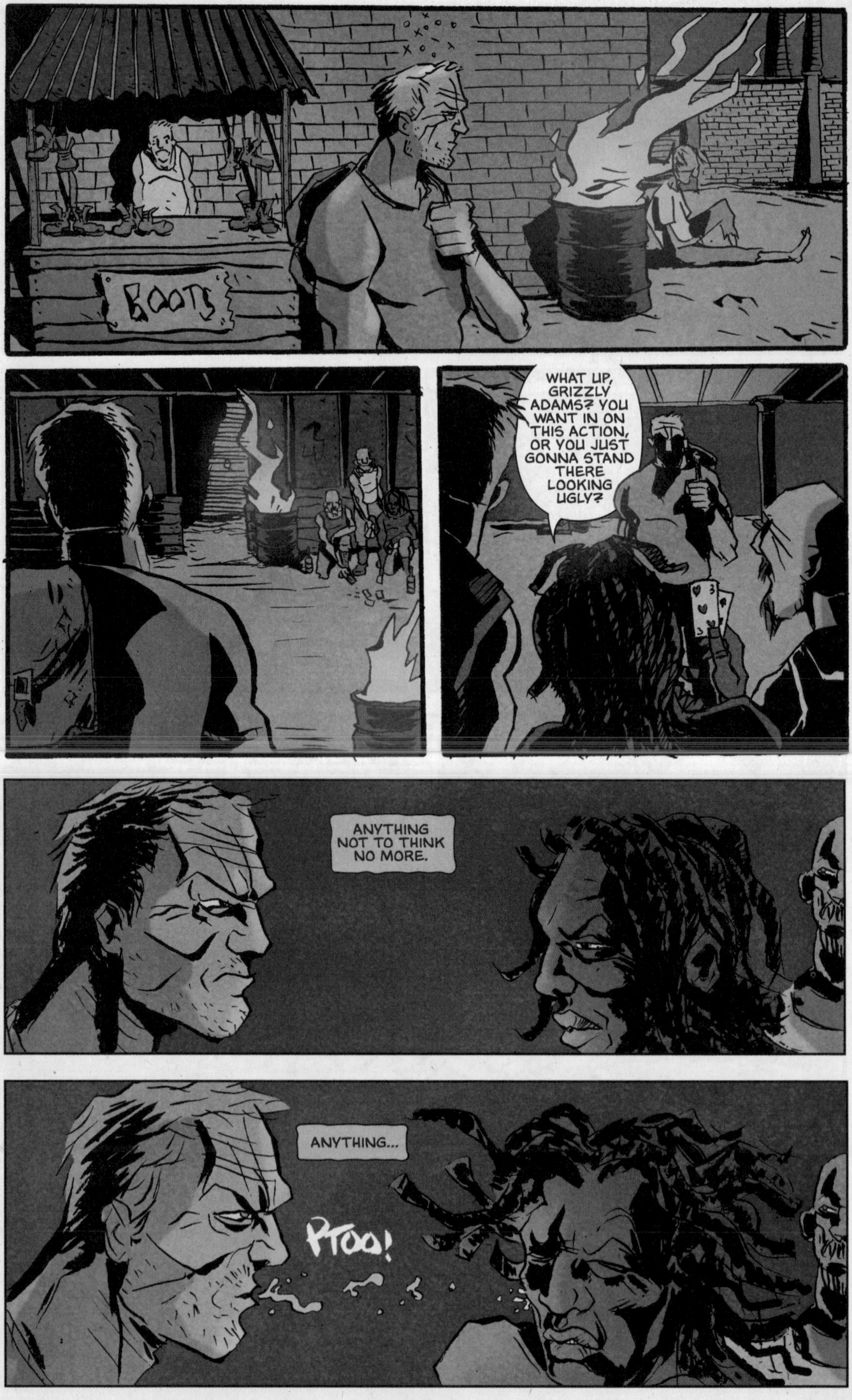
BOOTS
WHAT UP, GRIZZLY ADAMS? YOU WANT IN ON THIS ACTION, OR YOU JUST GONNA STAND THERE LOOKING UGLY?
ANYTHING NOT TO THINK NO MORE.
ANYTHING...
PTOO!

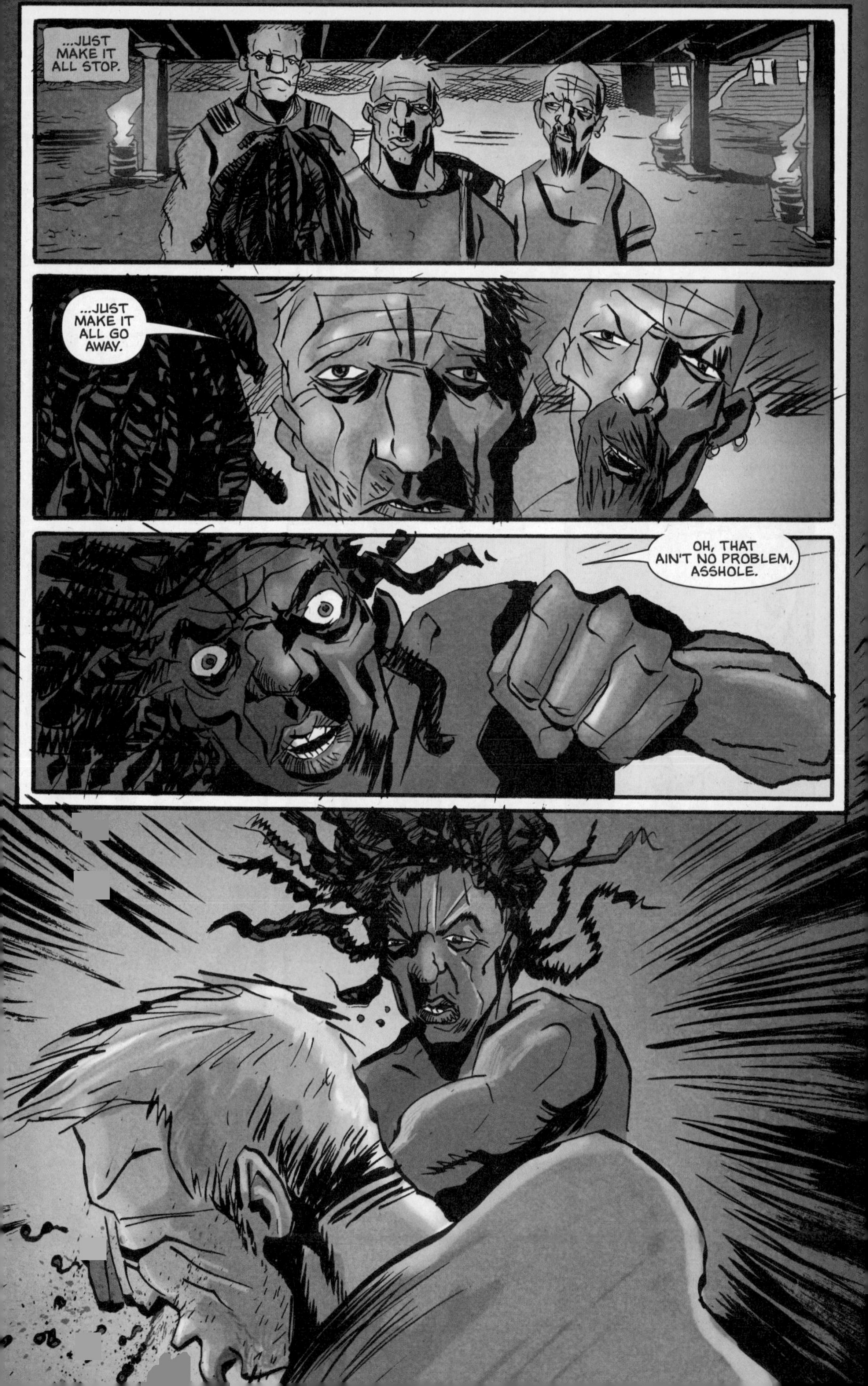
...JUST MAKE IT ALL STOP.
...JUST MAKE IT ALL GO AWAY.
OH, THAT AIN'T NO PROBLEM, ASSHOLE.

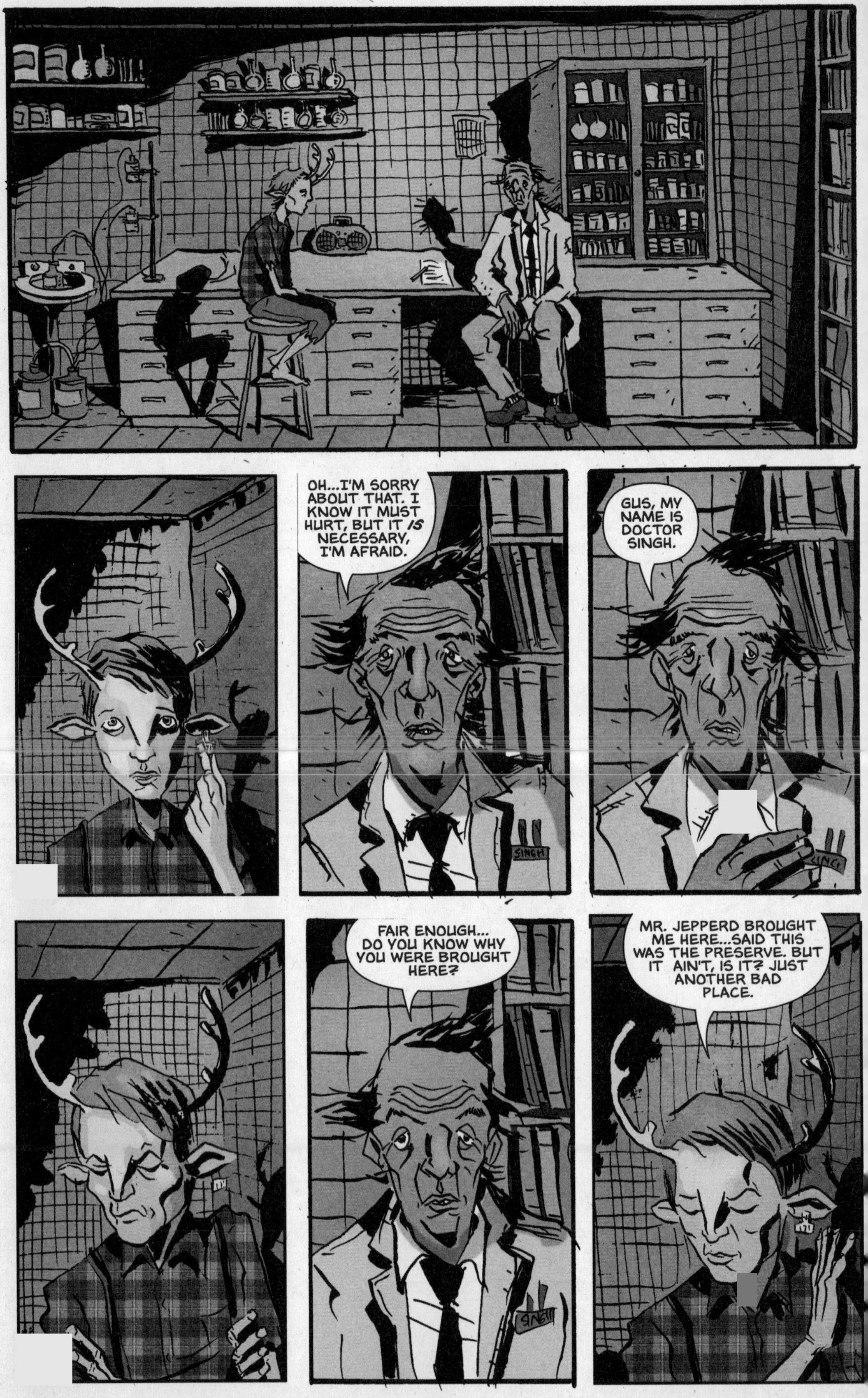
OH...I'M SORRY ABOUT THAT. I KNOW IT MUST HURT, BUT IT *IS* NECESSARY, I'M AFRAID.
GUS, MY NAME IS DOCTOR SINGH.
SINGH
FAIR ENOUGH... DO YOU KNOW WHY YOU WERE BROUGHT HERE?
MR. JEPPERD BROUGHT ME HERE...SAID THIS WAS THE PRESERVE. BUT IT AIN'T, IS IT? JUST ANOTHER BAD PLACE.

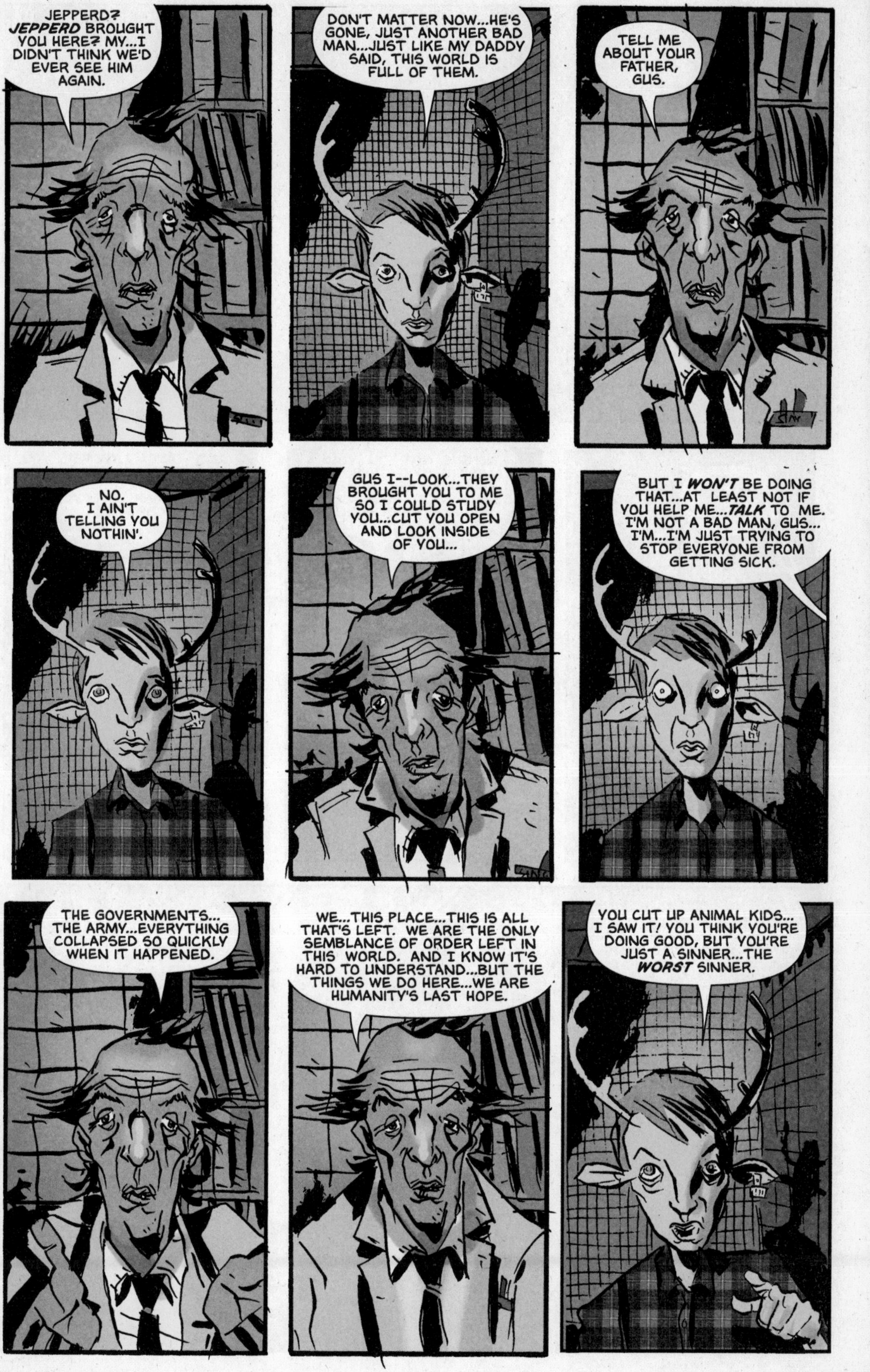
JEPPERD? *JEPPERD* BROUGHT YOU HERE? MY...I DIDN'T THINK WE'D EVER SEE HIM AGAIN.
DON'T MATTER NOW...HE'S GONE, JUST ANOTHER BAD MAN...JUST LIKE MY DADDY SAID, THIS WORLD IS FULL OF THEM.
TELL ME ABOUT YOUR FATHER, GUS.
NO. I AIN'T TELLING YOU NOTHIN'.
GUS I--LOOK...THEY BROUGHT YOU TO ME SO I COULD STUDY YOU...CUT YOU OPEN AND LOOK INSIDE OF YOU...
BUT I *WON'T* BE DOING THAT...AT LEAST NOT IF YOU HELP ME...*TALK* TO ME. I'M NOT A BAD MAN, GUS... I'M...I'M JUST TRYING TO STOP EVERYONE FROM GETTING SICK.
THE GOVERNMENTS... THE ARMY...EVERYTHING COLLAPSED SO QUICKLY WHEN IT HAPPENED.
WE...THIS PLACE...THIS IS ALL THAT'S LEFT. WE ARE THE ONLY SEMBLANCE OF ORDER LEFT IN THIS WORLD. AND I KNOW IT'S HARD TO UNDERSTAND...BUT THE THINGS WE DO HERE...WE ARE HUMANITY'S LAST HOPE.
YOU CUT UP ANIMAL KIDS... I SAW IT! YOU THINK YOU'RE DOING GOOD, BUT YOU'RE JUST A SINNER...THE *WORST* SINNER.

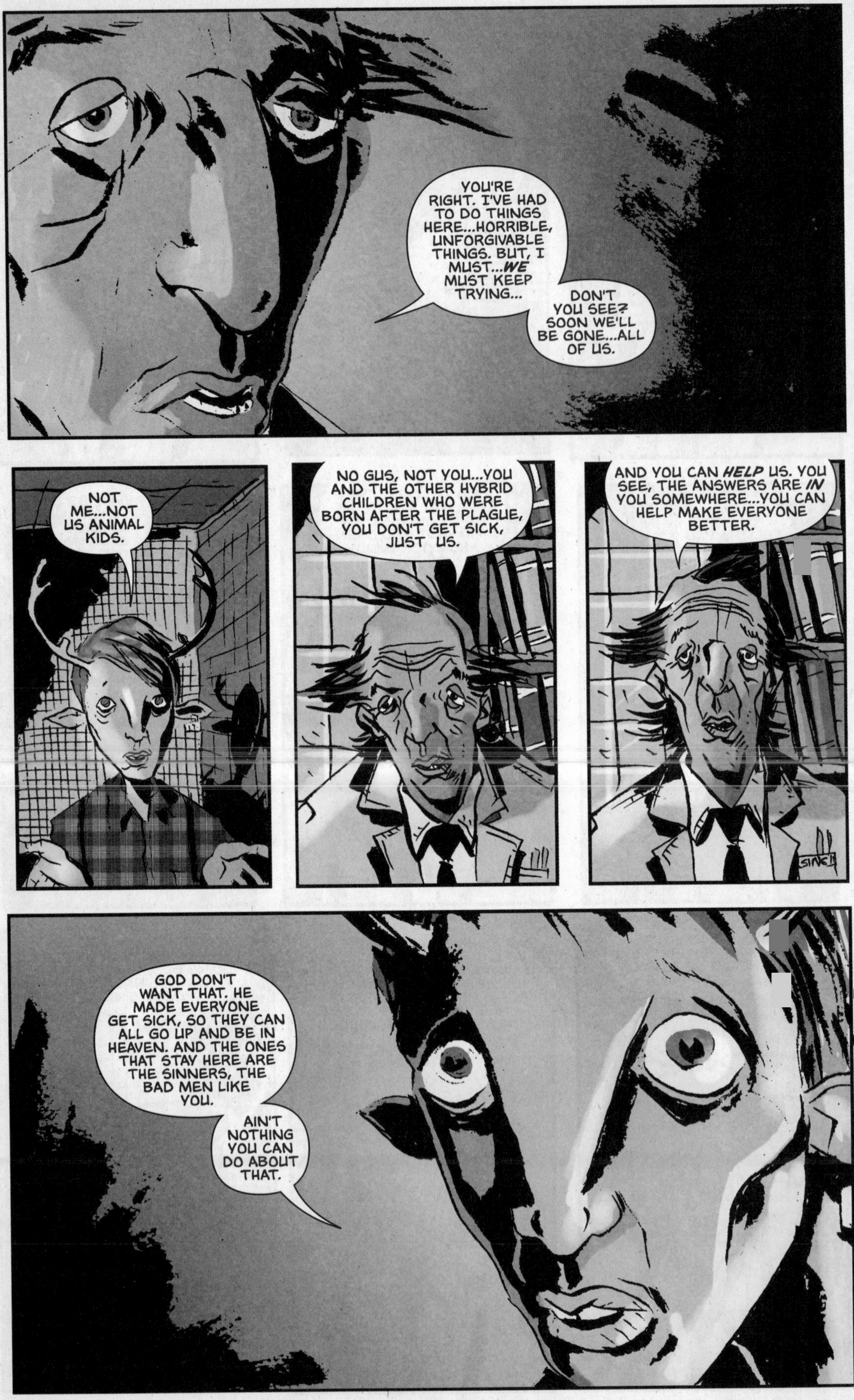
YOU'RE RIGHT. I'VE HAD TO DO THINGS HERE...HORRIBLE, UNFORGIVABLE THINGS. BUT, I MUST...*WE* MUST KEEP TRYING...
DON'T YOU SEE? SOON WE'LL BE GONE...ALL OF US.
NOT ME...NOT US ANIMAL KIDS.
NO GUS, NOT YOU...YOU AND THE OTHER HYBRID CHILDREN WHO WERE BORN AFTER THE PLAGUE, YOU DON'T GET SICK, JUST US.
AND YOU CAN *HELP* US. YOU SEE, THE ANSWERS ARE *IN* YOU SOMEWHERE...YOU CAN HELP MAKE EVERYONE BETTER.
GOD DON'T WANT THAT. HE MADE EVERYONE GET SICK, SO THEY CAN ALL GO UP AND BE IN HEAVEN. AND THE ONES THAT STAY HERE ARE THE SINNERS, THE BAD MEN LIKE YOU.
AIN'T NOTHING YOU CAN DO ABOUT THAT.

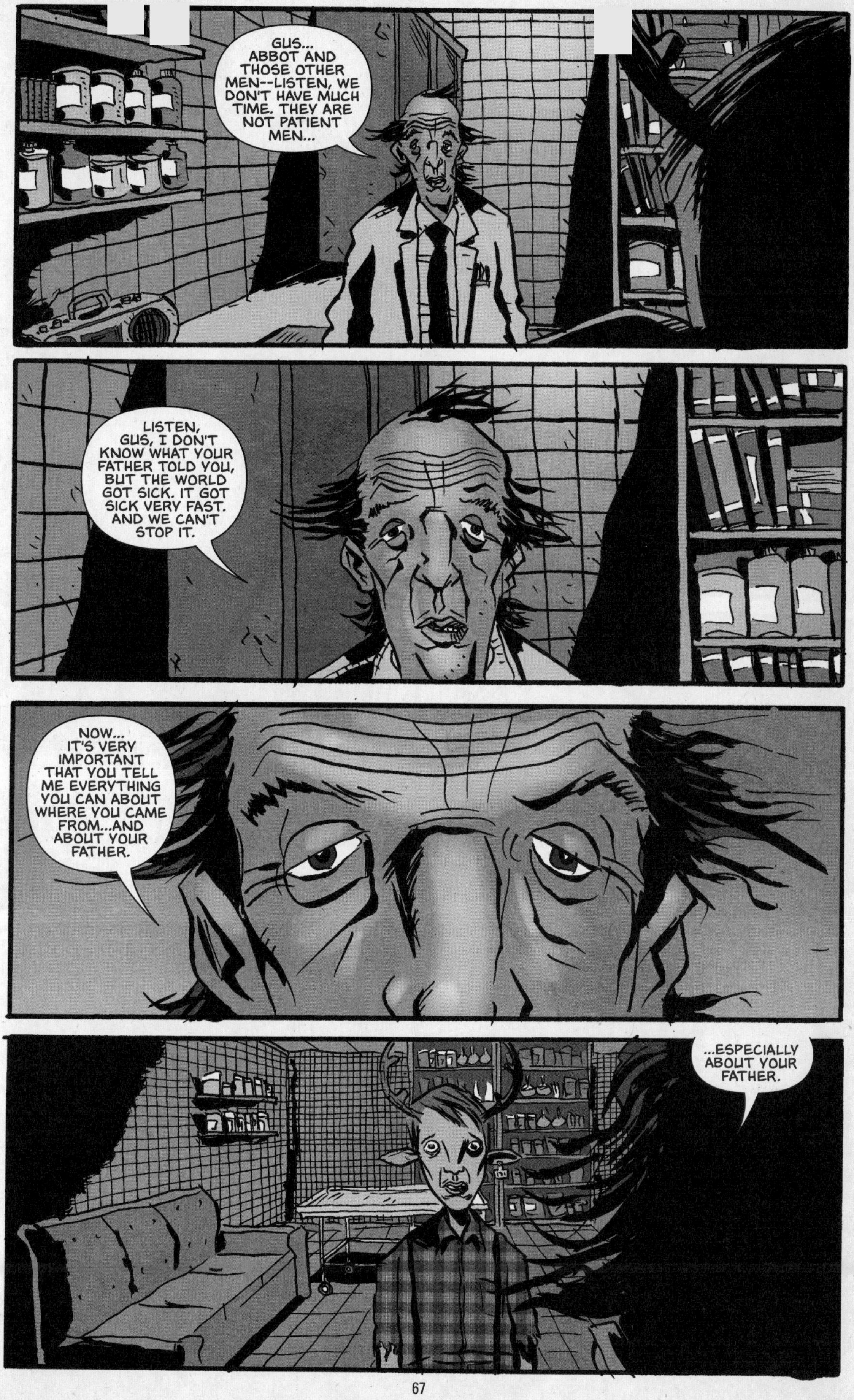
GUS... ABBOT AND THOSE OTHER MEN--LISTEN, WE DON'T HAVE MUCH TIME. THEY ARE NOT PATIENT MEN...
LISTEN, GUS, I DON'T KNOW WHAT YOUR FATHER TOLD YOU, BUT THE WORLD GOT SICK. IT GOT SICK VERY FAST. AND WE CAN'T STOP IT.
NOW... IT'S VERY IMPORTANT THAT YOU TELL ME EVERYTHING YOU CAN ABOUT WHERE YOU CAME FROM...AND ABOUT YOUR FATHER.
...ESPECIALLY ABOUT YOUR FATHER.

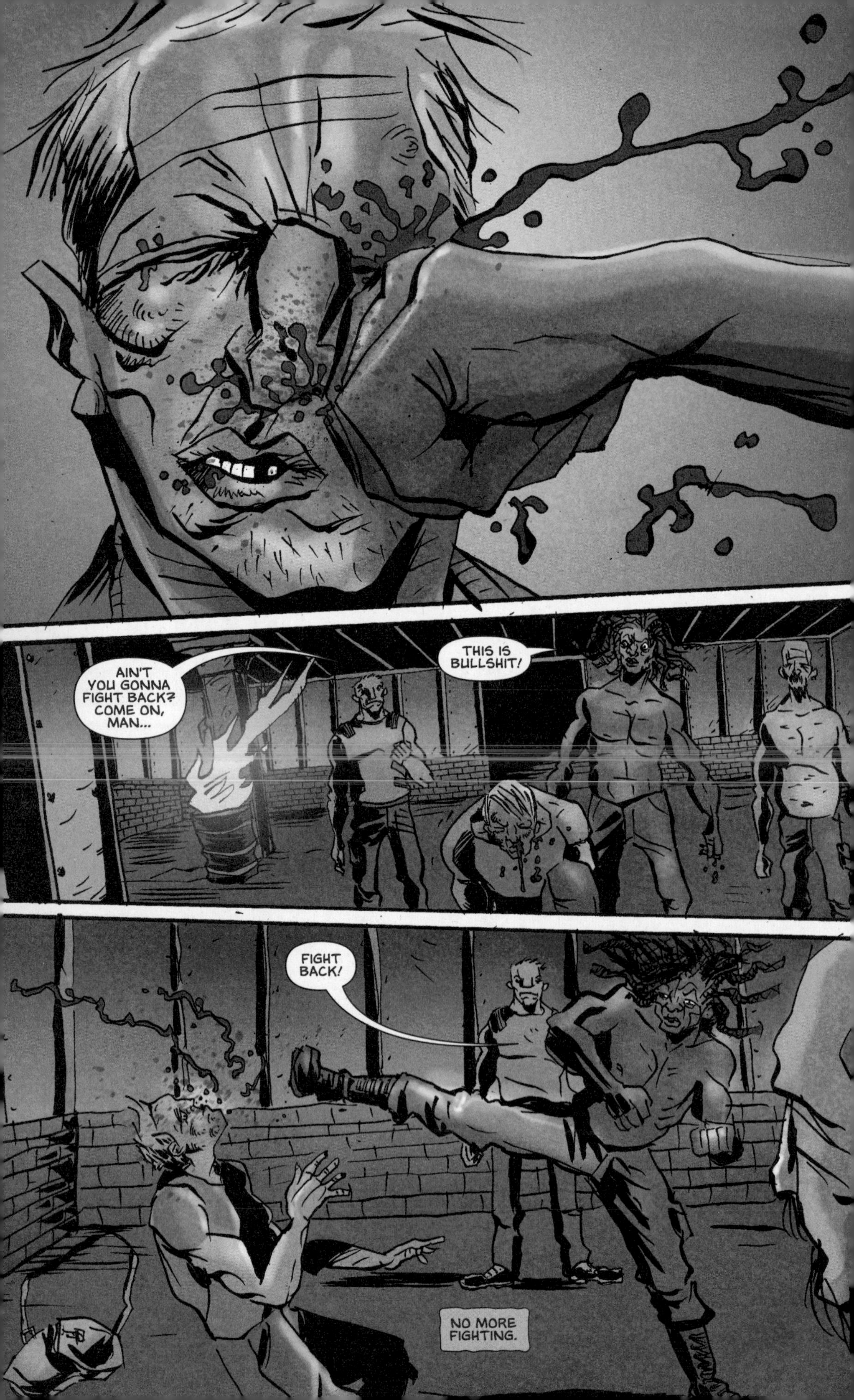
AIN'T YOU GONNA FIGHT BACK? COME ON, MAN...
THIS IS BULLSHIT!
FIGHT BACK!
NO MORE FIGHTING.

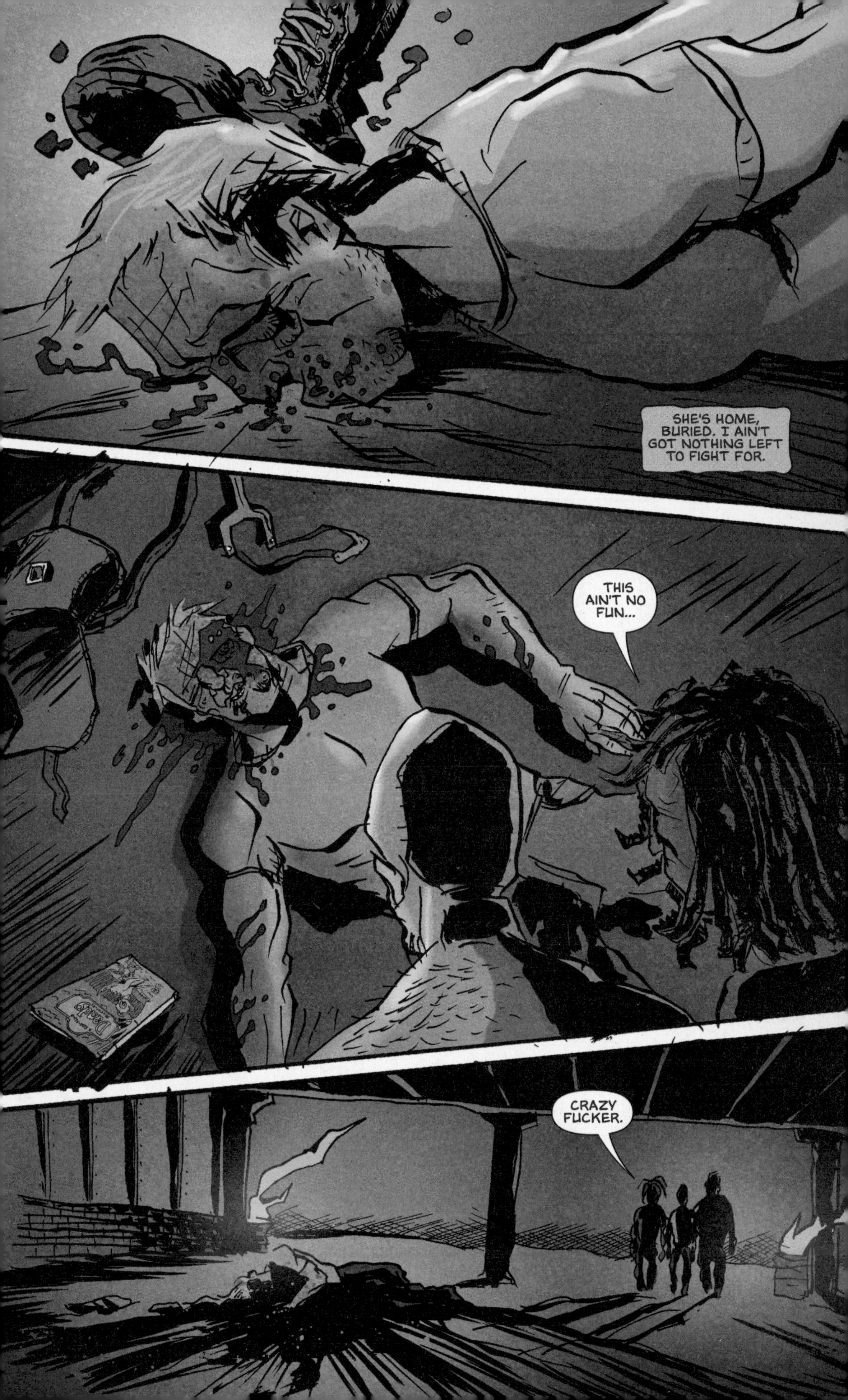
SHE'S HOME, BURIED. I AIN'T GOT NOTHING LEFT TO FIGHT FOR.
THIS AIN'T NO FUN...
CRAZY FUCKER.

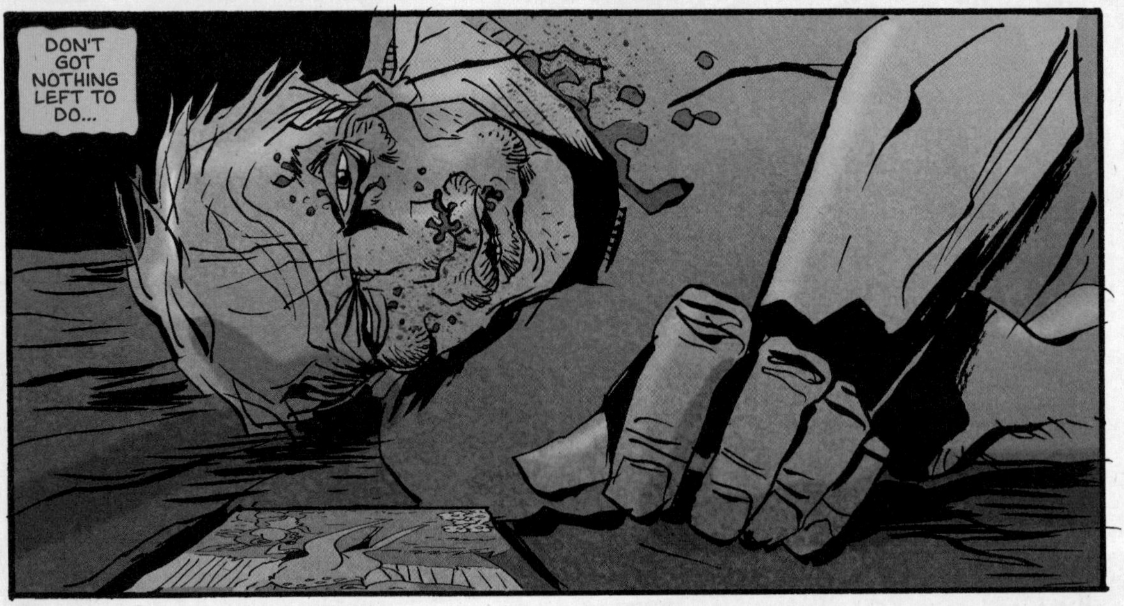
DON'T GOT NOTHING LEFT TO DO...

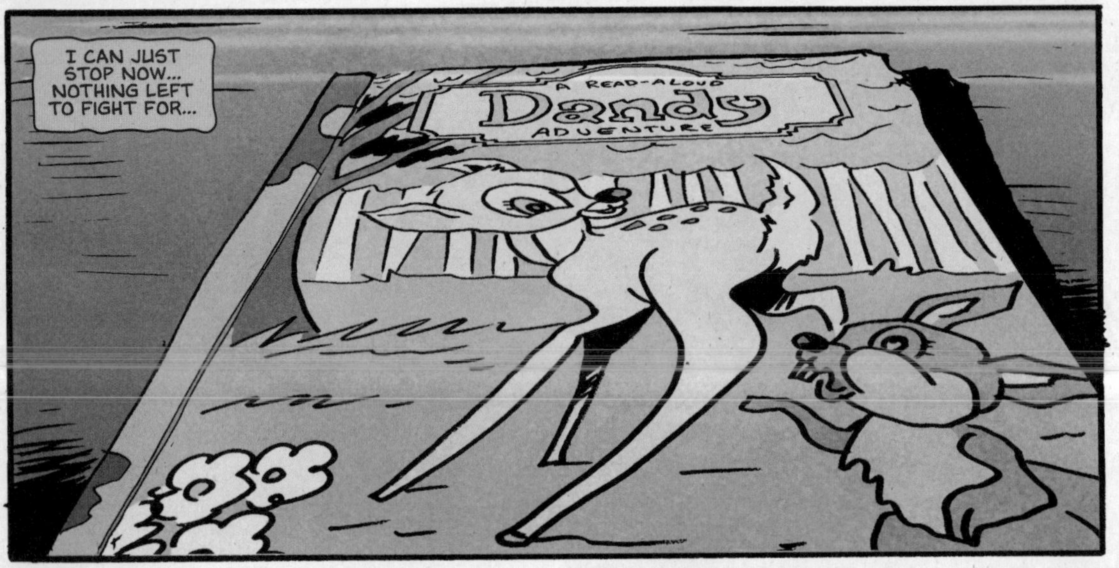
I CAN JUST STOP NOW... NOTHING LEFT TO FIGHT FOR...
A READ-ALOUD
Dandy
ADVENTURE

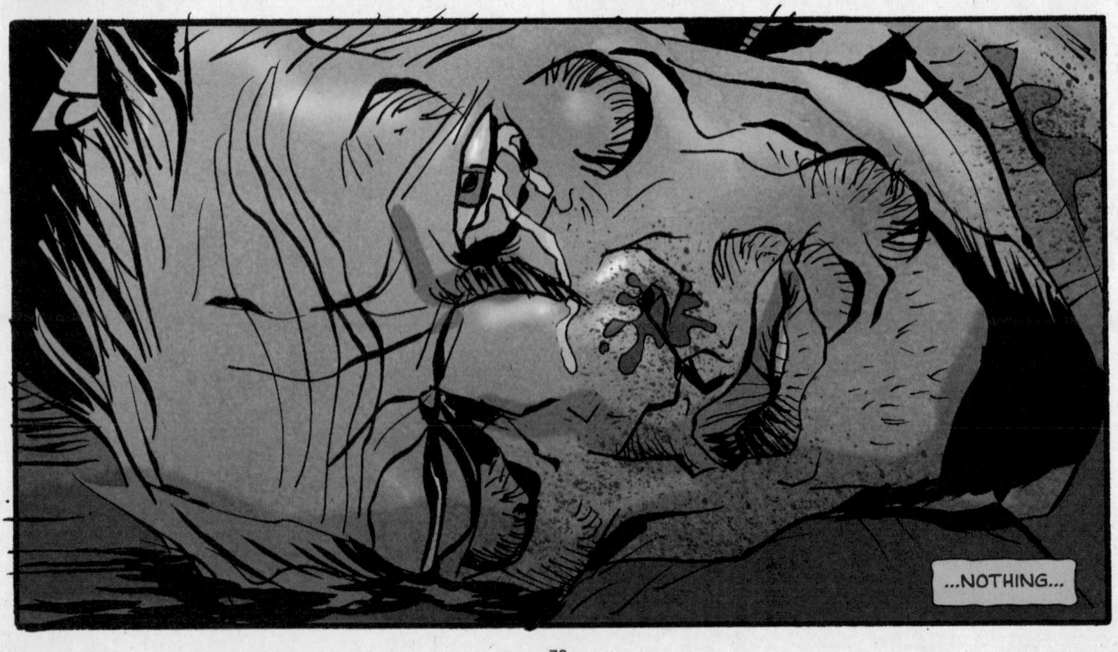
...NOTHING...

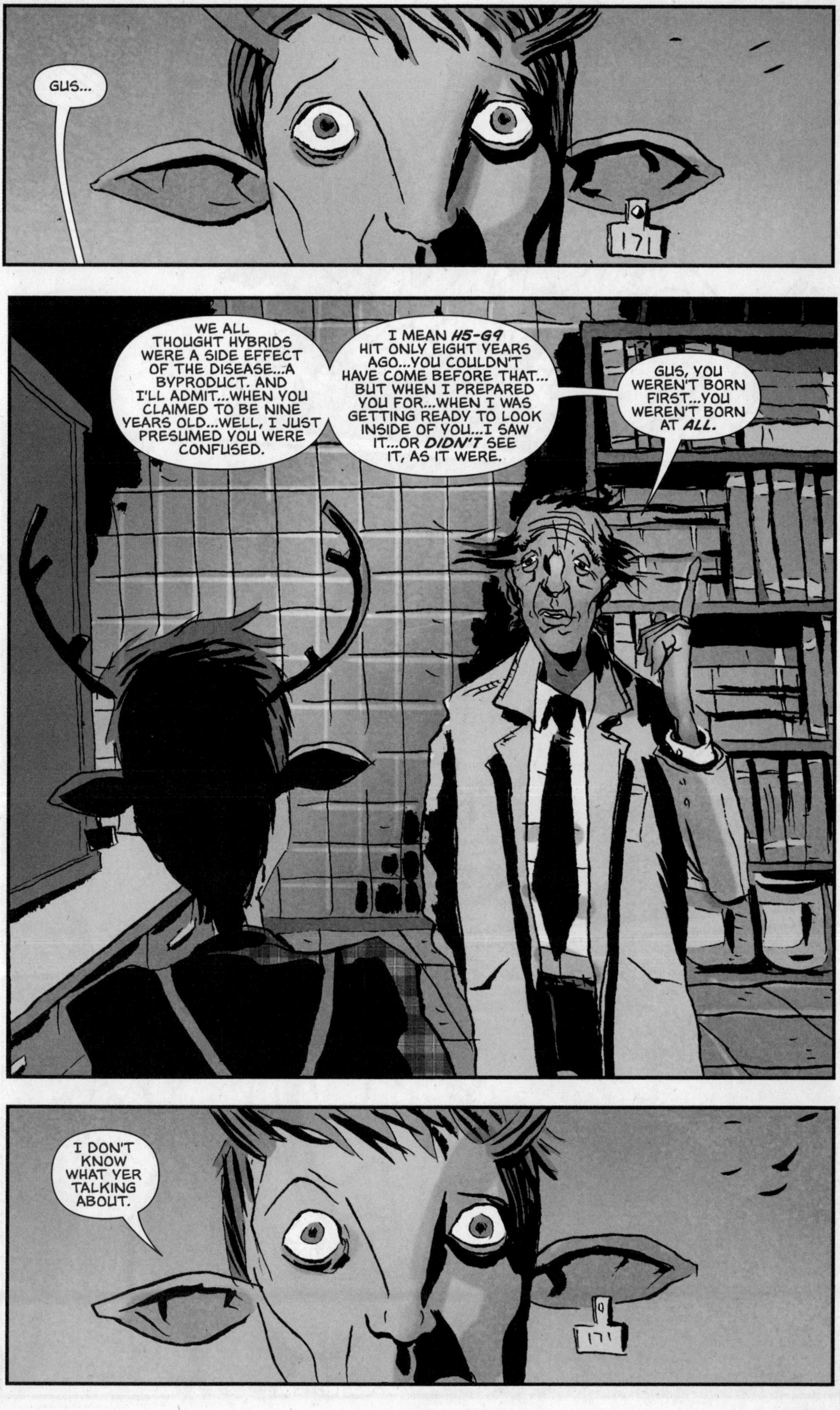
GUS...
171
WE ALL THOUGHT HYBRIDS WERE A SIDE EFFECT OF THE DISEASE...A BYPRODUCT. AND I'LL ADMIT...WHEN YOU CLAIMED TO BE NINE YEARS OLD...WELL, I JUST PRESUMED YOU WERE CONFUSED.
I MEAN *H5-G9* HIT ONLY EIGHT YEARS AGO...YOU COULDN'T HAVE COME BEFORE THAT... BUT WHEN I PREPARED YOU FOR...WHEN I WAS GETTING READY TO LOOK INSIDE OF YOU...I SAW IT...OR *DIDN'T* SEE IT, AS IT WERE.
GUS, YOU WEREN'T BORN FIRST...YOU WEREN'T BORN AT *ALL*.
I DON'T KNOW WHAT YER TALKING ABOUT.
171

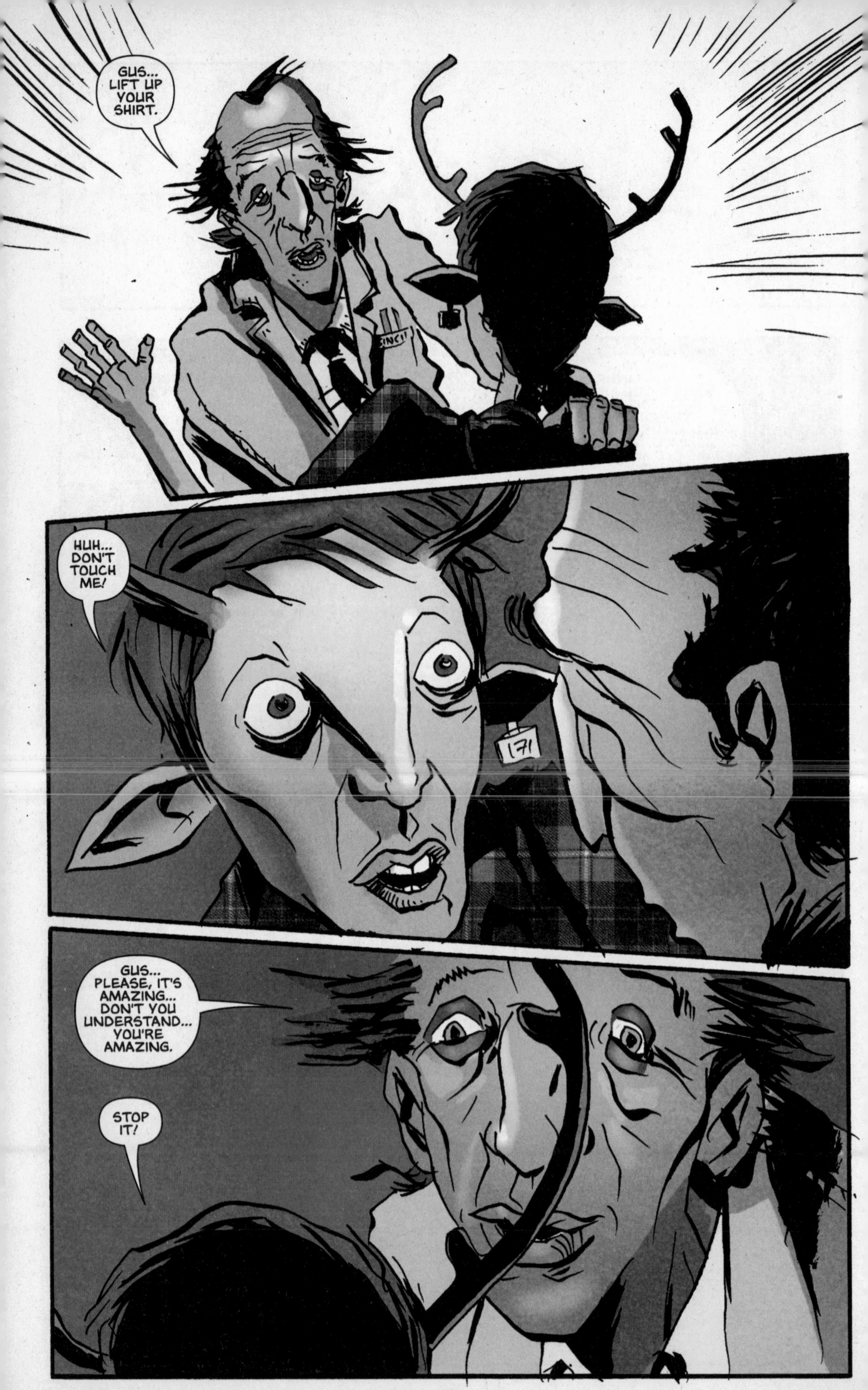

GUS... LIFT UP YOUR SHIRT.
HUH... DON'T TOUCH ME!
GUS... PLEASE, IT'S AMAZING... DON'T YOU UNDERSTAND... YOU'RE AMAZING.
STOP IT!

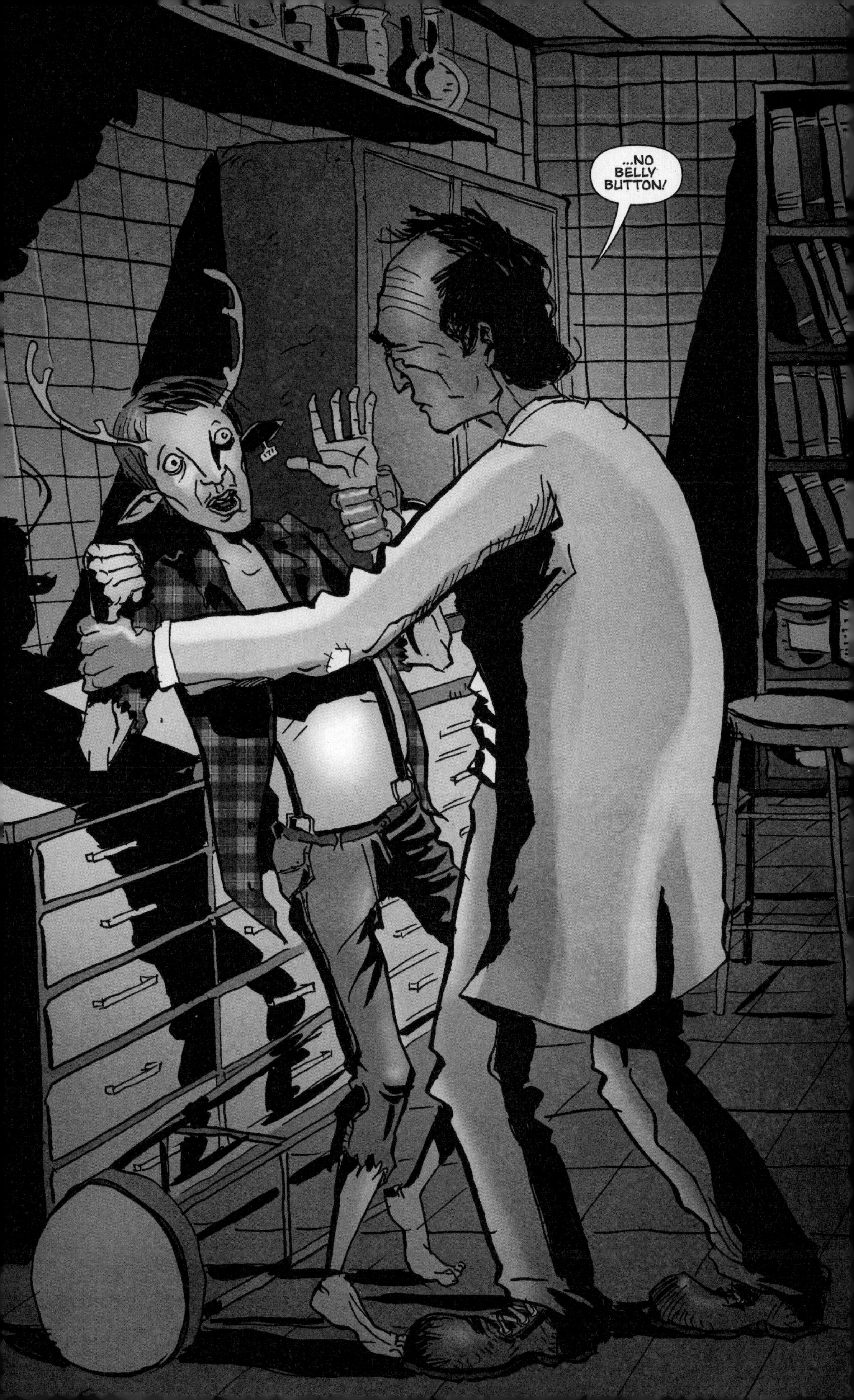
...NO BELLY BUTTON!

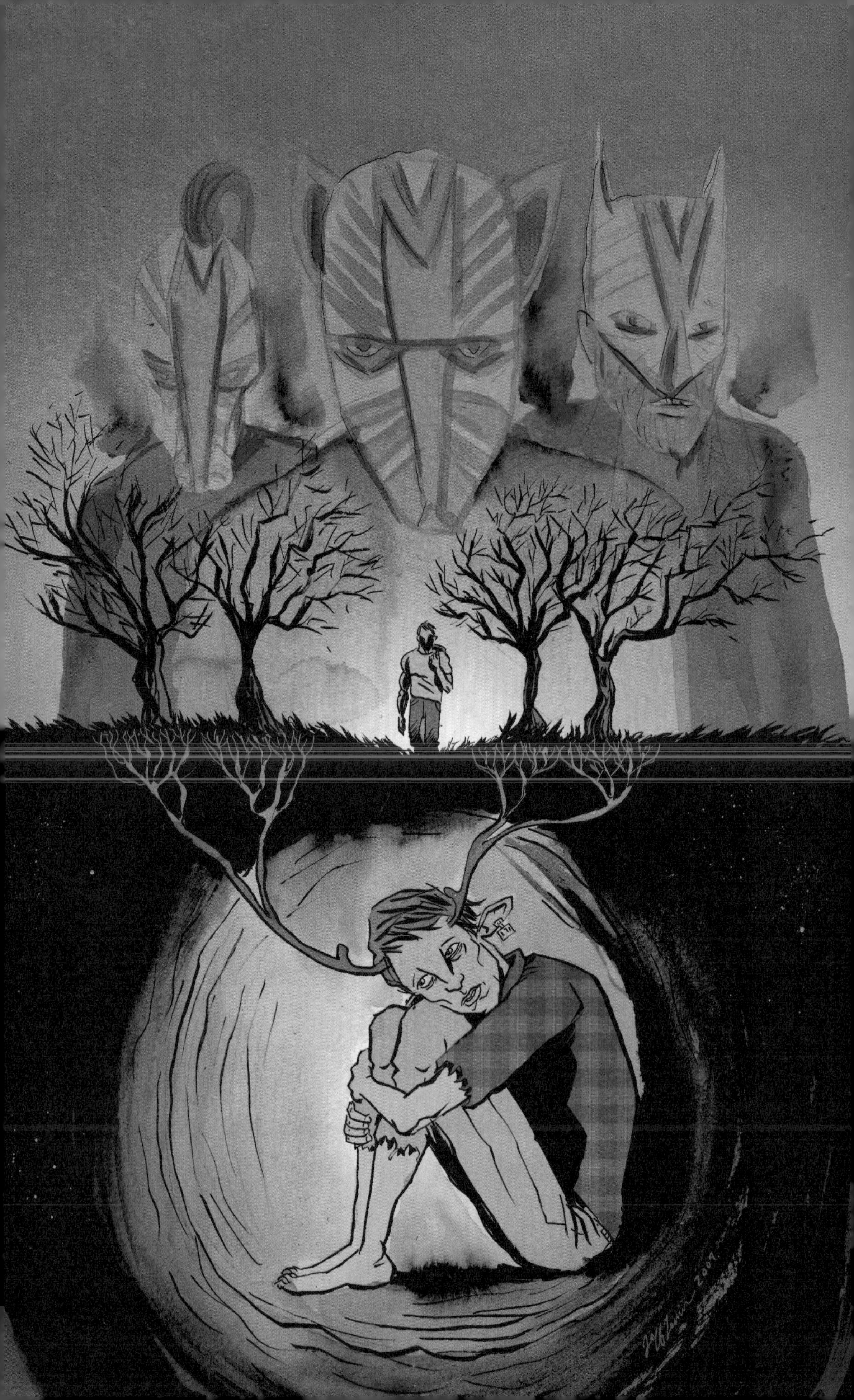

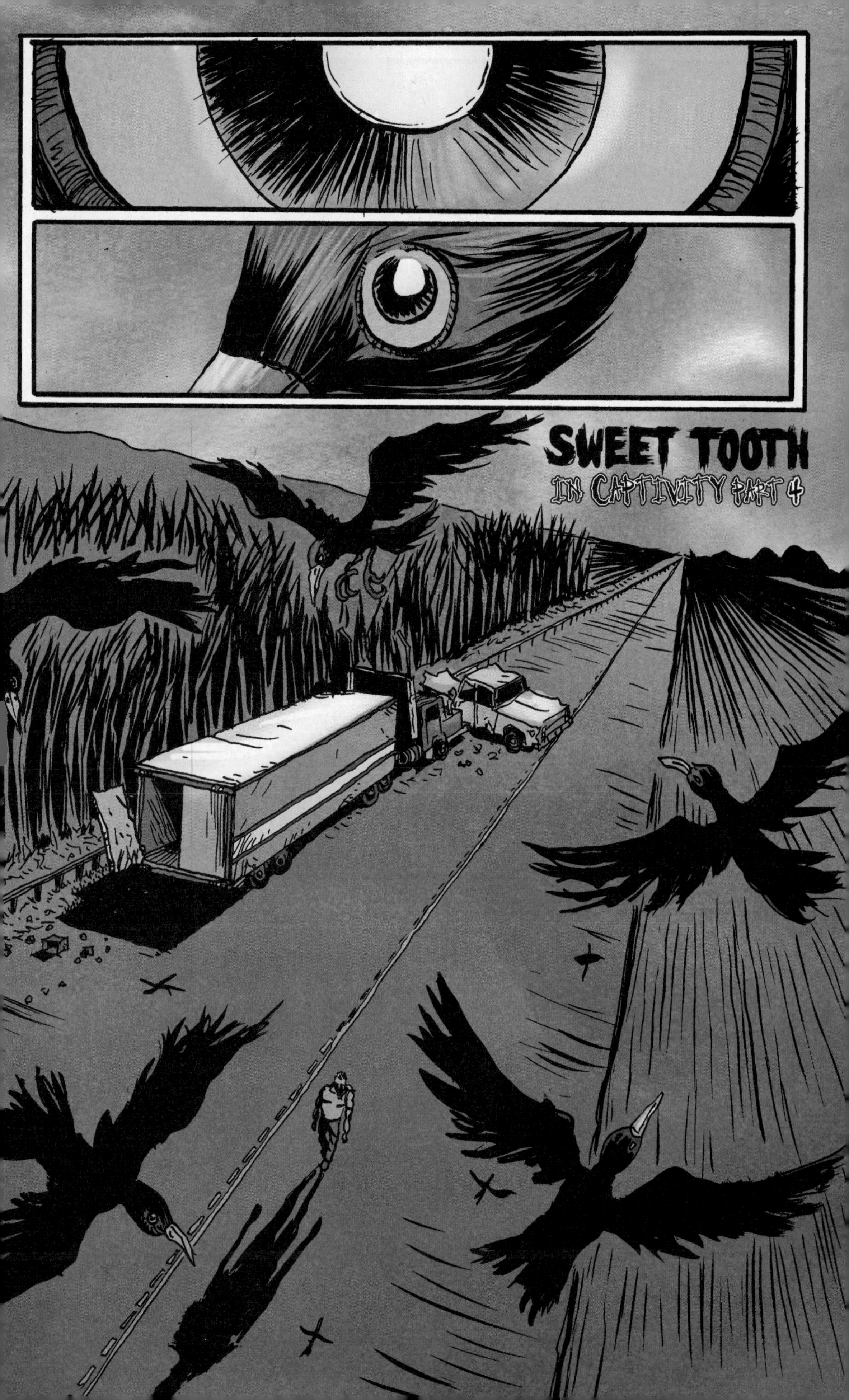
SWEET TOOTH
IN CAPTIVITY PART 4

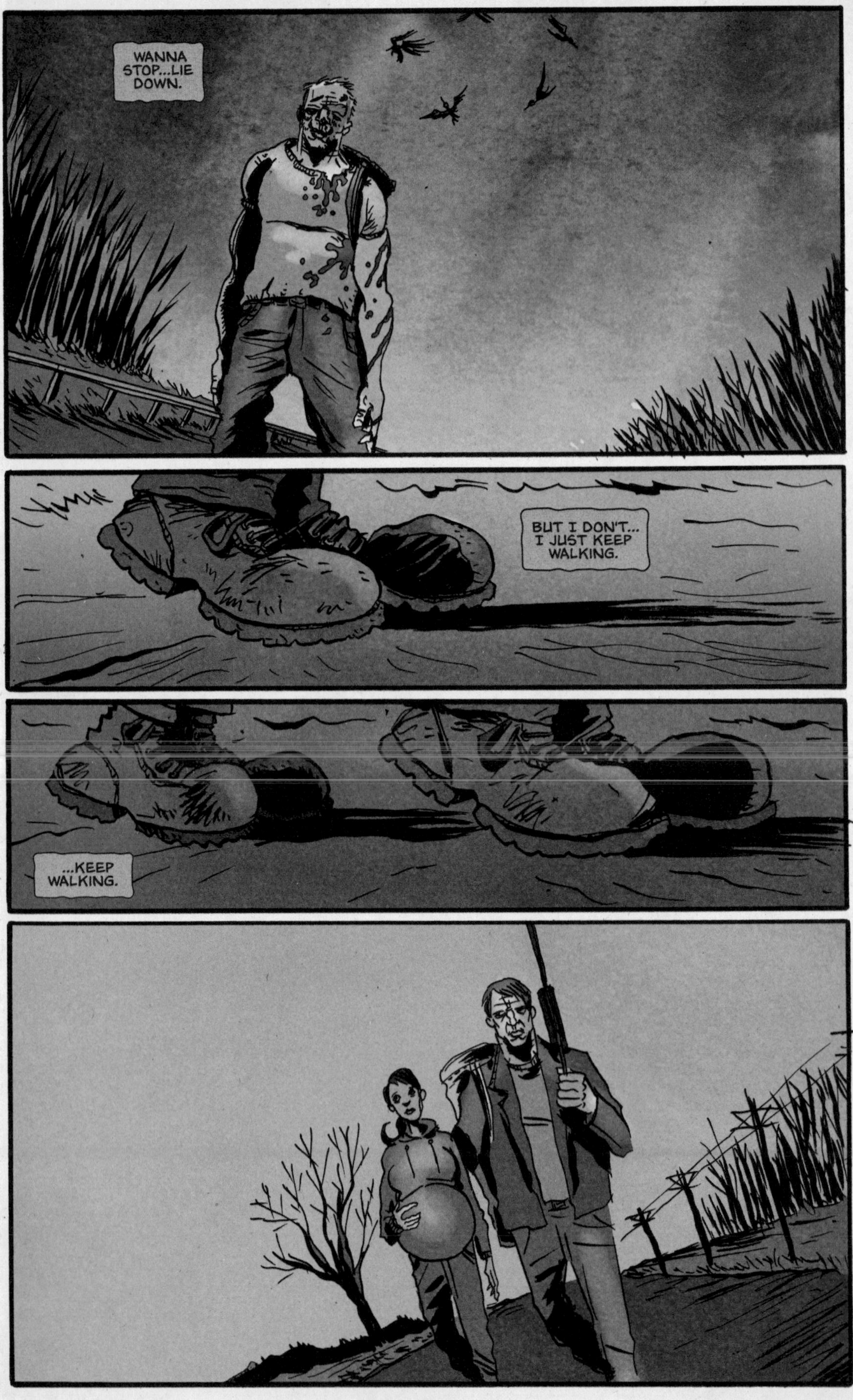
WANNA STOP...LIE DOWN.
BUT I DON'T... I JUST KEEP WALKING.
...KEEP WALKING.

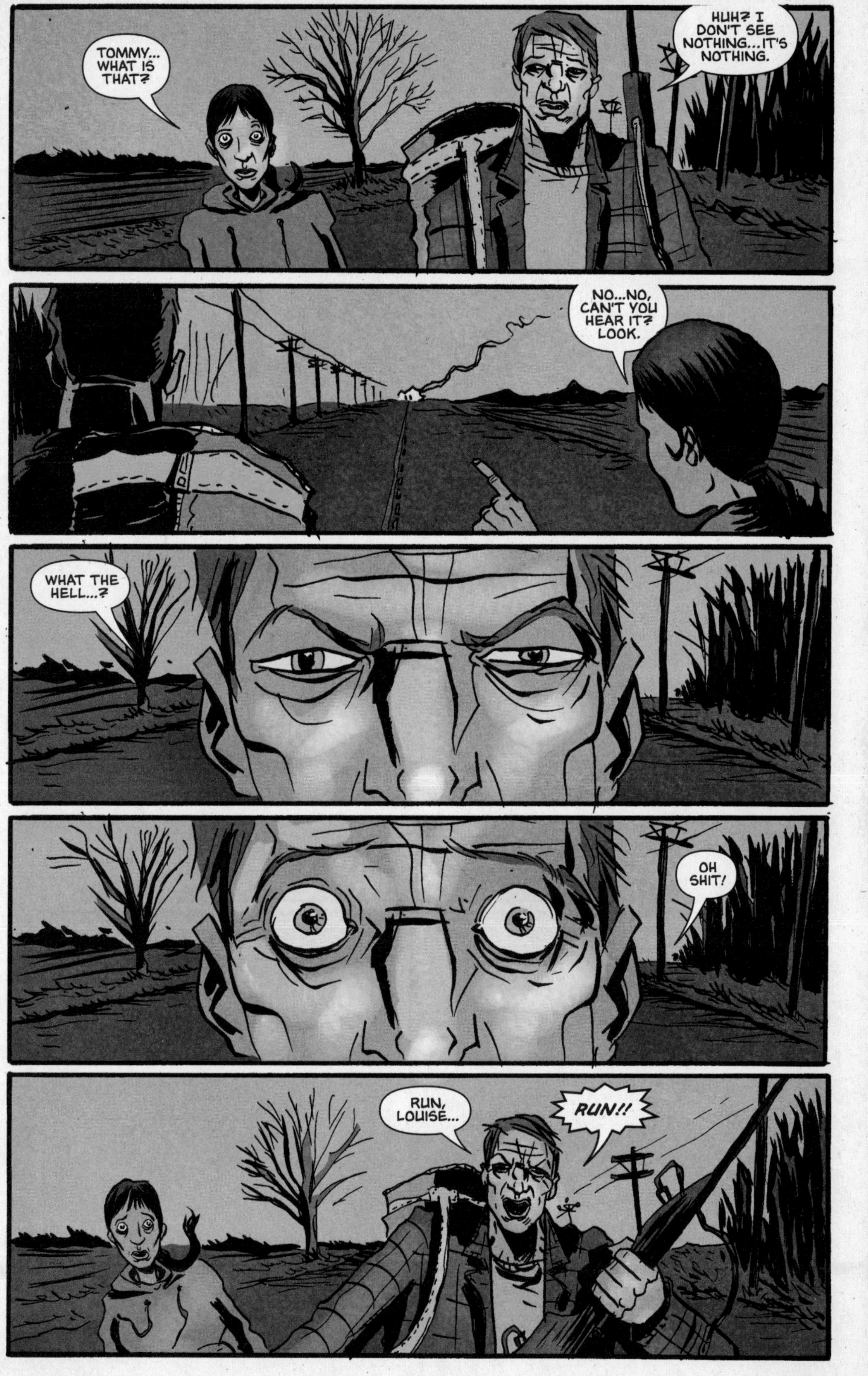
TOMMY... WHAT IS THAT?
HUH? I DON'T SEE NOTHING...IT'S NOTHING.
NO...NO, CAN'T YOU HEAR IT? LOOK.
WHAT THE HELL...?
OH SHIT!
RUN, LOUISE...
RUN!!

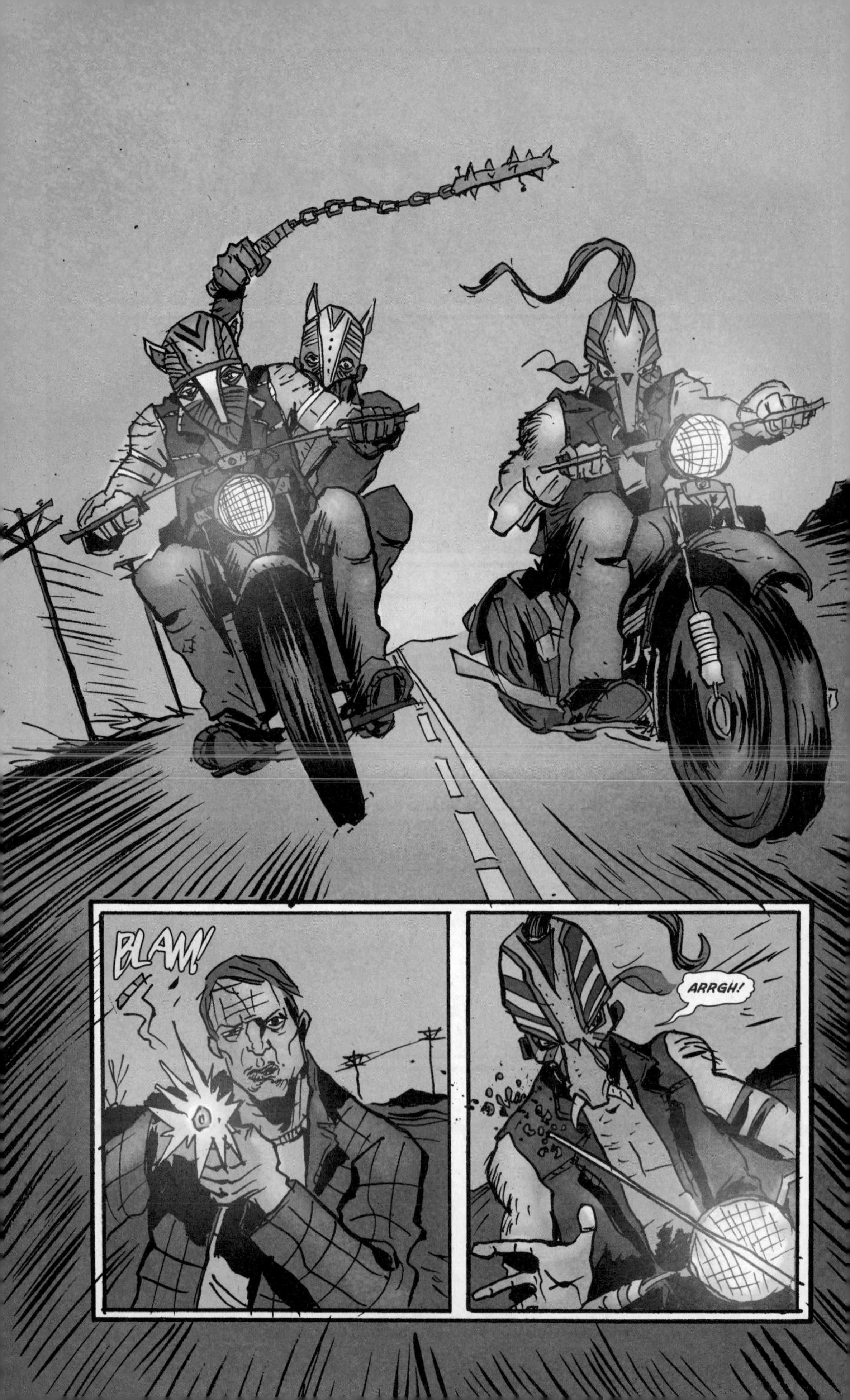
BLAM!
ARRGH!

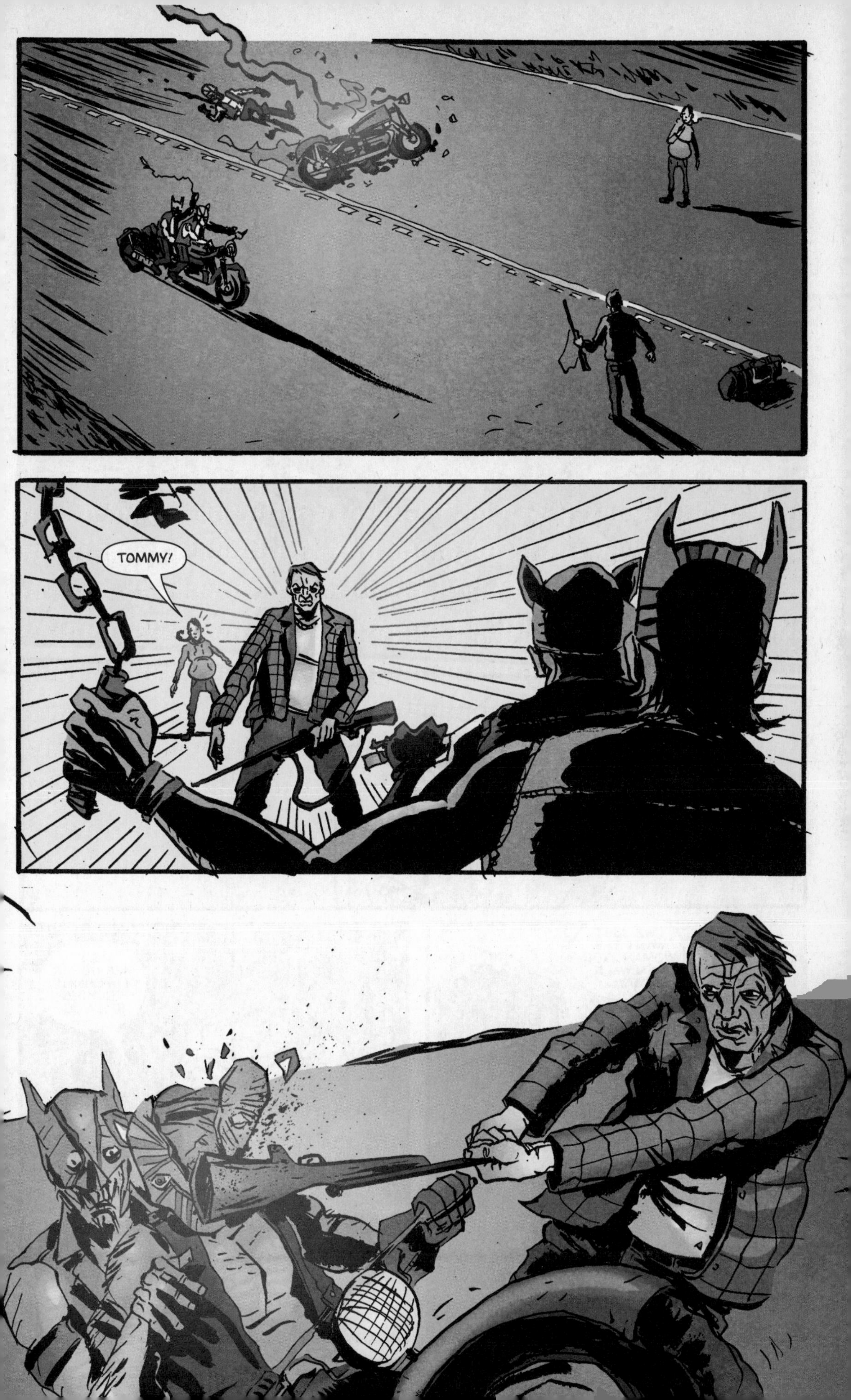
TOMMY!

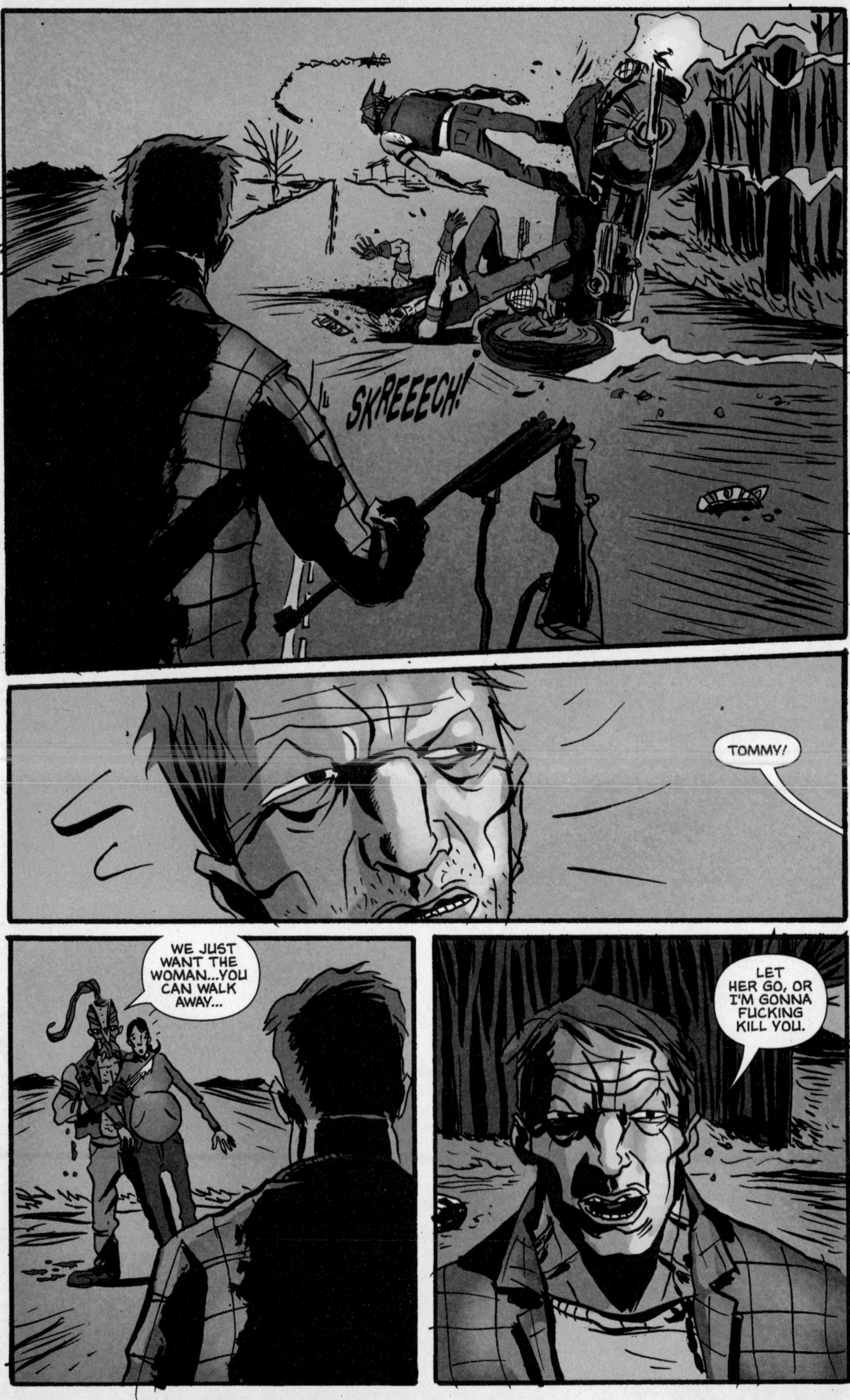
SKREEECH!
TOMMY!
WE JUST WANT THE WOMAN...YOU CAN WALK AWAY...
LET HER GO, OR I'M GONNA FUCKING KILL YOU.

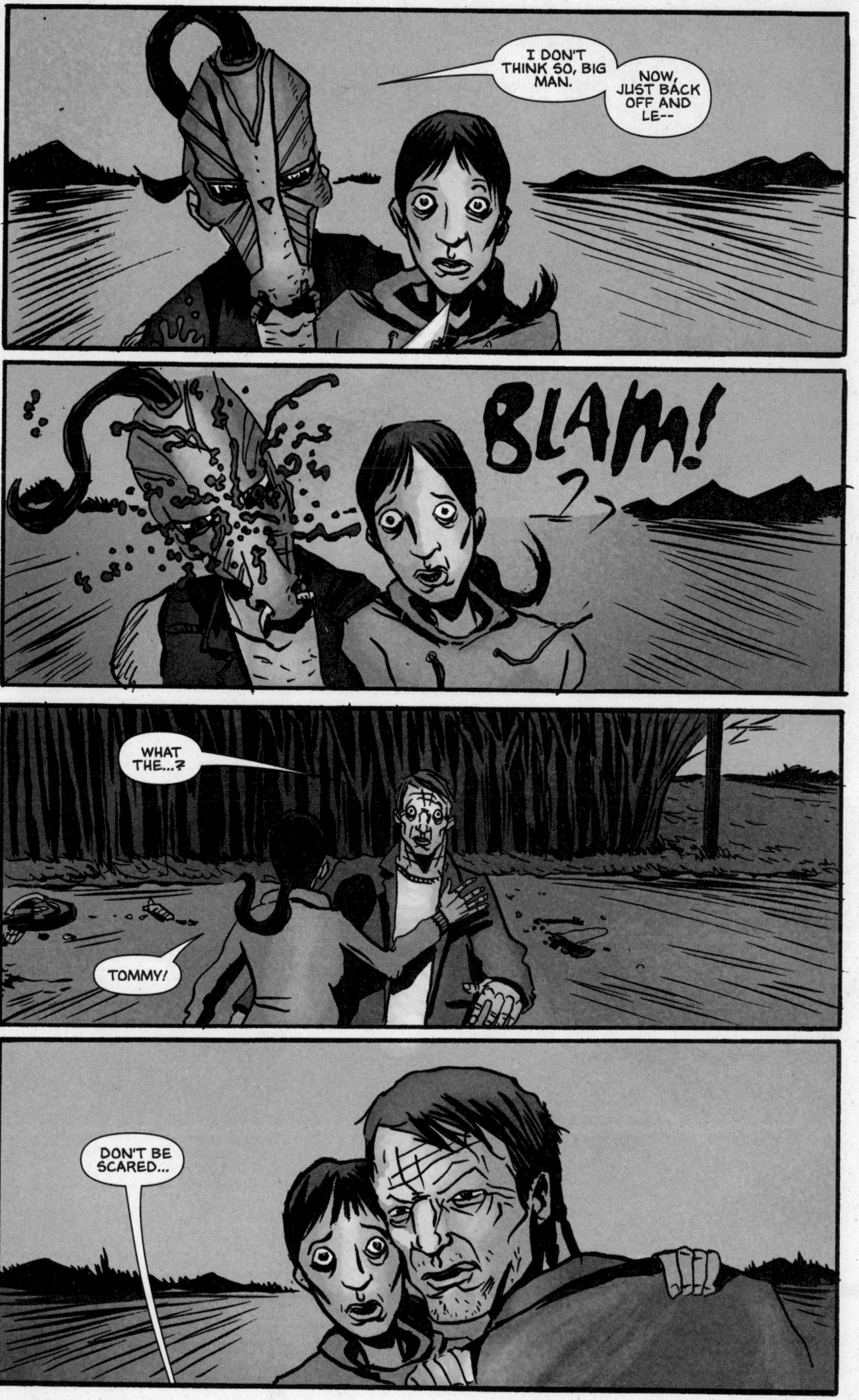
I DON'T THINK SO, BIG MAN.
NOW, JUST BACK OFF AND LE--
BLAM!
WHAT THE...?
TOMMY!
DON'T BE SCARED...

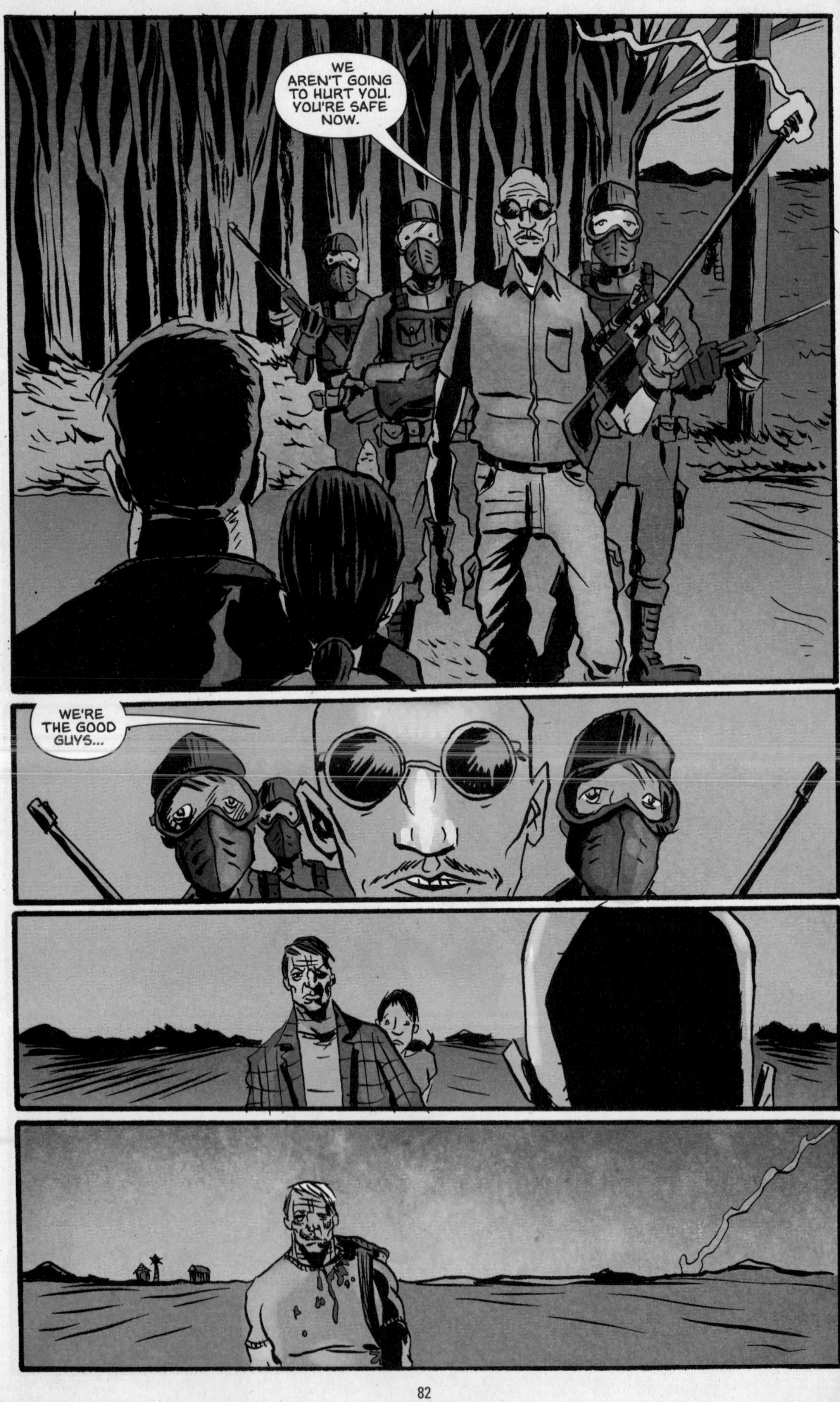
WE AREN'T GOING TO HURT YOU. YOU'RE SAFE NOW.
WE'RE THE GOOD GUYS...

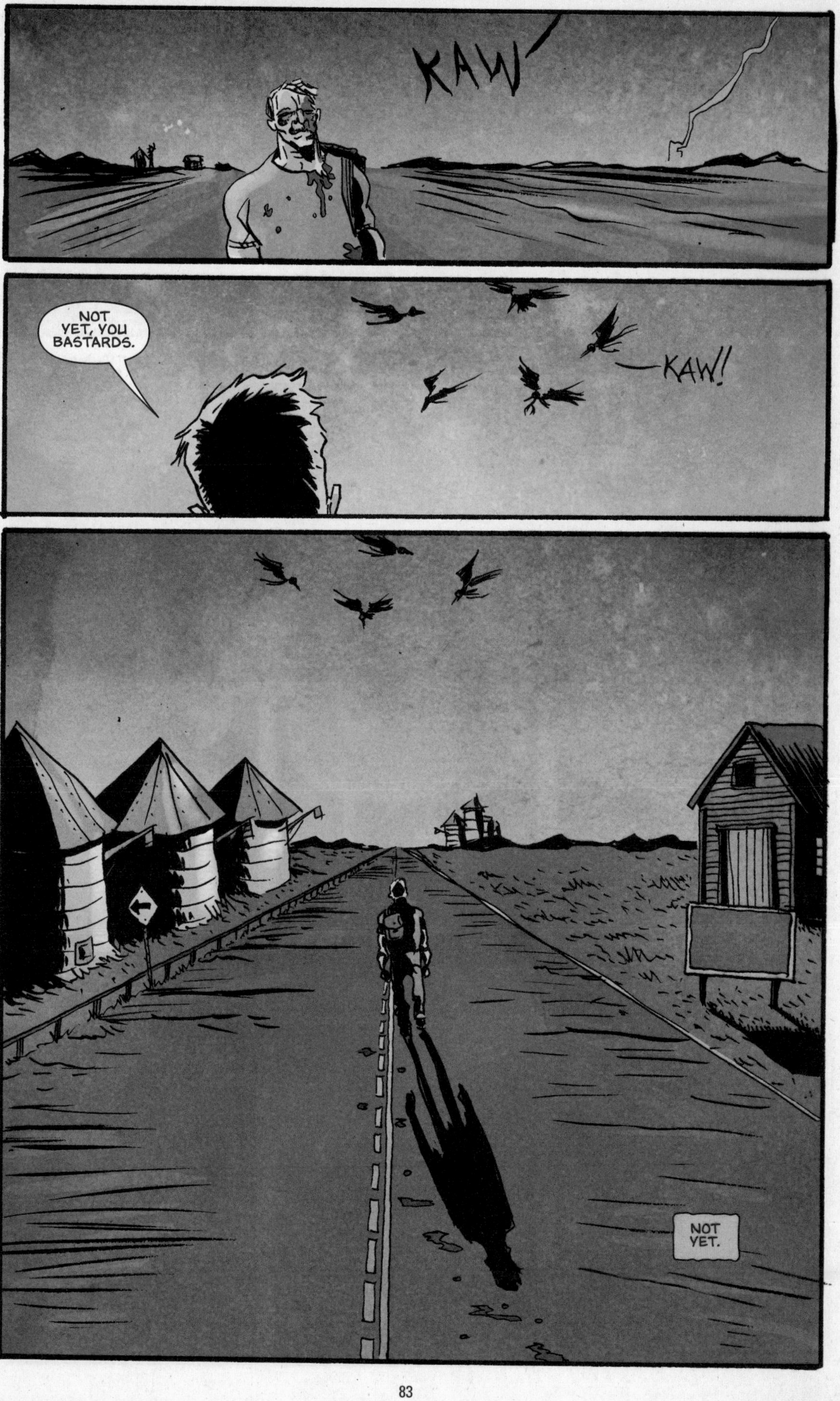
KAW
NOT YET, YOU BASTARDS.
KAW!
NOT YET.

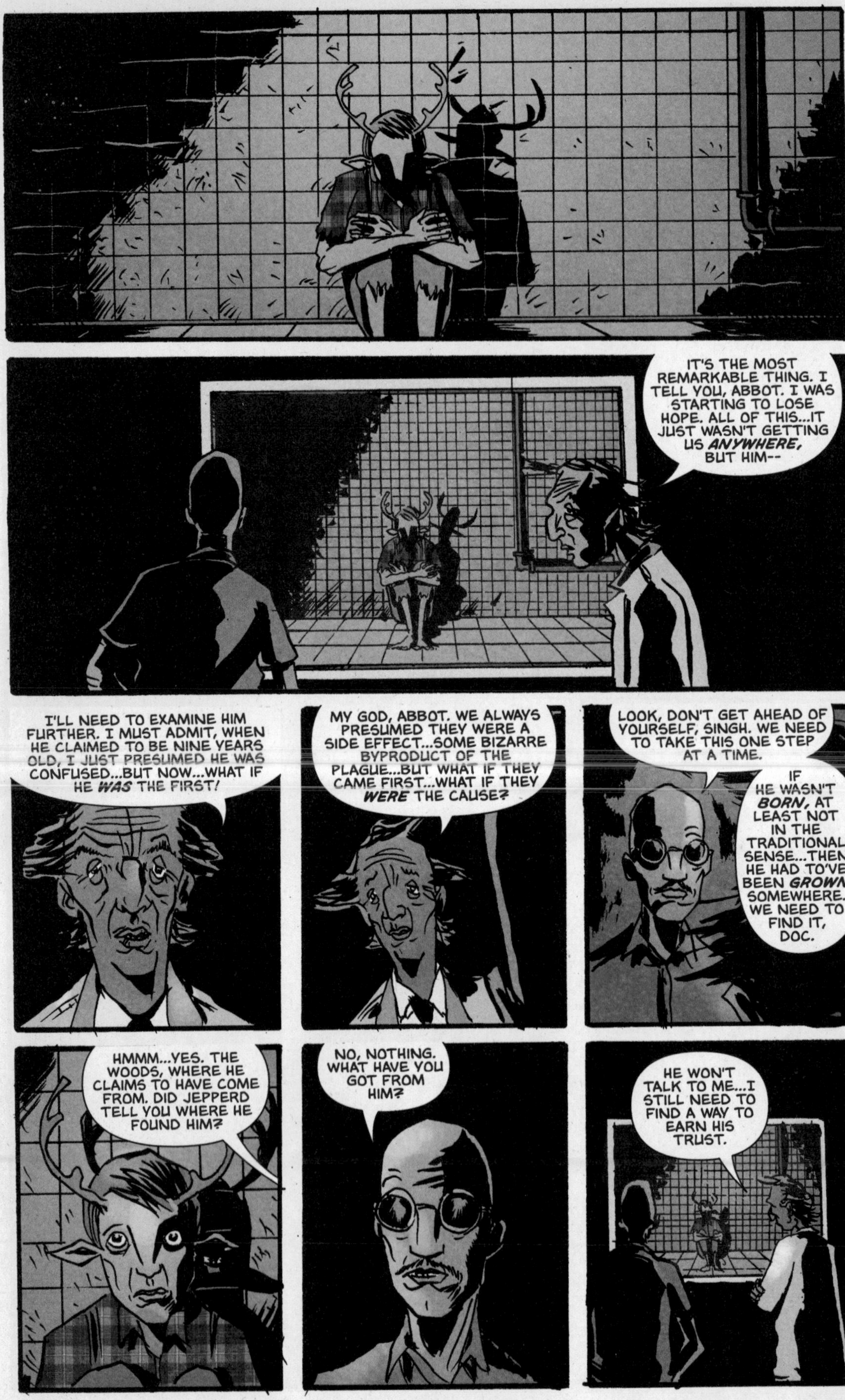

IT'S THE MOST REMARKABLE THING. I TELL YOU, ABBOT. I WAS STARTING TO LOSE HOPE. ALL OF THIS...IT JUST WASN'T GETTING US *ANYWHERE,* BUT HIM--
I'LL NEED TO EXAMINE HIM FURTHER. I MUST ADMIT, WHEN HE CLAIMED TO BE NINE YEARS OLD, I JUST PRESUMED HE WAS CONFUSED...BUT NOW...WHAT IF HE *WAS* THE FIRST!
MY GOD, ABBOT. WE ALWAYS PRESUMED THEY WERE A SIDE EFFECT...SOME BIZARRE BYPRODUCT OF THE PLAGUE...BUT WHAT IF THEY CAME FIRST...WHAT IF THEY *WERE* THE CAUSE?
LOOK, DON'T GET AHEAD OF YOURSELF, SINGH. WE NEED TO TAKE THIS ONE STEP AT A TIME.
IF HE WASN'T *BORN,* AT LEAST NOT IN THE TRADITIONAL SENSE...THEN HE HAD TO'VE BEEN *GROWN* SOMEWHERE. WE NEED TO FIND IT, DOC.
HMMM...YES. THE WOODS, WHERE HE CLAIMS TO HAVE COME FROM. DID JEPPERD TELL YOU WHERE HE FOUND HIM?
NO, NOTHING. WHAT HAVE YOU GOT FROM HIM?
HE WON'T TALK TO ME...I STILL NEED TO FIND A WAY TO EARN HIS TRUST.

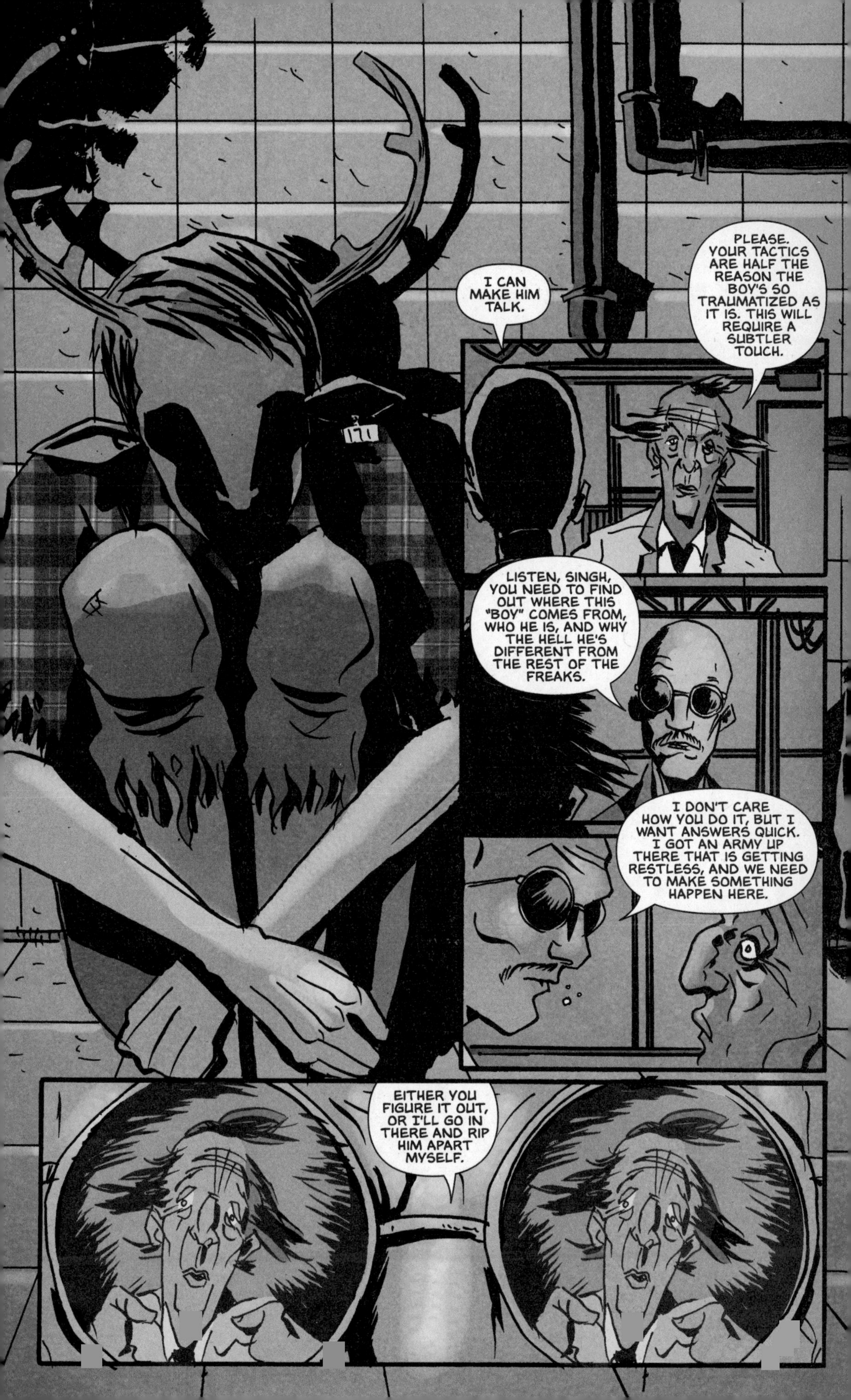
I CAN MAKE HIM TALK.
PLEASE. YOUR TACTICS ARE HALF THE REASON THE BOY'S SO TRAUMATIZED AS IT IS. THIS WILL REQUIRE A SUBTLER TOUCH.
LISTEN, SINGH, YOU NEED TO FIND OUT WHERE THIS "BOY" COMES FROM, WHO HE IS, AND WHY THE HELL HE'S DIFFERENT FROM THE REST OF THE FREAKS.
I DON'T CARE HOW YOU DO IT, BUT I WANT ANSWERS QUICK. I GOT AN ARMY UP THERE THAT IS GETTING RESTLESS, AND WE NEED TO MAKE SOMETHING HAPPEN HERE.
EITHER YOU FIGURE IT OUT, OR I'LL GO IN THERE AND RIP HIM APART MYSELF.

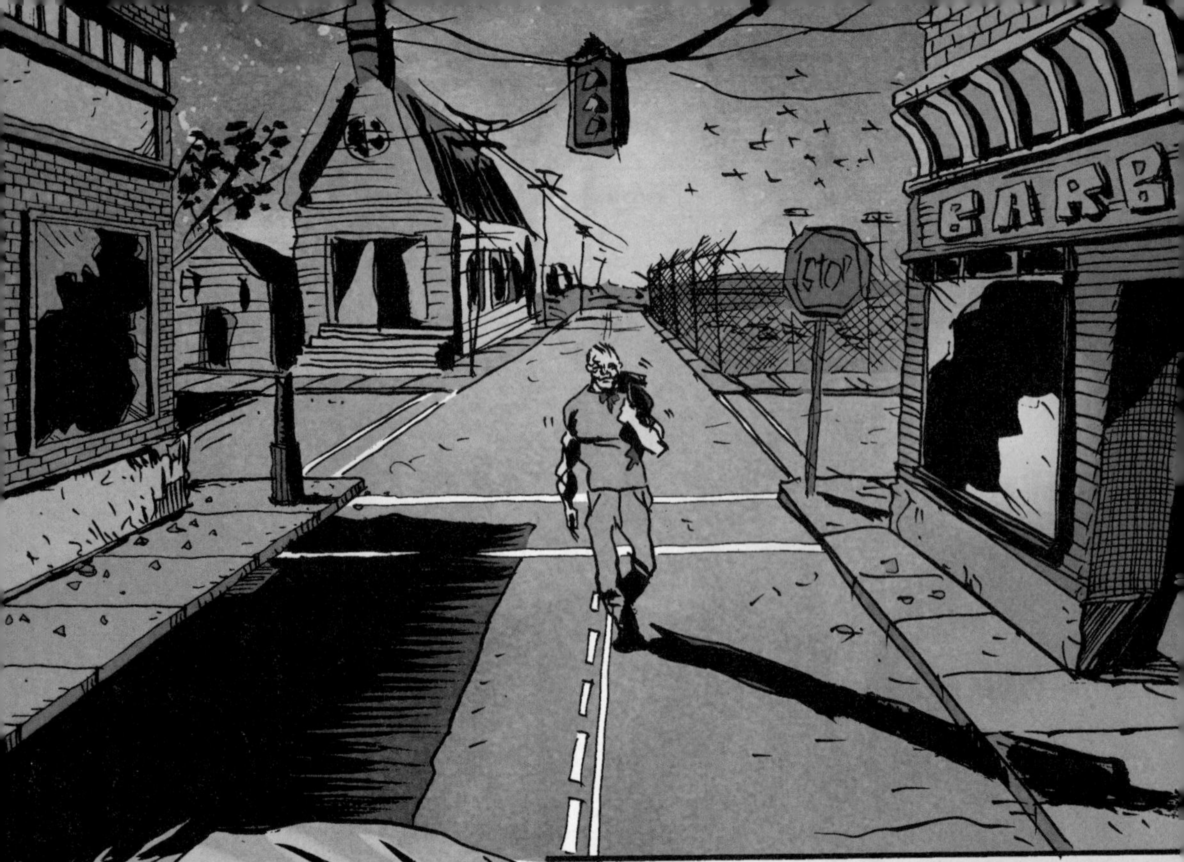
STOP
CARB

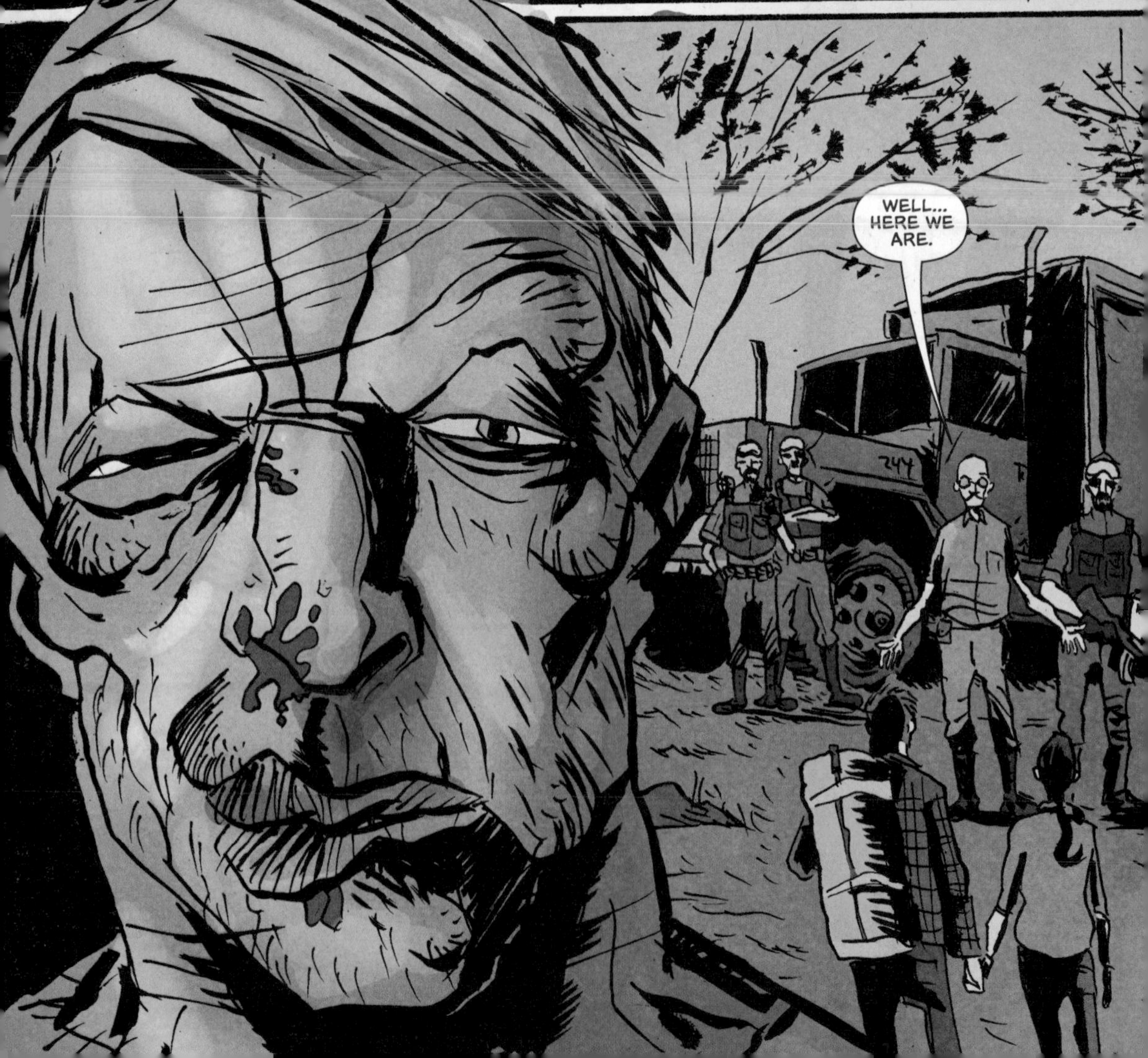
WELL... HERE WE ARE.
244

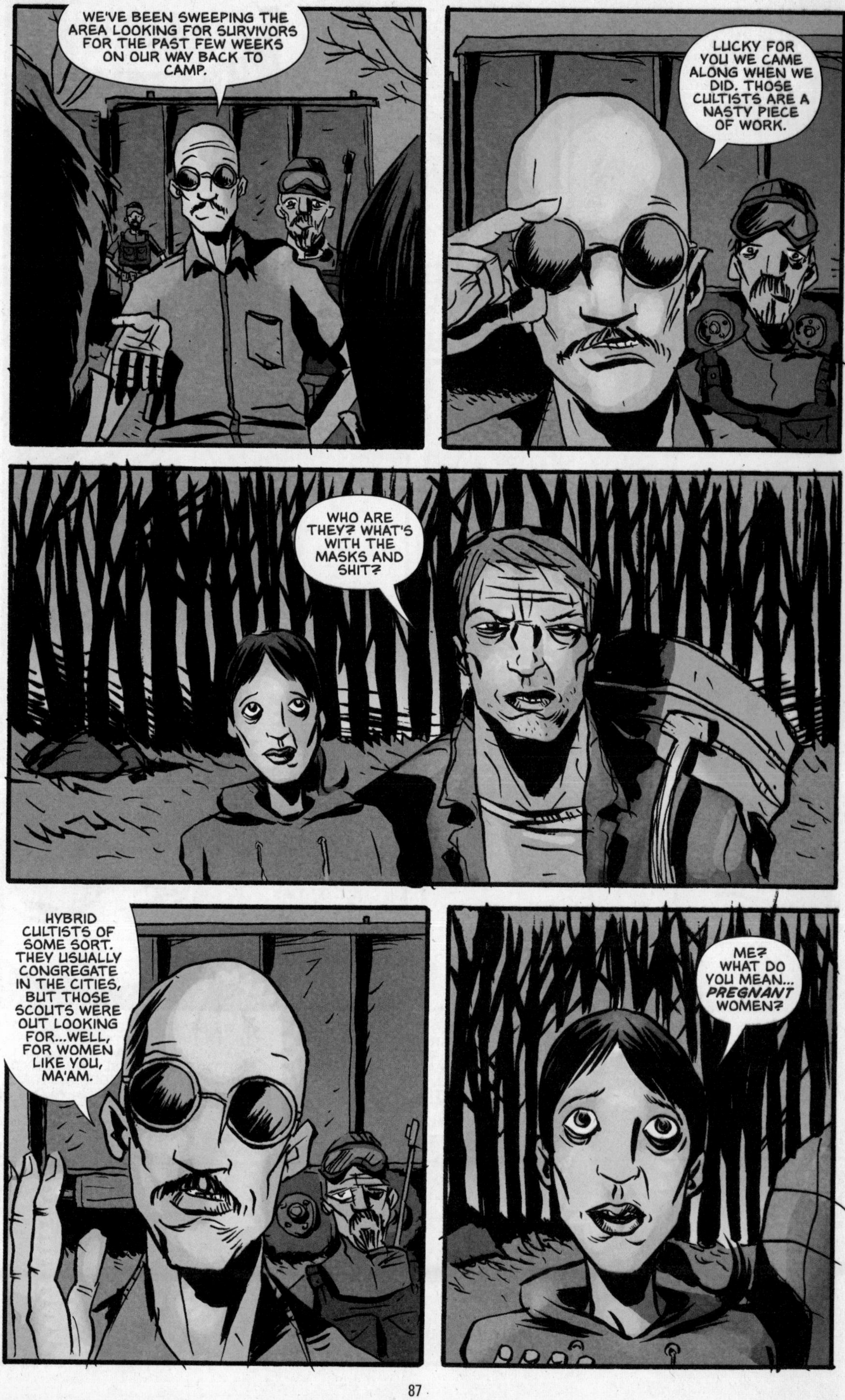
WE'VE BEEN SWEEPING THE AREA LOOKING FOR SURVIVORS FOR THE PAST FEW WEEKS ON OUR WAY BACK TO CAMP.
LUCKY FOR YOU WE CAME ALONG WHEN WE DID. THOSE CULTISTS ARE A NASTY PIECE OF WORK.
WHO ARE THEY? WHAT'S WITH THE MASKS AND SHIT?
HYBRID CULTISTS OF SOME SORT. THEY USUALLY CONGREGATE IN THE CITIES, BUT THOSE SCOUTS WERE OUT LOOKING FOR...WELL, FOR WOMEN LIKE YOU, MA'AM.
ME? WHAT DO YOU MEAN... *PREGNANT* WOMEN?

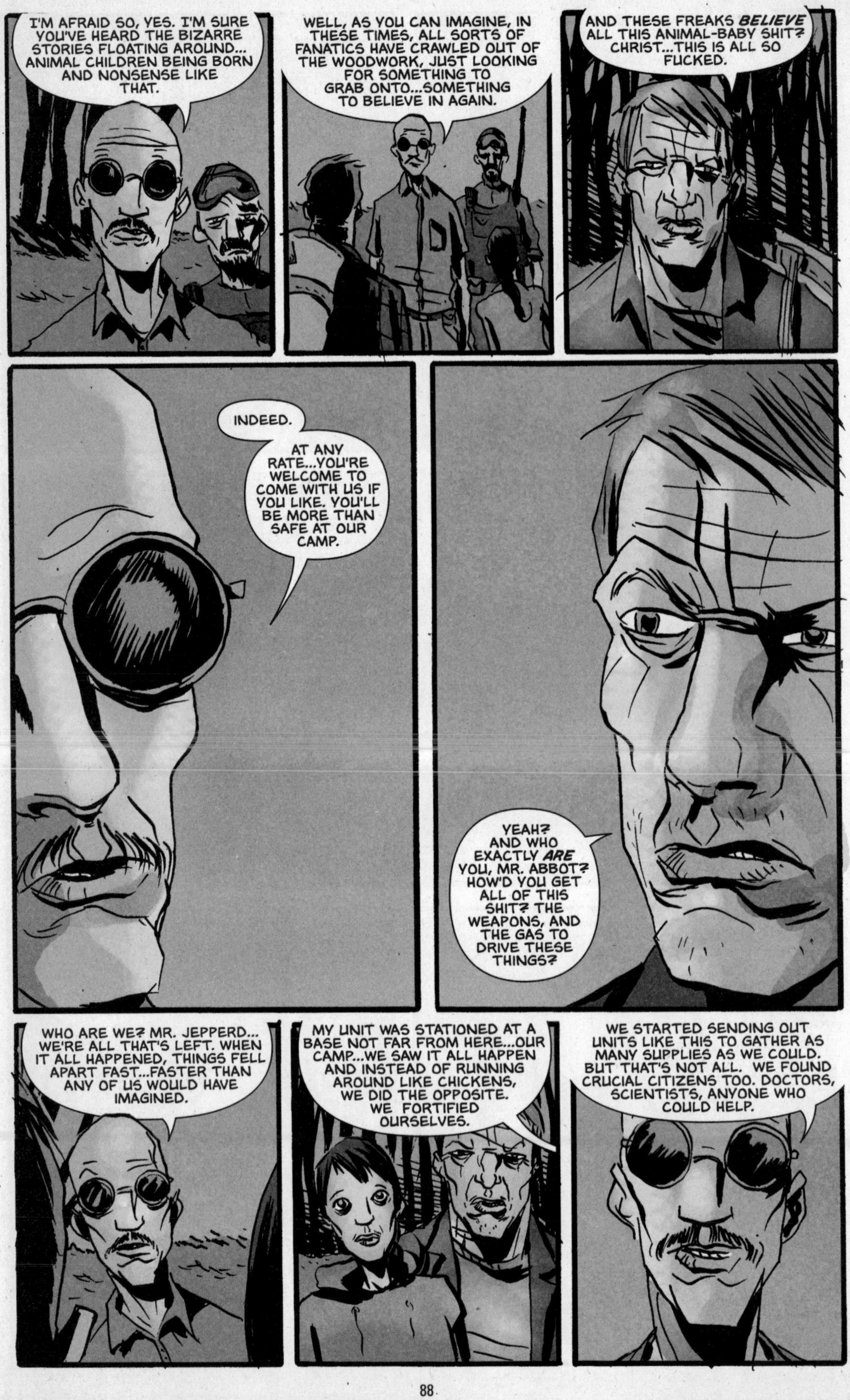
I'M AFRAID SO, YES. I'M SURE YOU'VE HEARD THE BIZARRE STORIES FLOATING AROUND... ANIMAL CHILDREN BEING BORN AND NONSENSE LIKE THAT.
WELL, AS YOU CAN IMAGINE, IN THESE TIMES, ALL SORTS OF FANATICS HAVE CRAWLED OUT OF THE WOODWORK, JUST LOOKING FOR SOMETHING TO GRAB ONTO...SOMETHING TO BELIEVE IN AGAIN.
AND THESE FREAKS *BELIEVE* ALL THIS ANIMAL-BABY SHIT? CHRIST...THIS IS ALL SO FUCKED.
INDEED.
AT ANY RATE...YOU'RE WELCOME TO COME WITH US IF YOU LIKE. YOU'LL BE MORE THAN SAFE AT OUR CAMP.
YEAH? AND WHO EXACTLY *ARE* YOU, MR. ABBOT? HOW'D YOU GET ALL OF THIS SHIT? THE WEAPONS, AND THE GAS TO DRIVE THESE THINGS?
WHO ARE WE? MR. JEPPERD... WE'RE ALL THAT'S LEFT. WHEN IT ALL HAPPENED, THINGS FELL APART FAST...FASTER THAN ANY OF US WOULD HAVE IMAGINED.
MY UNIT WAS STATIONED AT A BASE NOT FAR FROM HERE...OUR CAMP...WE SAW IT ALL HAPPEN AND INSTEAD OF RUNNING AROUND LIKE CHICKENS, WE DID THE OPPOSITE. WE FORTIFIED OURSELVES.
WE STARTED SENDING OUT UNITS LIKE THIS TO GATHER AS MANY SUPPLIES AS WE COULD. BUT THAT'S NOT ALL. WE FOUND CRUCIAL CITIZENS TOO. DOCTORS, SCIENTISTS, ANYONE WHO COULD HELP.

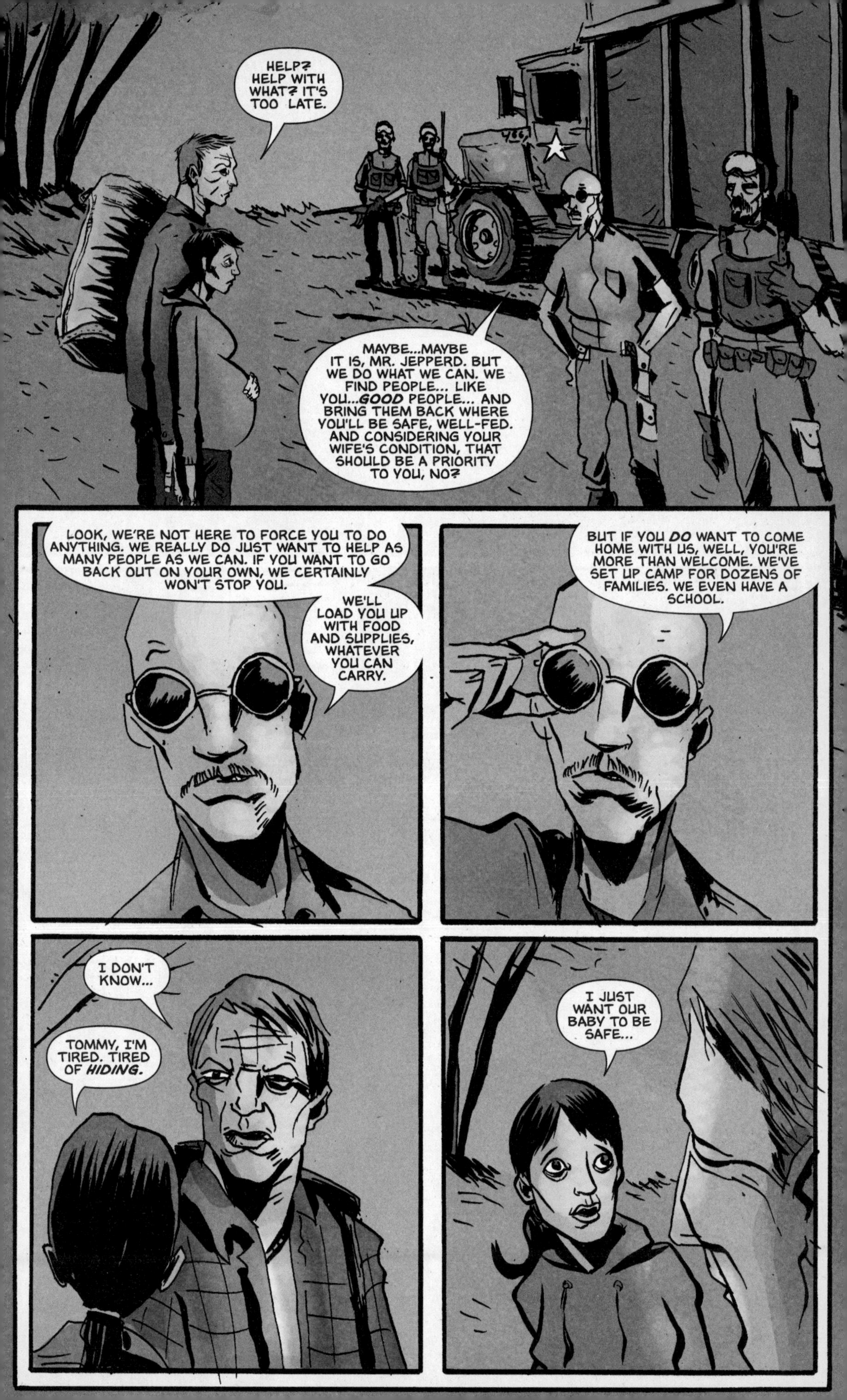
HELP? HELP WITH WHAT? IT'S TOO LATE.
MAYBE...MAYBE IT IS, MR. JEPPERD. BUT WE DO WHAT WE CAN. WE FIND PEOPLE... LIKE YOU...GOOD PEOPLE... AND BRING THEM BACK WHERE YOU'LL BE SAFE, WELL-FED. AND CONSIDERING YOUR WIFE'S CONDITION, THAT SHOULD BE A PRIORITY TO YOU, NO?
LOOK, WE'RE NOT HERE TO FORCE YOU TO DO ANYTHING. WE REALLY DO JUST WANT TO HELP AS MANY PEOPLE AS WE CAN. IF YOU WANT TO GO BACK OUT ON YOUR OWN, WE CERTAINLY WON'T STOP YOU.
WE'LL LOAD YOU UP WITH FOOD AND SUPPLIES, WHATEVER YOU CAN CARRY.
BUT IF YOU DO WANT TO COME HOME WITH US, WELL, YOU'RE MORE THAN WELCOME. WE'VE SET UP CAMP FOR DOZENS OF FAMILIES. WE EVEN HAVE A SCHOOL.
I DON'T KNOW...
TOMMY, I'M TIRED. TIRED OF HIDING.
I JUST WANT OUR BABY TO BE SAFE...

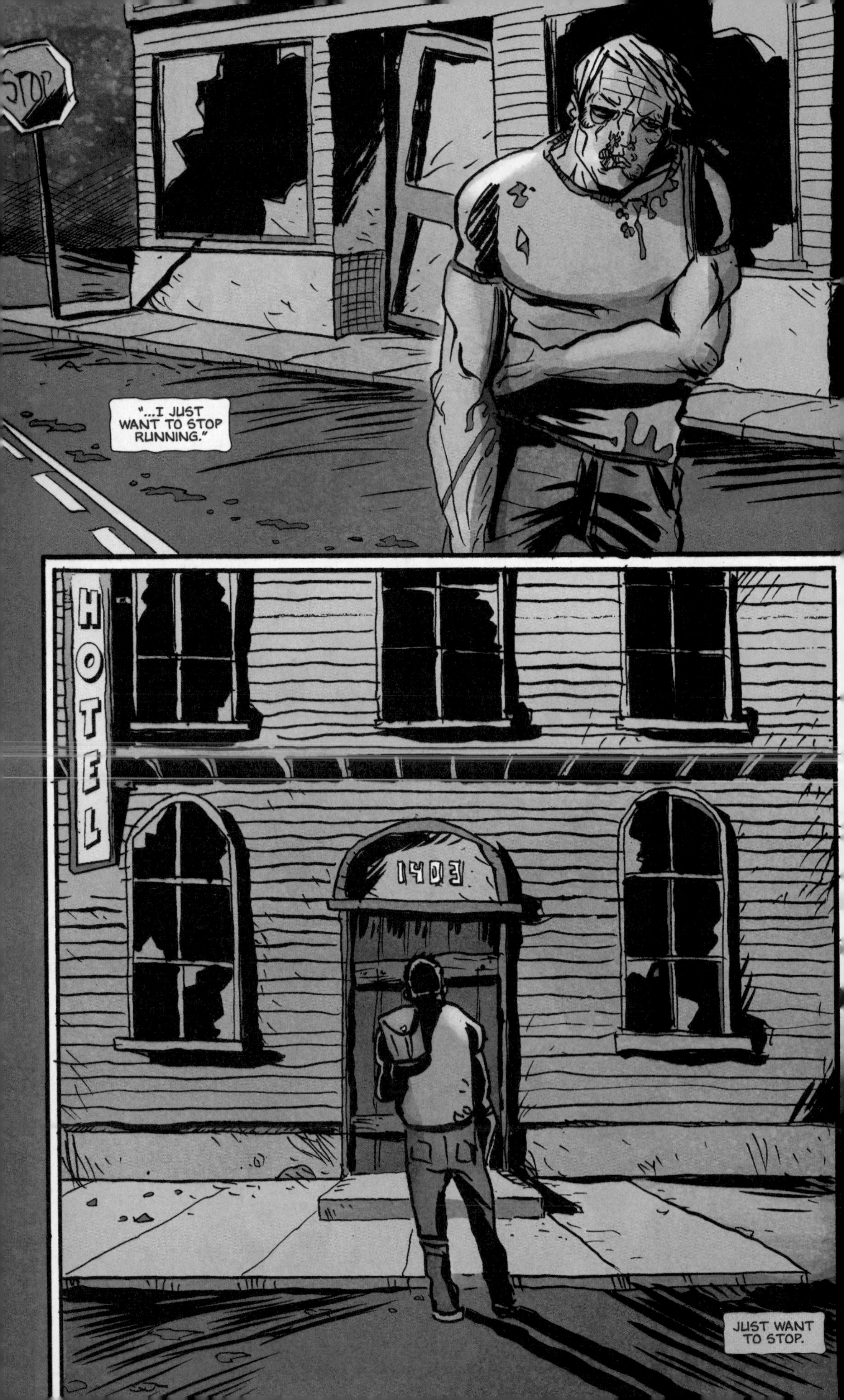
STOP
"...I JUST WANT TO STOP RUNNING."
HOTEL
1403
JUST WANT TO STOP.

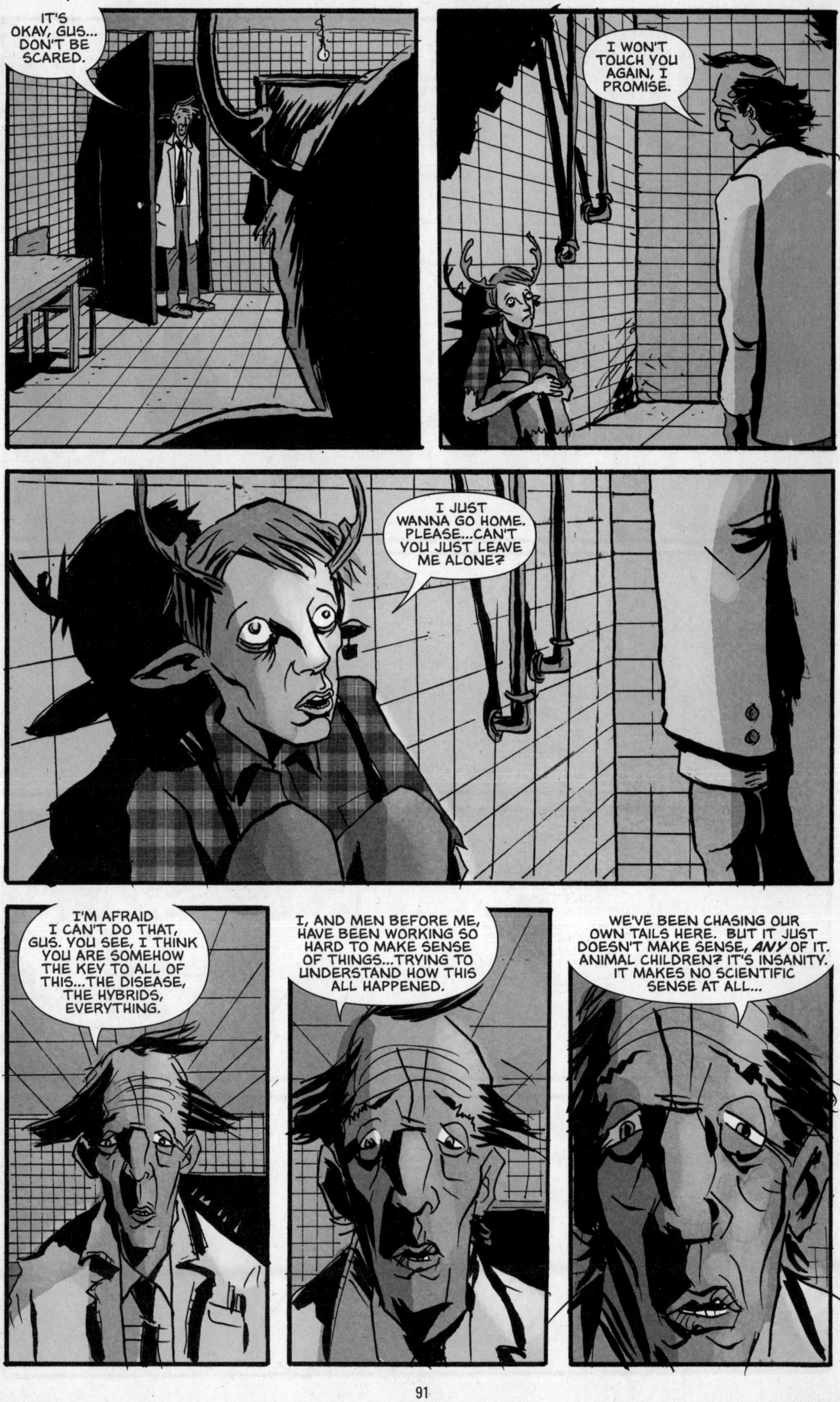
IT'S OKAY, GUS... DON'T BE SCARED.
I WON'T TOUCH YOU AGAIN, I PROMISE.
I JUST WANNA GO HOME. PLEASE...CAN'T YOU JUST LEAVE ME ALONE?
I'M AFRAID I CAN'T DO THAT, GUS. YOU SEE, I THINK YOU ARE SOMEHOW THE KEY TO ALL OF THIS...THE DISEASE, THE HYBRIDS, EVERYTHING.
I, AND MEN BEFORE ME, HAVE BEEN WORKING SO HARD TO MAKE SENSE OF THINGS...TRYING TO UNDERSTAND HOW THIS ALL HAPPENED.
WE'VE BEEN CHASING OUR OWN TAILS HERE. BUT IT JUST DOESN'T MAKE SENSE, ANY OF IT. ANIMAL CHILDREN? IT'S INSANITY. IT MAKES NO SCIENTIFIC SENSE AT ALL...

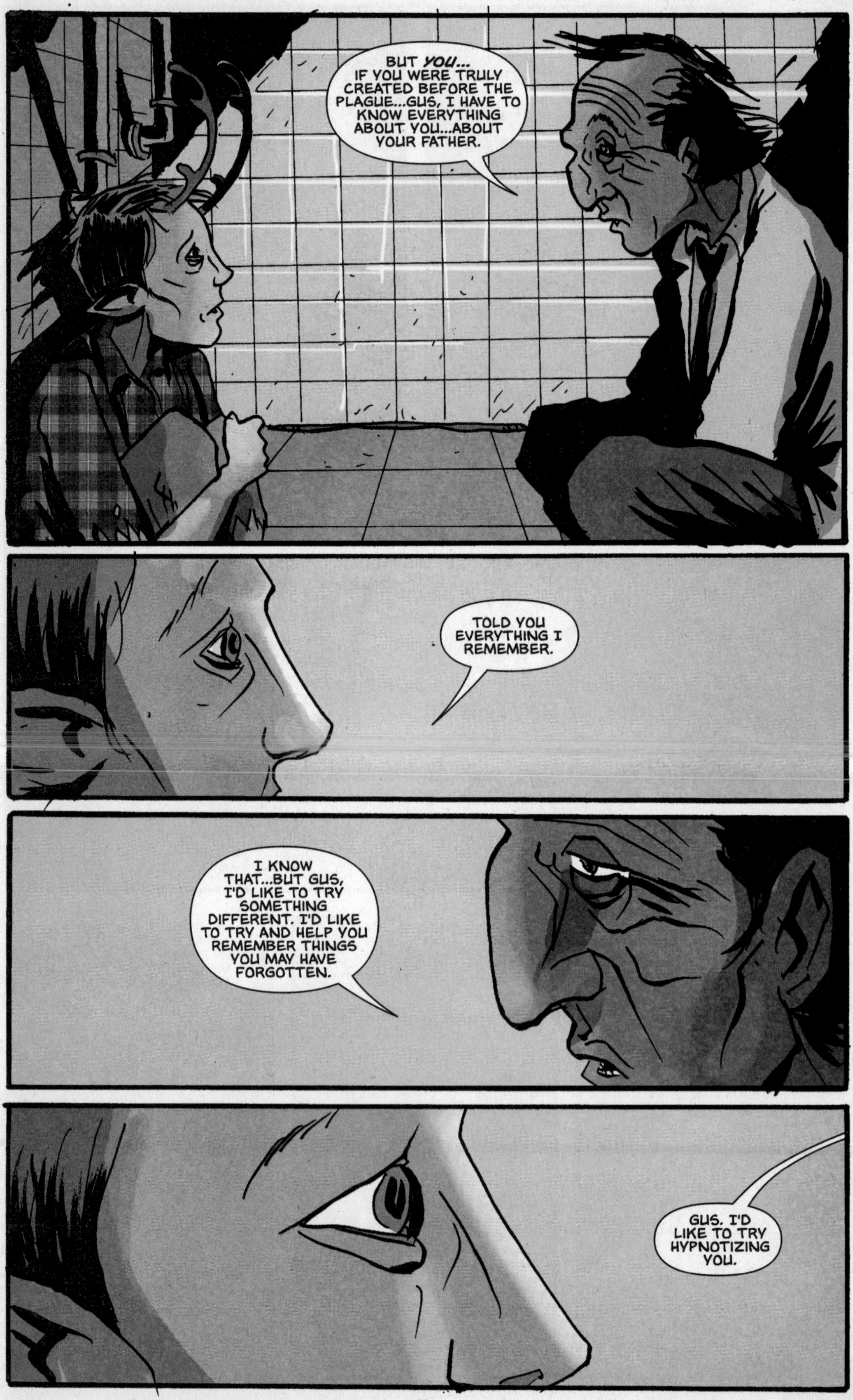

BUT YOU... IF YOU WERE TRULY CREATED BEFORE THE PLAGUE...GUS, I HAVE TO KNOW EVERYTHING ABOUT YOU...ABOUT YOUR FATHER.
TOLD YOU EVERYTHING I REMEMBER.
I KNOW THAT...BUT GUS, I'D LIKE TO TRY SOMETHING DIFFERENT. I'D LIKE TO TRY AND HELP YOU REMEMBER THINGS YOU MAY HAVE FORGOTTEN.
GUS. I'D LIKE TO TRY HYPNOTIZING YOU.

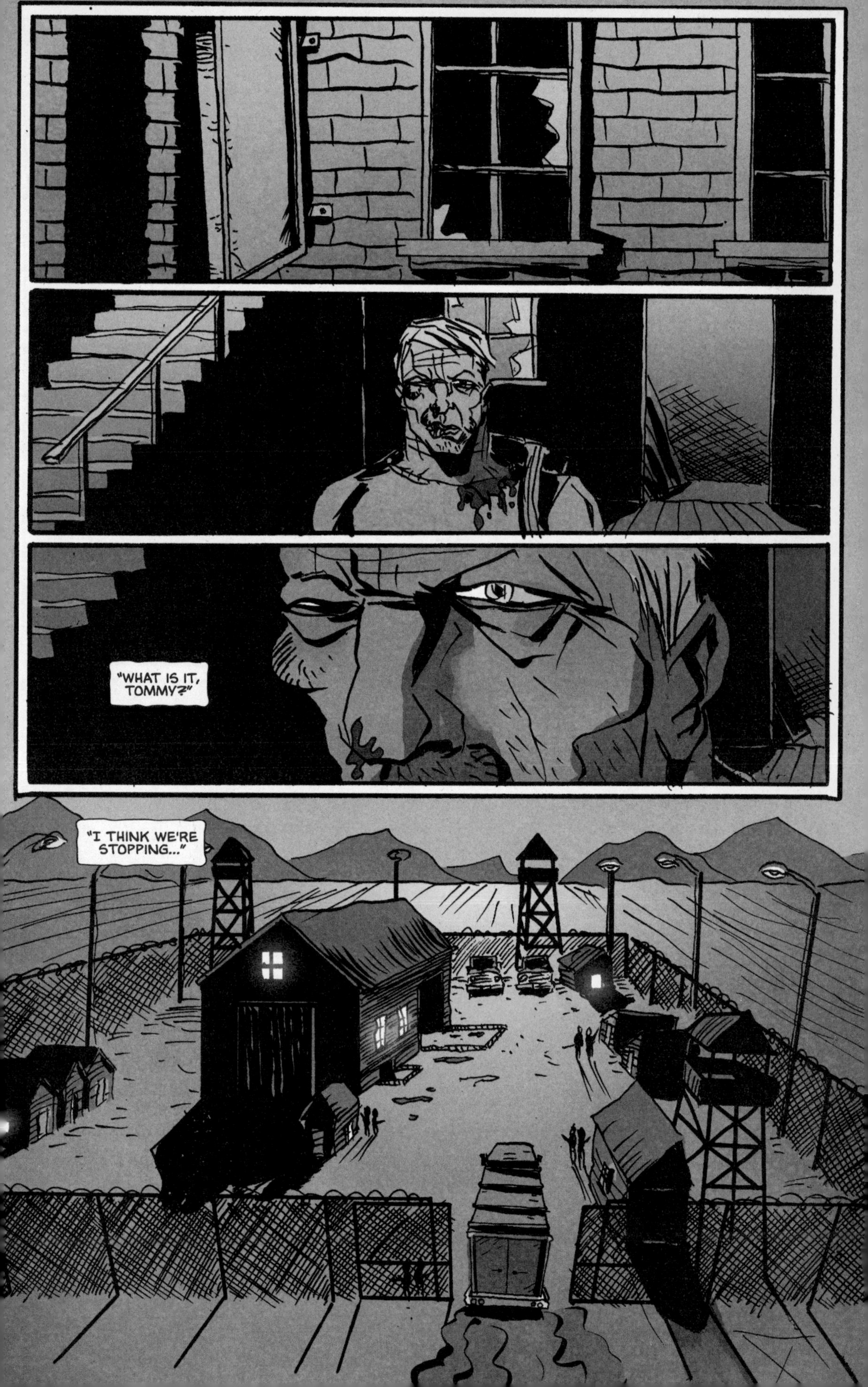
"WHAT IS IT, TOMMY?"
"I THINK WE'RE STOPPING..."

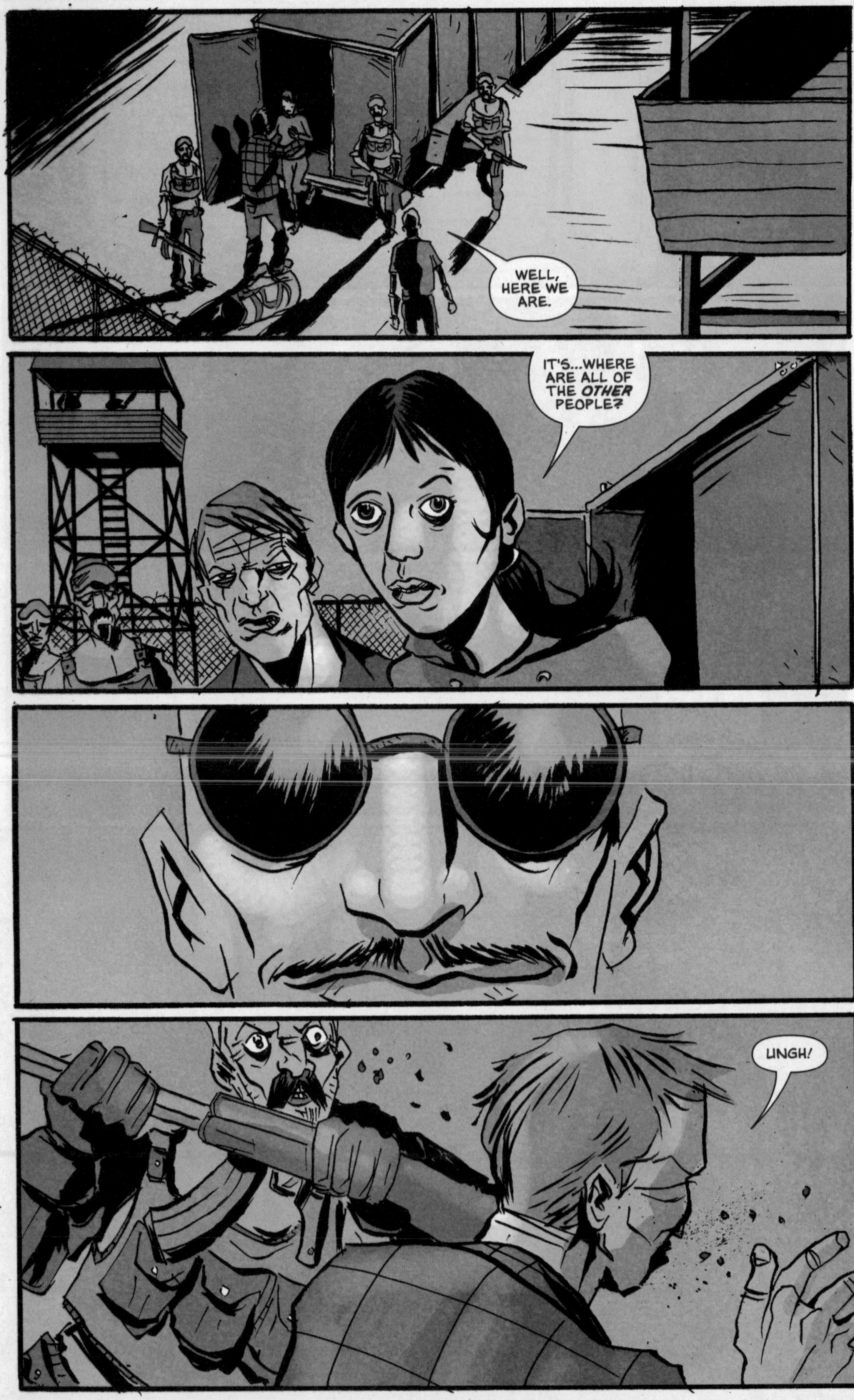
WELL, HERE WE ARE.
IT'S...WHERE ARE ALL OF THE *OTHER* PEOPLE?
UNGH!

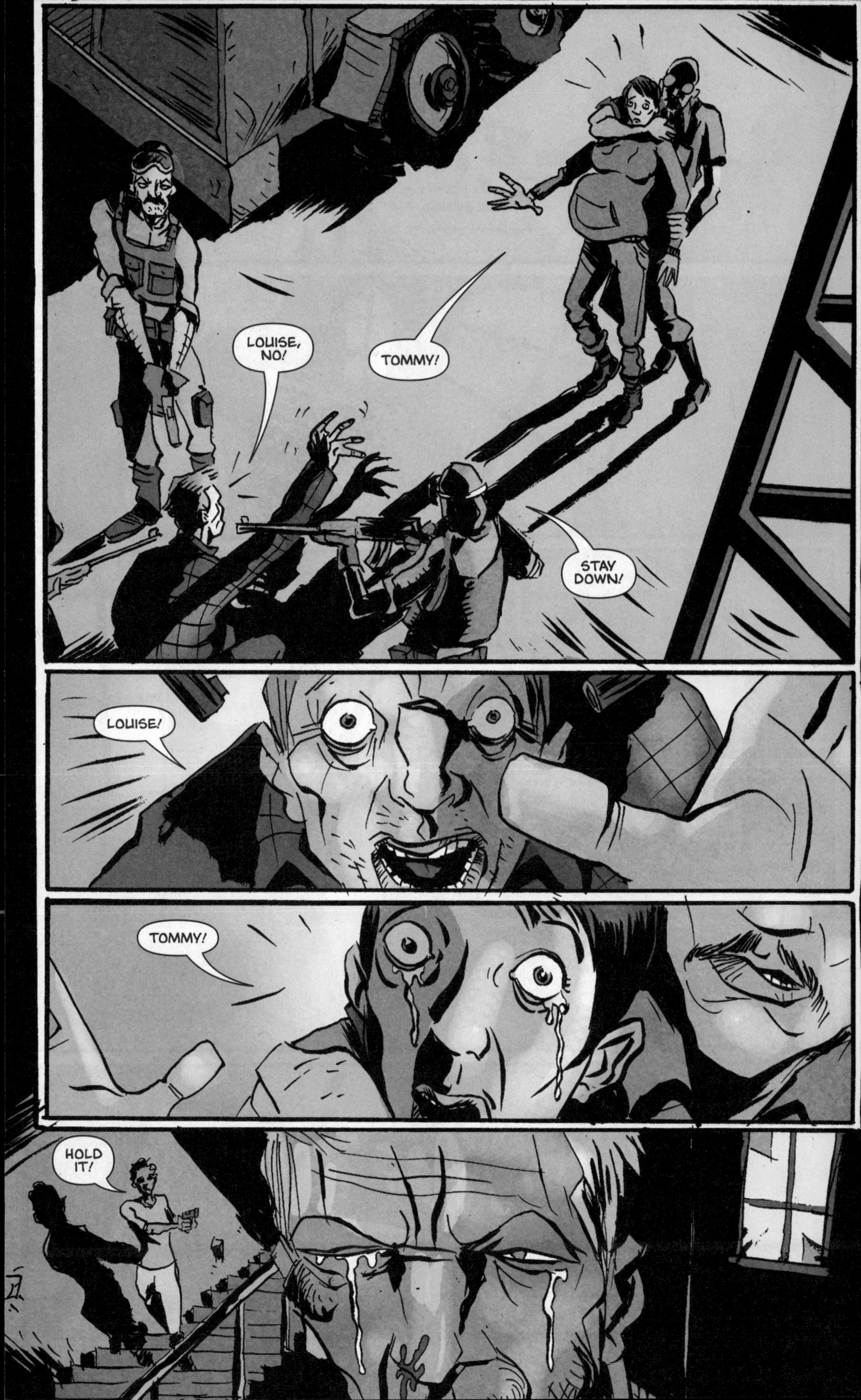
LOUISE, NO!
TOMMY!
STAY DOWN!
LOUISE!
TOMMY!
HOLD IT!

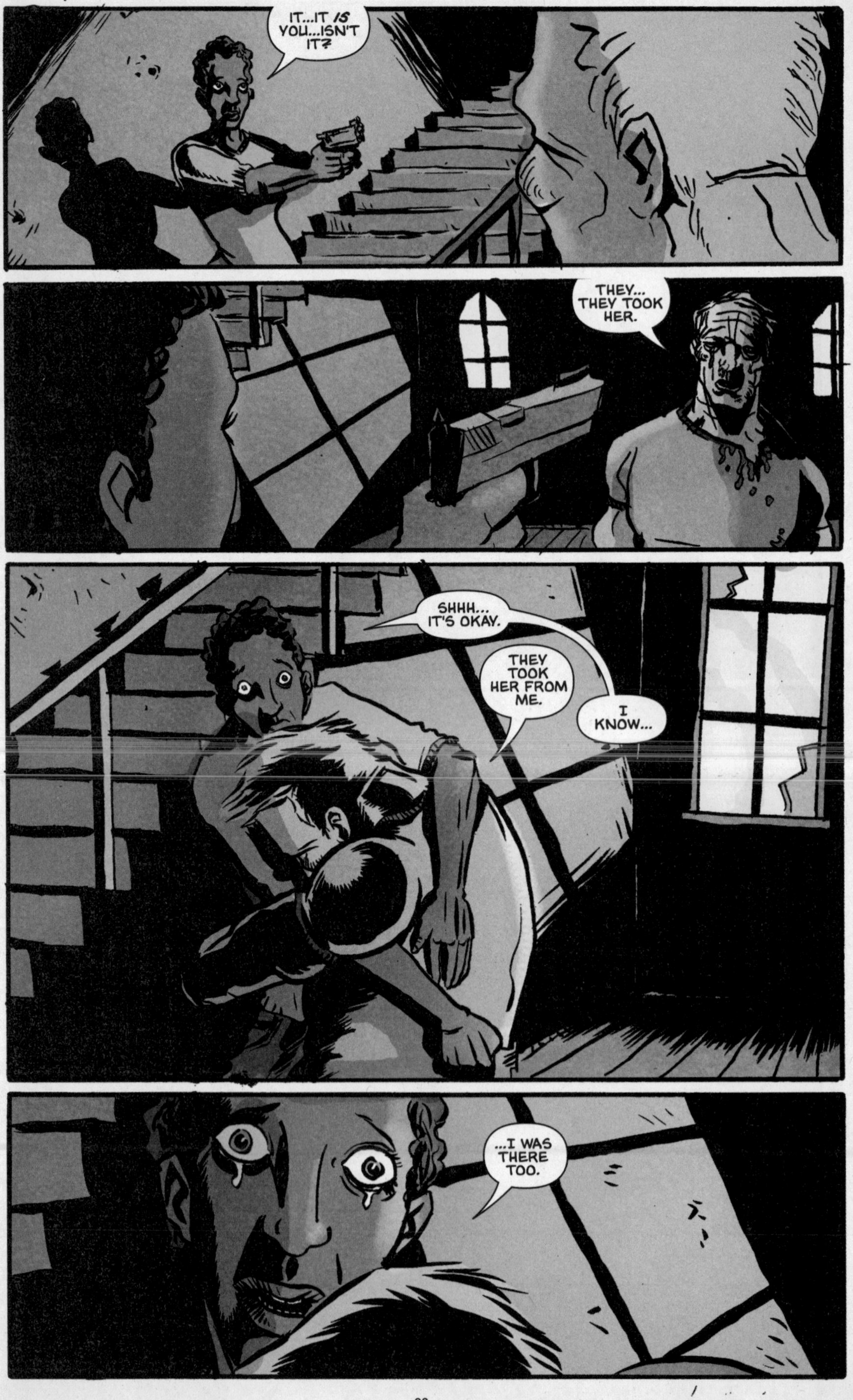
IT...IT IS YOU...ISN'T IT?
THEY... THEY TOOK HER.
SHHH... IT'S OKAY.
THEY TOOK HER FROM ME.
I KNOW...
...I WAS THERE TOO.

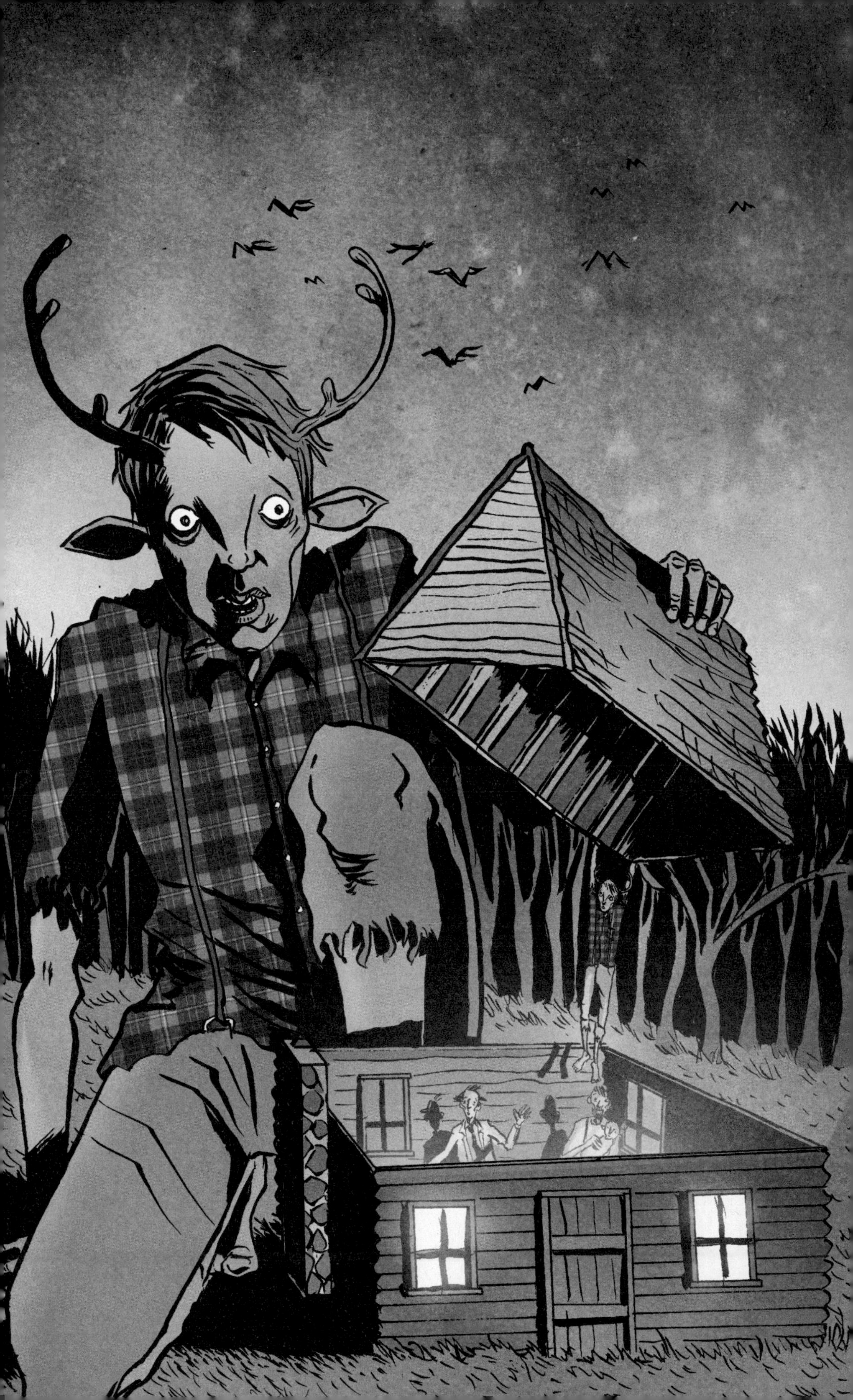

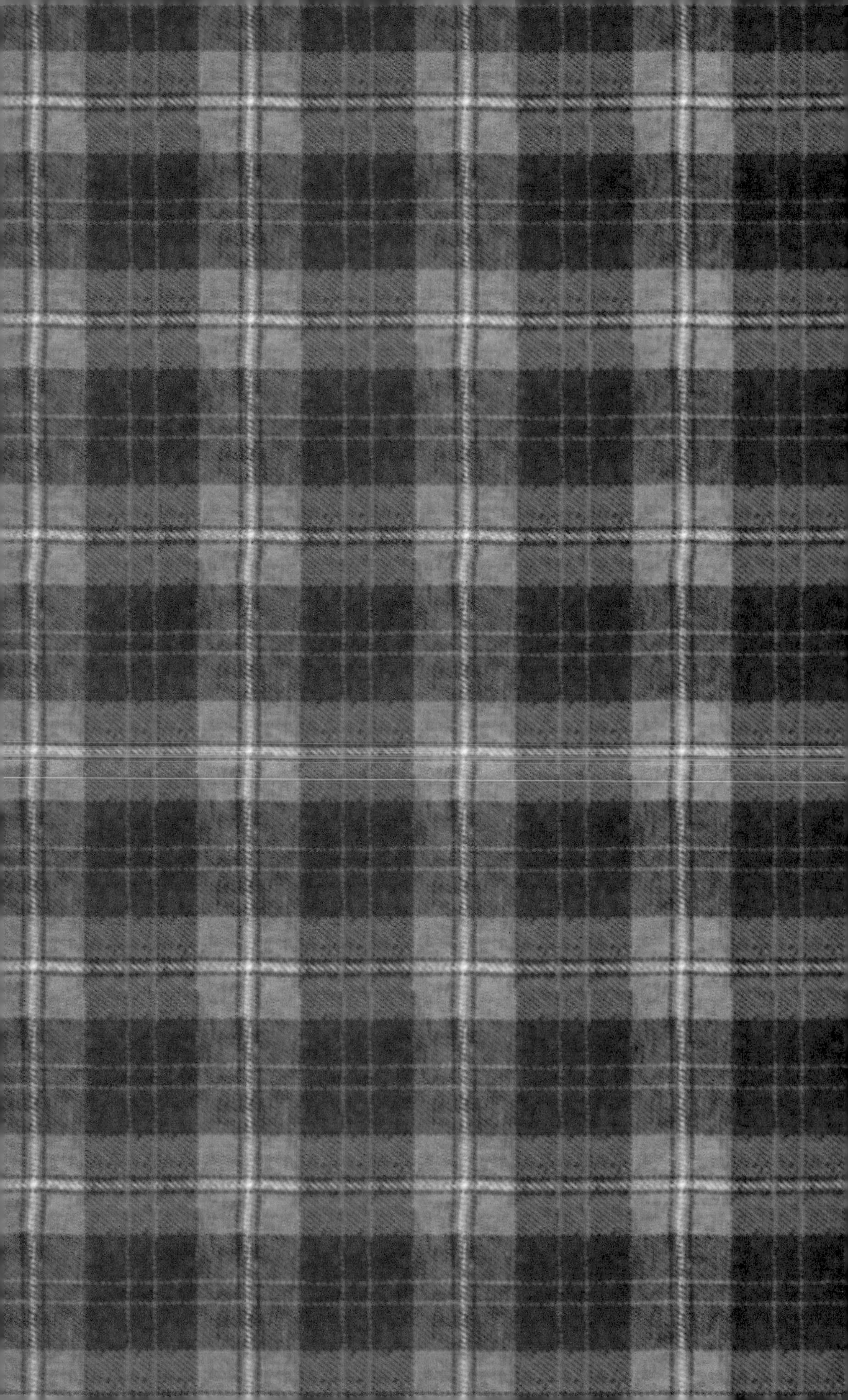

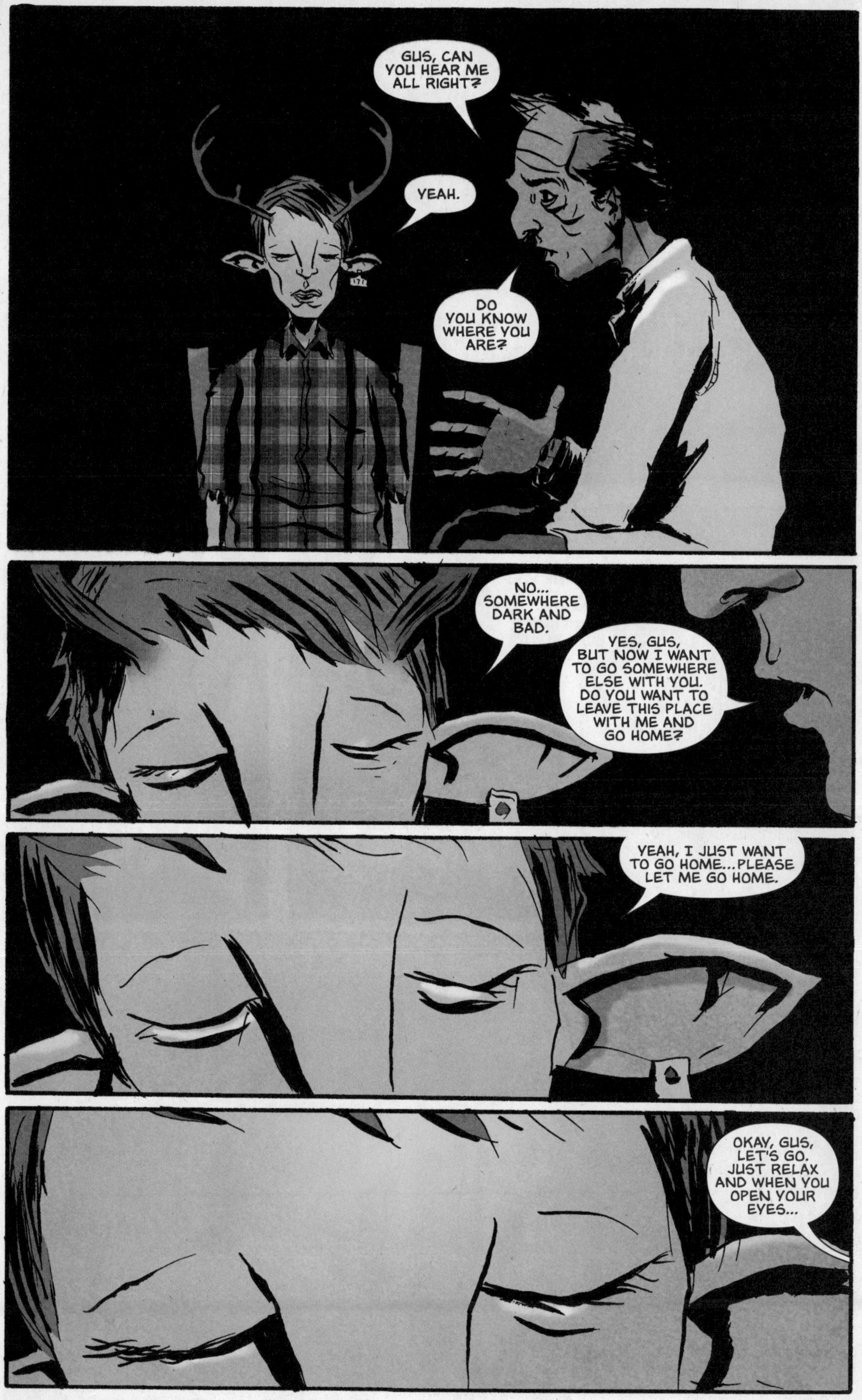
GUS, CAN YOU HEAR ME ALL RIGHT?
YEAH.
DO YOU KNOW WHERE YOU ARE?
NO... SOMEWHERE DARK AND BAD.
YES, GUS, BUT NOW I WANT TO GO SOMEWHERE ELSE WITH YOU. DO YOU WANT TO LEAVE THIS PLACE WITH ME AND GO HOME?
YEAH, I JUST WANT TO GO HOME... PLEASE LET ME GO HOME.
OKAY, GUS, LET'S GO. JUST RELAX AND WHEN YOU OPEN YOUR EYES...

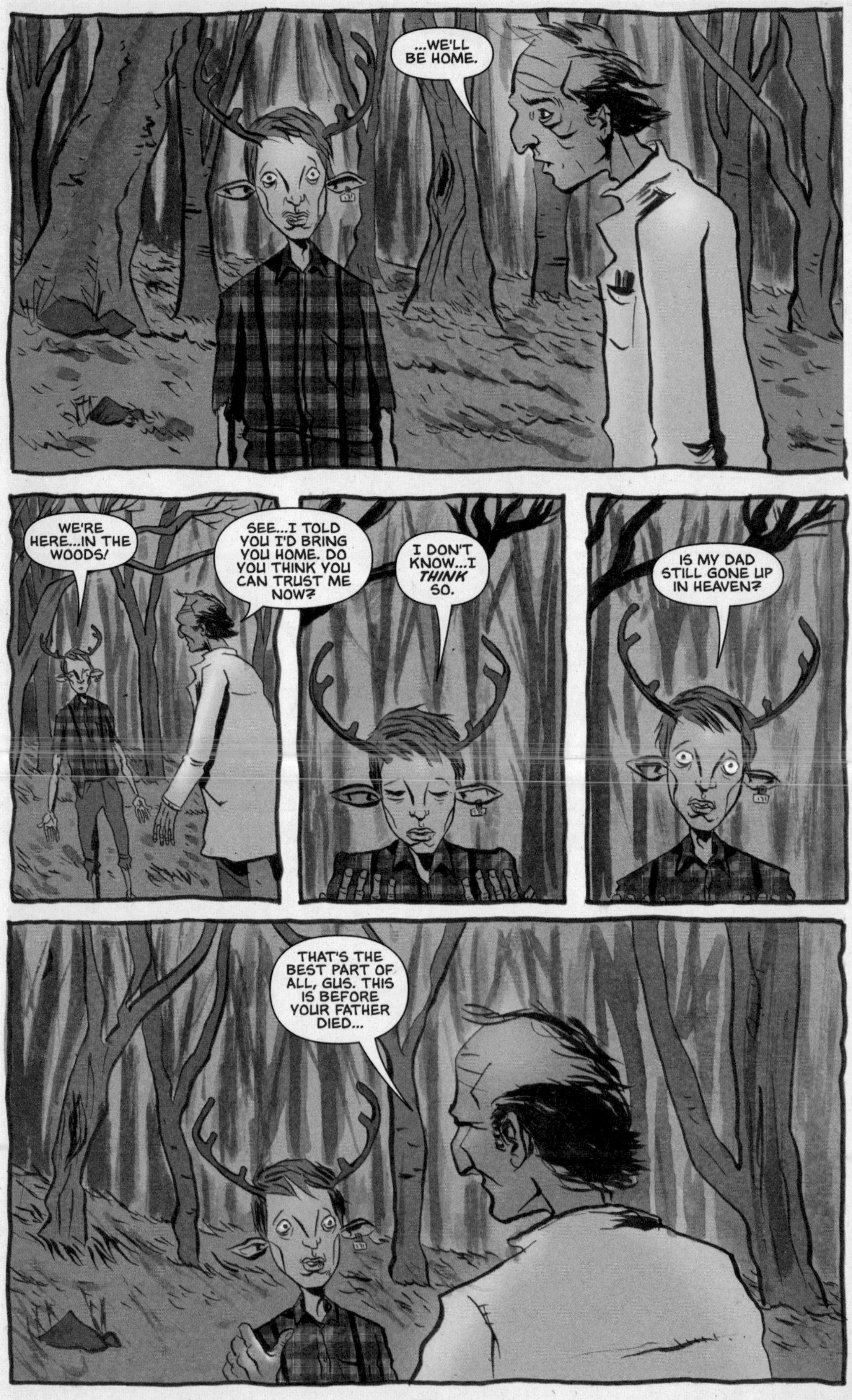
...WE'LL BE HOME.
WE'RE HERE...IN THE WOODS!
SEE...I TOLD YOU I'D BRING YOU HOME. DO YOU THINK YOU CAN TRUST ME NOW?
I DON'T KNOW...I *THINK* SO.
IS MY DAD STILL GONE UP IN HEAVEN?
THAT'S THE BEST PART OF ALL, GUS. THIS IS BEFORE YOUR FATHER DIED...

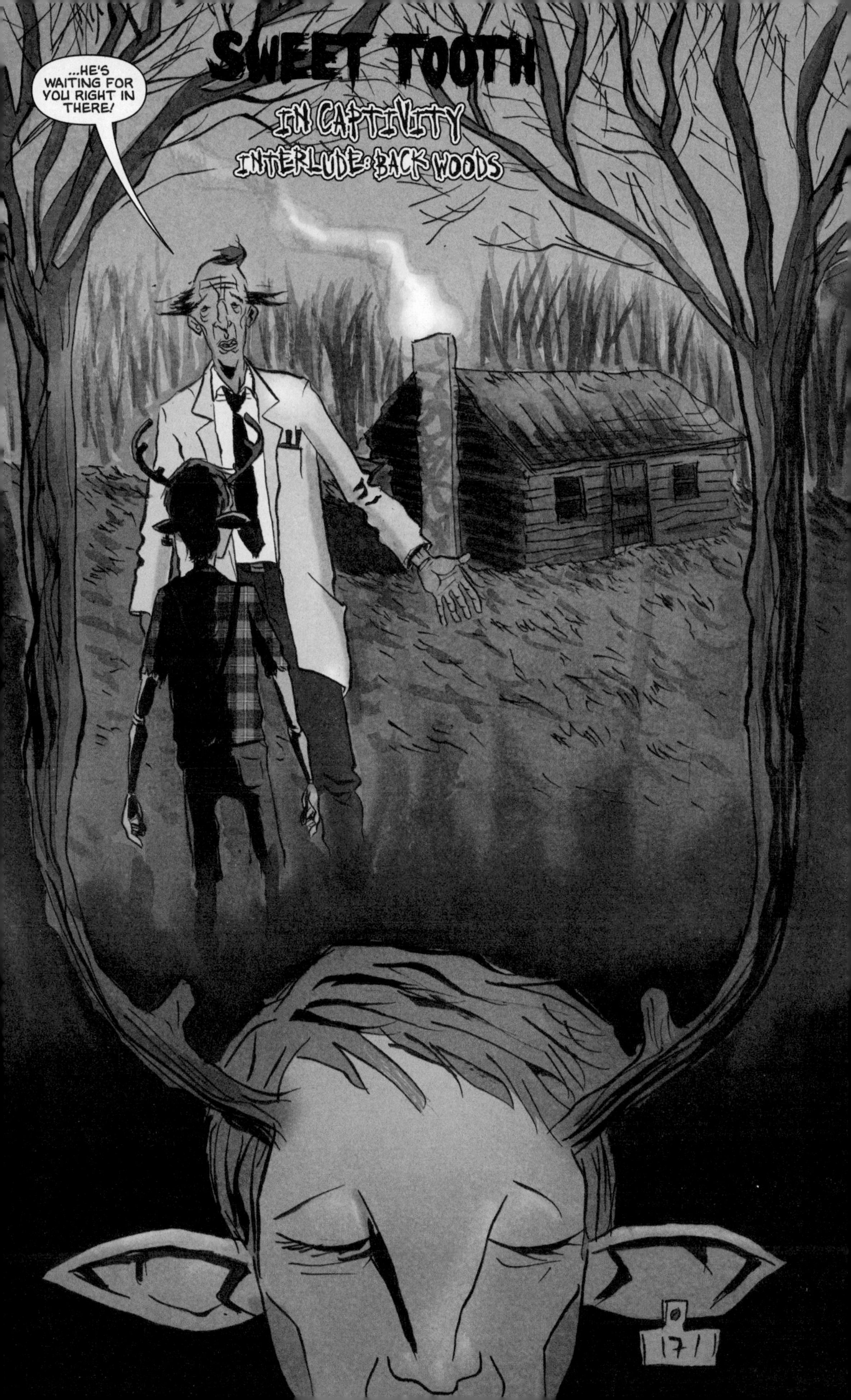
SWEET TOOTH
IN CAPTIVITY
INTERLUDE: BACK WOODS
...HE'S WAITING FOR YOU RIGHT IN THERE!
17

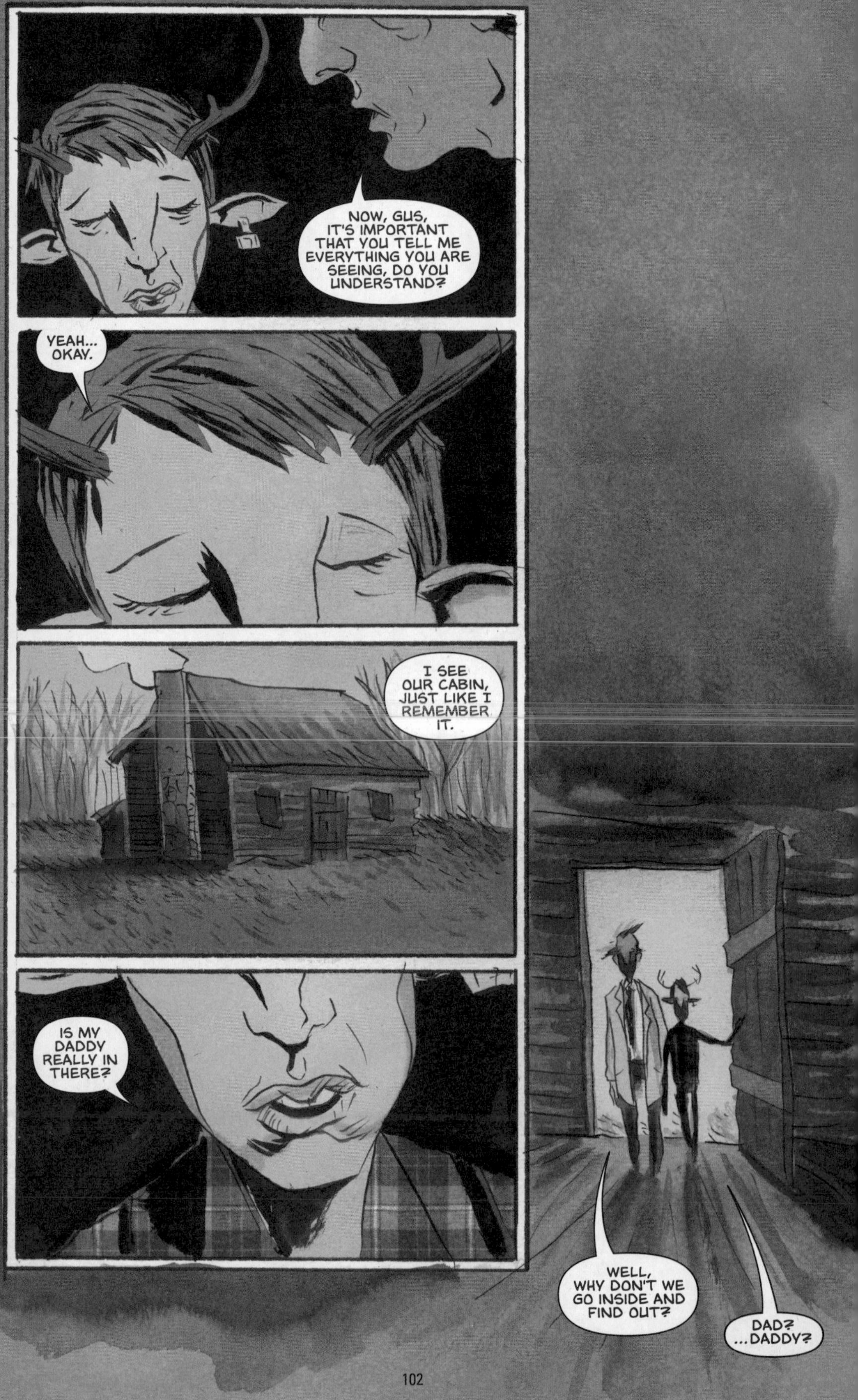
NOW, GUS, IT'S IMPORTANT THAT YOU TELL ME EVERYTHING YOU ARE SEEING, DO YOU UNDERSTAND?
YEAH... OKAY.
I SEE OUR CABIN, JUST LIKE I REMEMBER IT.
IS MY DADDY REALLY IN THERE?
WELL, WHY DON'T WE GO INSIDE AND FIND OUT?
DAD? ...DADDY?

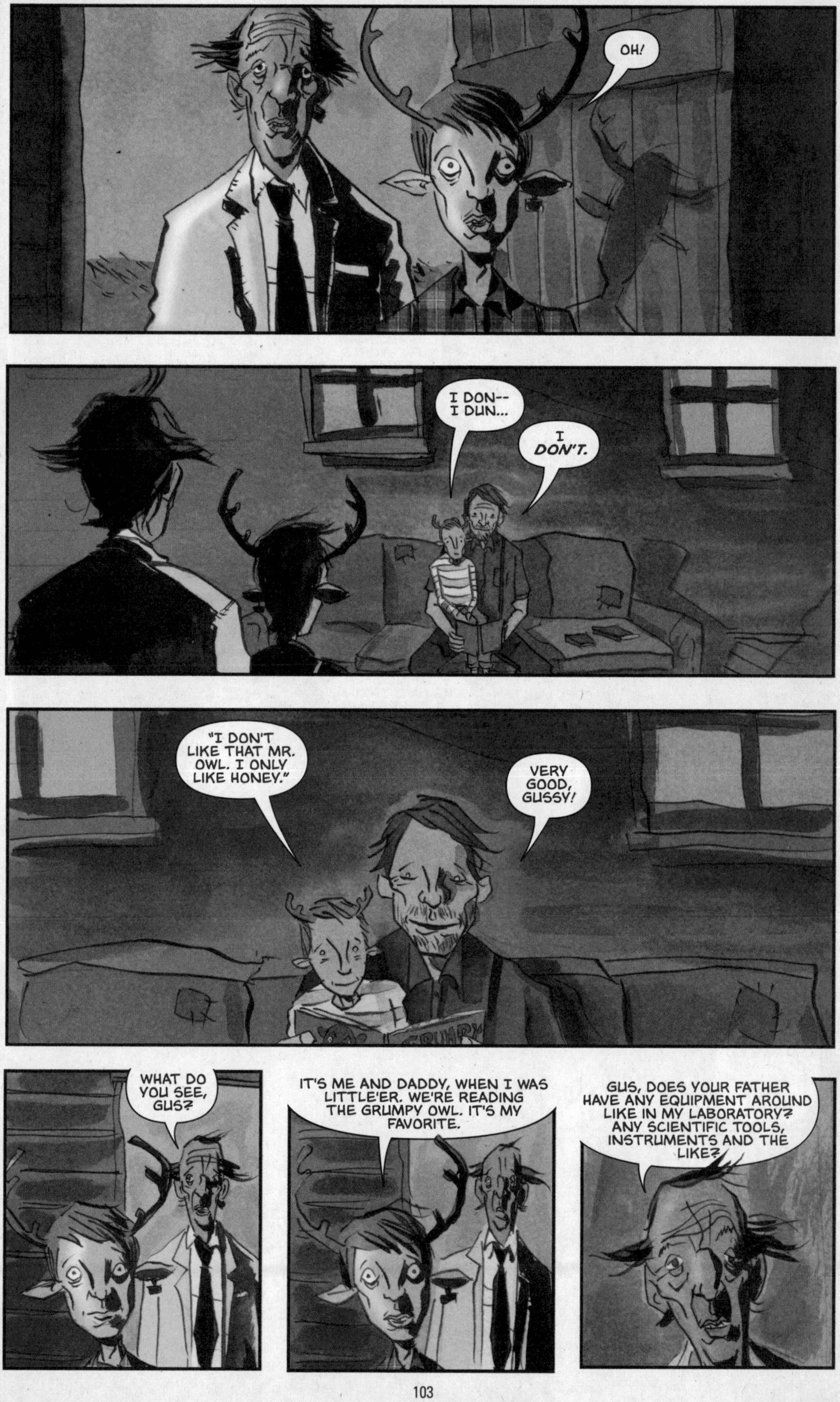
OH!
I DON--
I DUN...
I *DON'T.*
"I DON'T LIKE THAT MR. OWL. I ONLY LIKE HONEY."
VERY GOOD, GUSSY!
WHAT DO YOU SEE, GUS?
IT'S ME AND DADDY, WHEN I WAS LITTLE'ER. WE'RE READING THE GRUMPY OWL. IT'S MY FAVORITE.
GUS, DOES YOUR FATHER HAVE ANY EQUIPMENT AROUND LIKE IN MY LABORATORY? ANY SCIENTIFIC TOOLS, INSTRUMENTS AND THE LIKE?

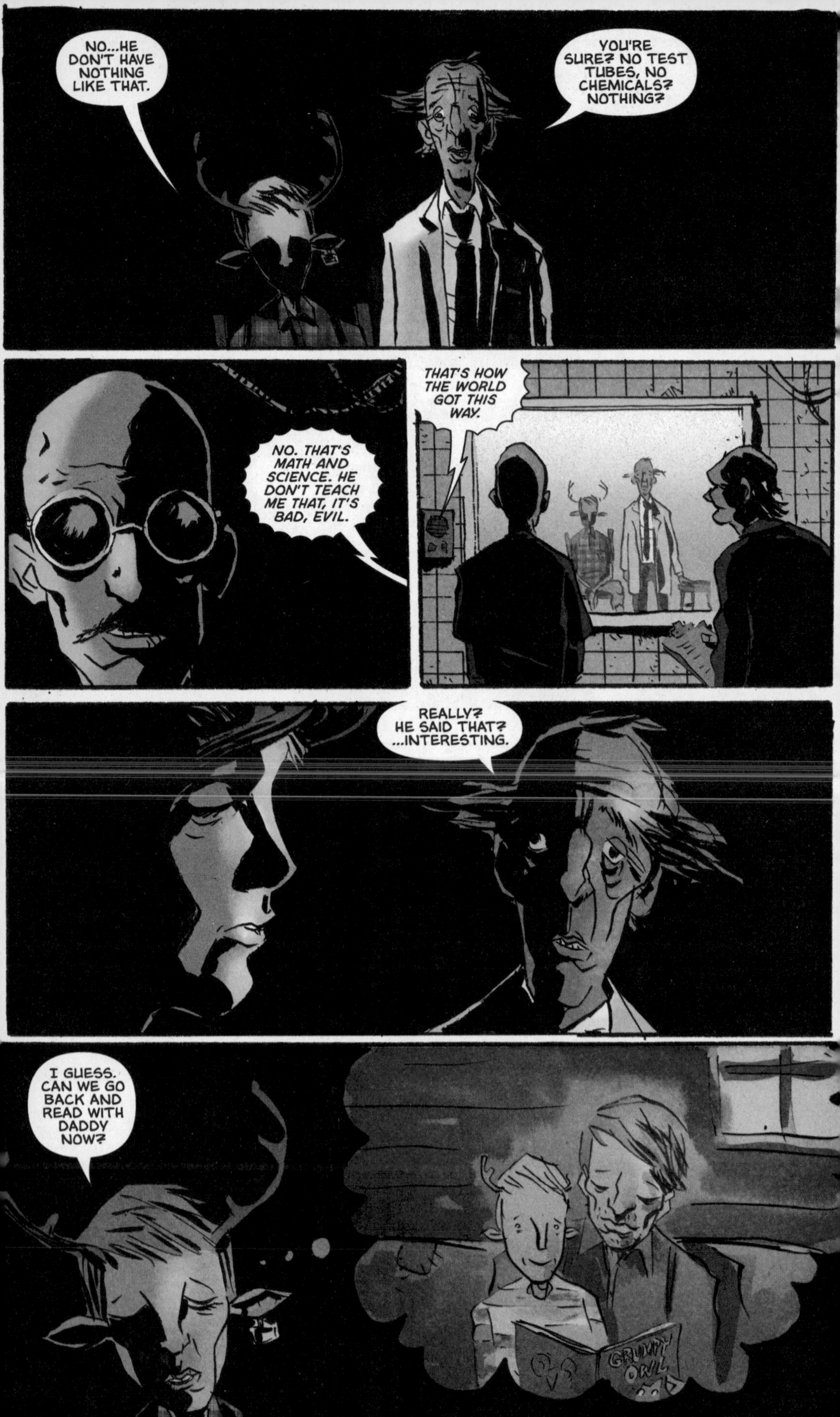
NO...HE DON'T HAVE NOTHING LIKE THAT.
YOU'RE SURE? NO TEST TUBES, NO CHEMICALS? NOTHING?
NO. THAT'S MATH AND SCIENCE. HE DON'T TEACH ME THAT, IT'S BAD, EVIL.
THAT'S HOW THE WORLD GOT THIS WAY.
REALLY? HE SAID THAT? ...INTERESTING.
I GUESS. CAN WE GO BACK AND READ WITH DADDY NOW?
GRUMPY OWL

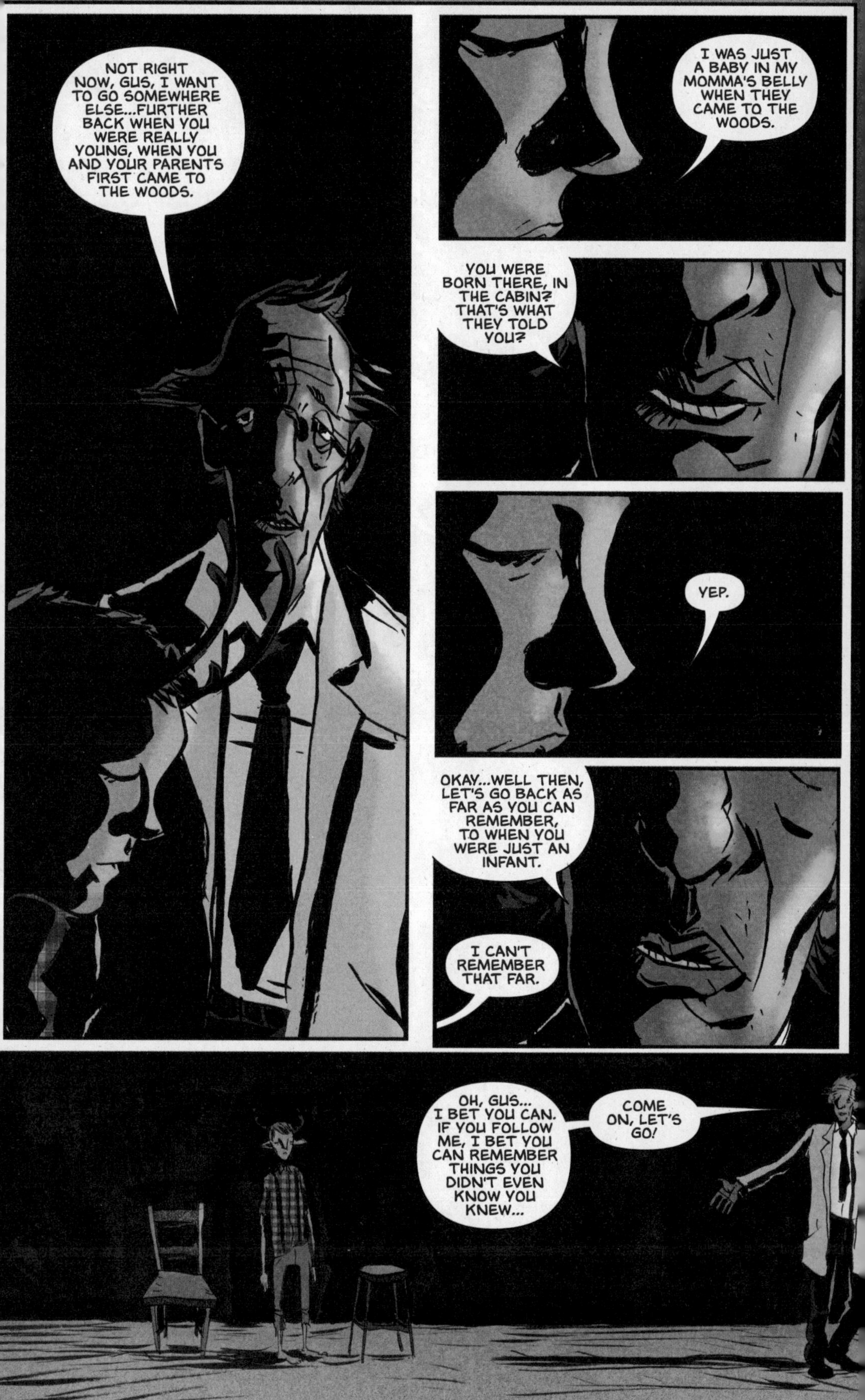
NOT RIGHT NOW, GUS, I WANT TO GO SOMEWHERE ELSE...FURTHER BACK WHEN YOU WERE REALLY YOUNG, WHEN YOU AND YOUR PARENTS FIRST CAME TO THE WOODS.
I WAS JUST A BABY IN MY MOMMA'S BELLY WHEN THEY CAME TO THE WOODS.
YOU WERE BORN THERE, IN THE CABIN? THAT'S WHAT THEY TOLD YOU?
YEP.
OKAY...WELL THEN, LET'S GO BACK AS FAR AS YOU CAN REMEMBER, TO WHEN YOU WERE JUST AN INFANT.
I CAN'T REMEMBER THAT FAR.
OH, GUS... I BET YOU CAN. IF YOU FOLLOW ME, I BET YOU CAN REMEMBER THINGS YOU DIDN'T EVEN KNOW YOU KNEW...
COME ON, LET'S GO!

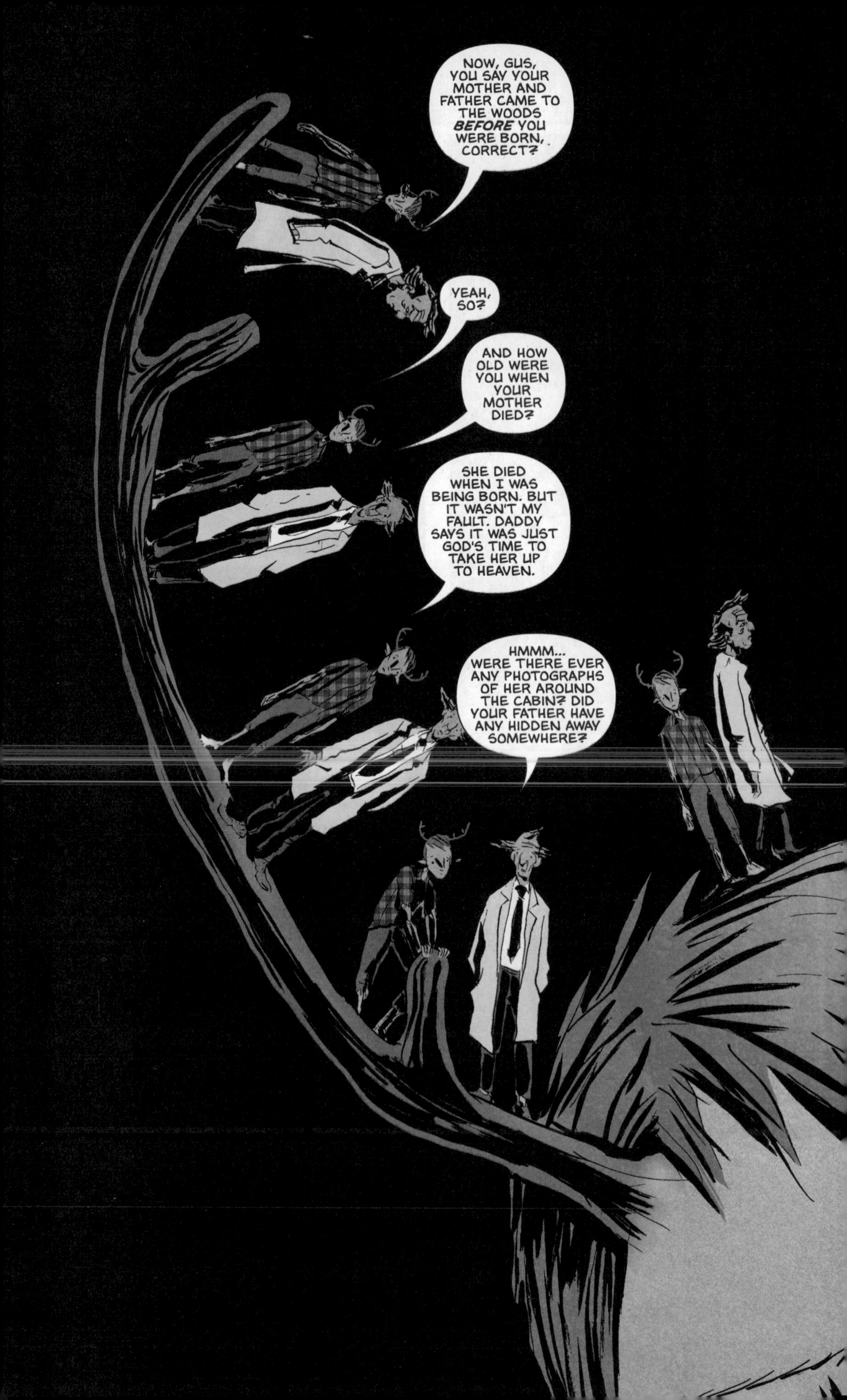
NOW, GUS, YOU SAY YOUR MOTHER AND FATHER CAME TO THE WOODS *BEFORE* YOU WERE BORN, CORRECT?
YEAH, SO?
AND HOW OLD WERE YOU WHEN YOUR MOTHER DIED?
SHE DIED WHEN I WAS BEING BORN. BUT IT WASN'T MY FAULT. DADDY SAYS IT WAS JUST GOD'S TIME TO TAKE HER UP TO HEAVEN.
HMMM... WERE THERE EVER ANY PHOTOGRAPHS OF HER AROUND THE CABIN? DID YOUR FATHER HAVE ANY HIDDEN AWAY SOMEWHERE?

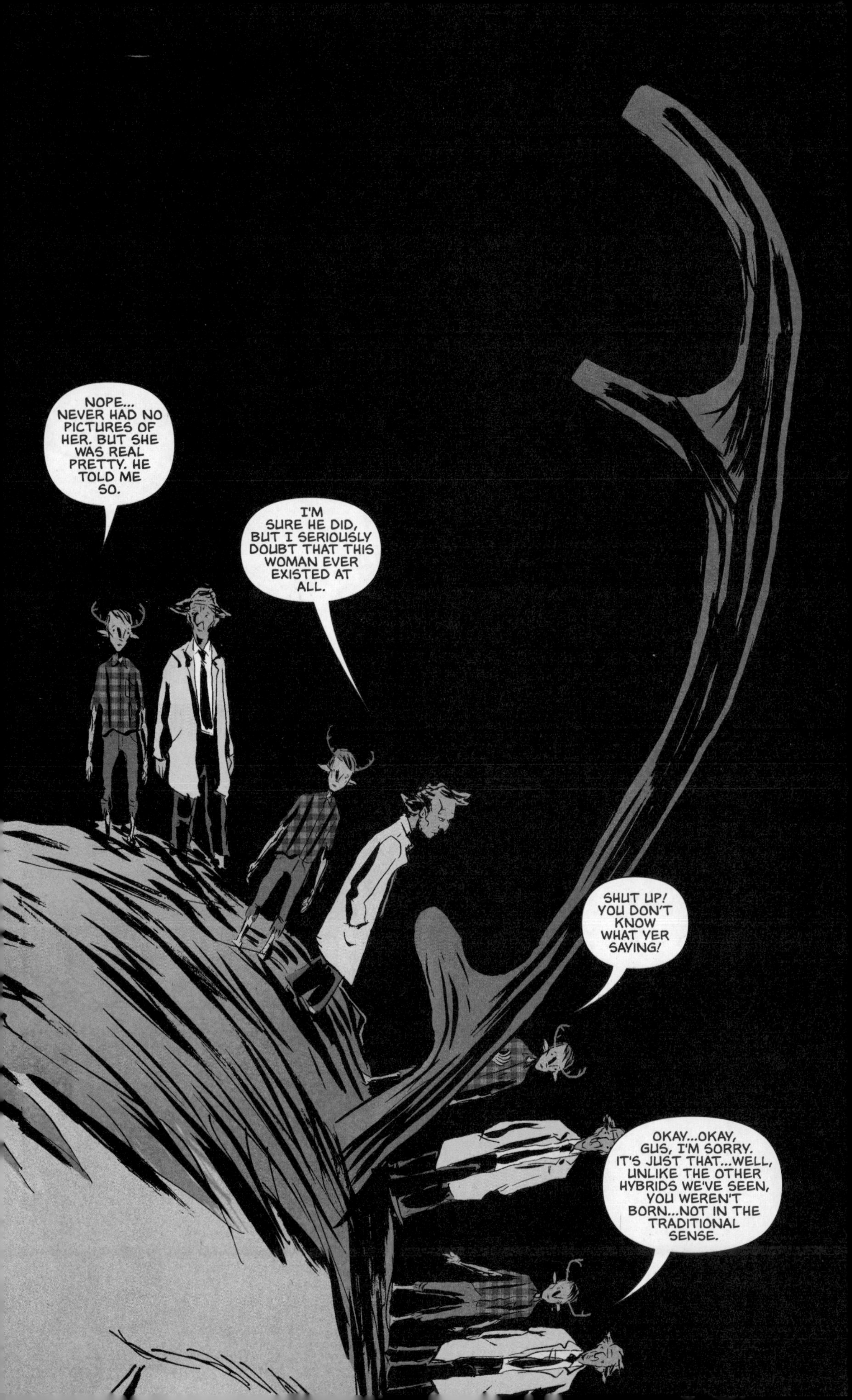
NOPE... NEVER HAD NO PICTURES OF HER. BUT SHE WAS REAL PRETTY. HE TOLD ME SO.
I'M SURE HE DID, BUT I SERIOUSLY DOUBT THAT THIS WOMAN EVER EXISTED AT ALL.
SHUT UP! YOU DON'T KNOW WHAT YER SAYING!
OKAY...OKAY, GUS, I'M SORRY. IT'S JUST THAT...WELL, UNLIKE THE OTHER HYBRIDS WE'VE SEEN, YOU WEREN'T BORN...NOT IN THE TRADITIONAL SENSE.

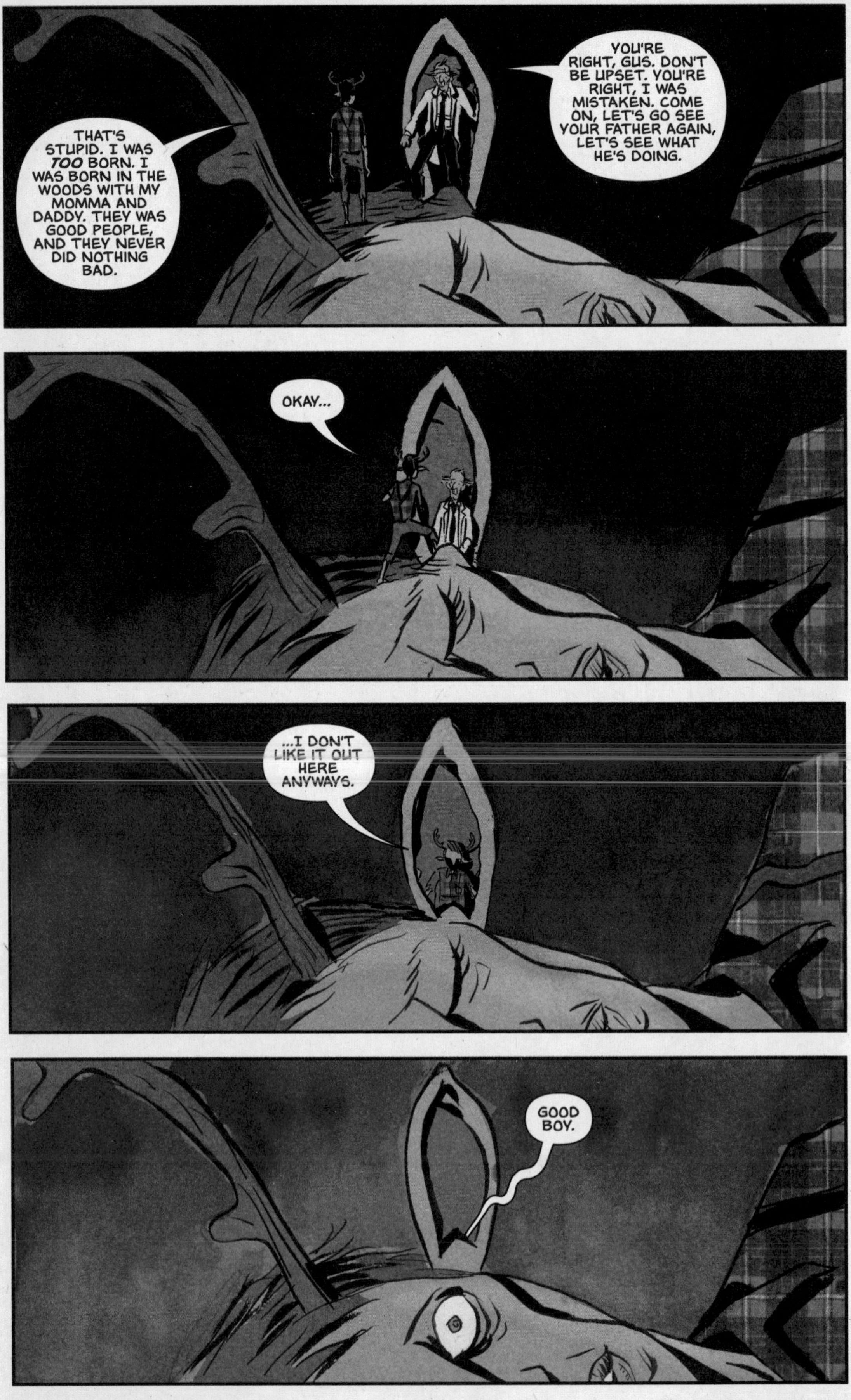
THAT'S STUPID. I WAS *TOO* BORN. I WAS BORN IN THE WOODS WITH MY MOMMA AND DADDY. THEY WAS GOOD PEOPLE, AND THEY NEVER DID NOTHING BAD.
YOU'RE RIGHT, GUS. DON'T BE UPSET. YOU'RE RIGHT, I WAS MISTAKEN. COME ON, LET'S GO SEE YOUR FATHER AGAIN, LET'S SEE WHAT HE'S DOING.
OKAY...
...I DON'T LIKE IT OUT HERE ANYWAYS.
GOOD BOY.

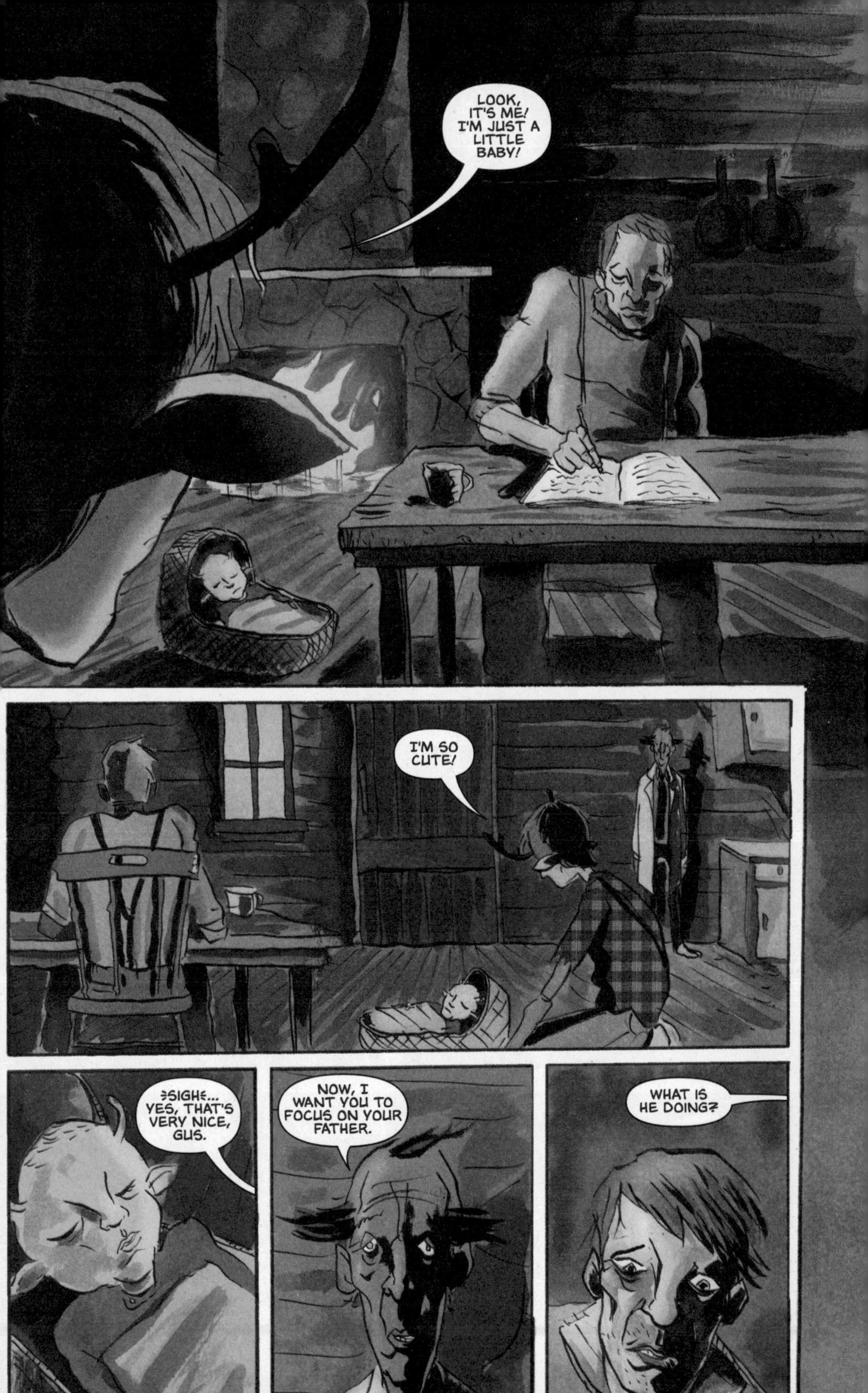
LOOK, IT'S ME! I'M JUST A LITTLE BABY!
I'M SO CUTE!
⋾SIGH⋲... YES, THAT'S VERY NICE, GUS.
NOW, I WANT YOU TO FOCUS ON YOUR FATHER.
WHAT IS HE DOING?

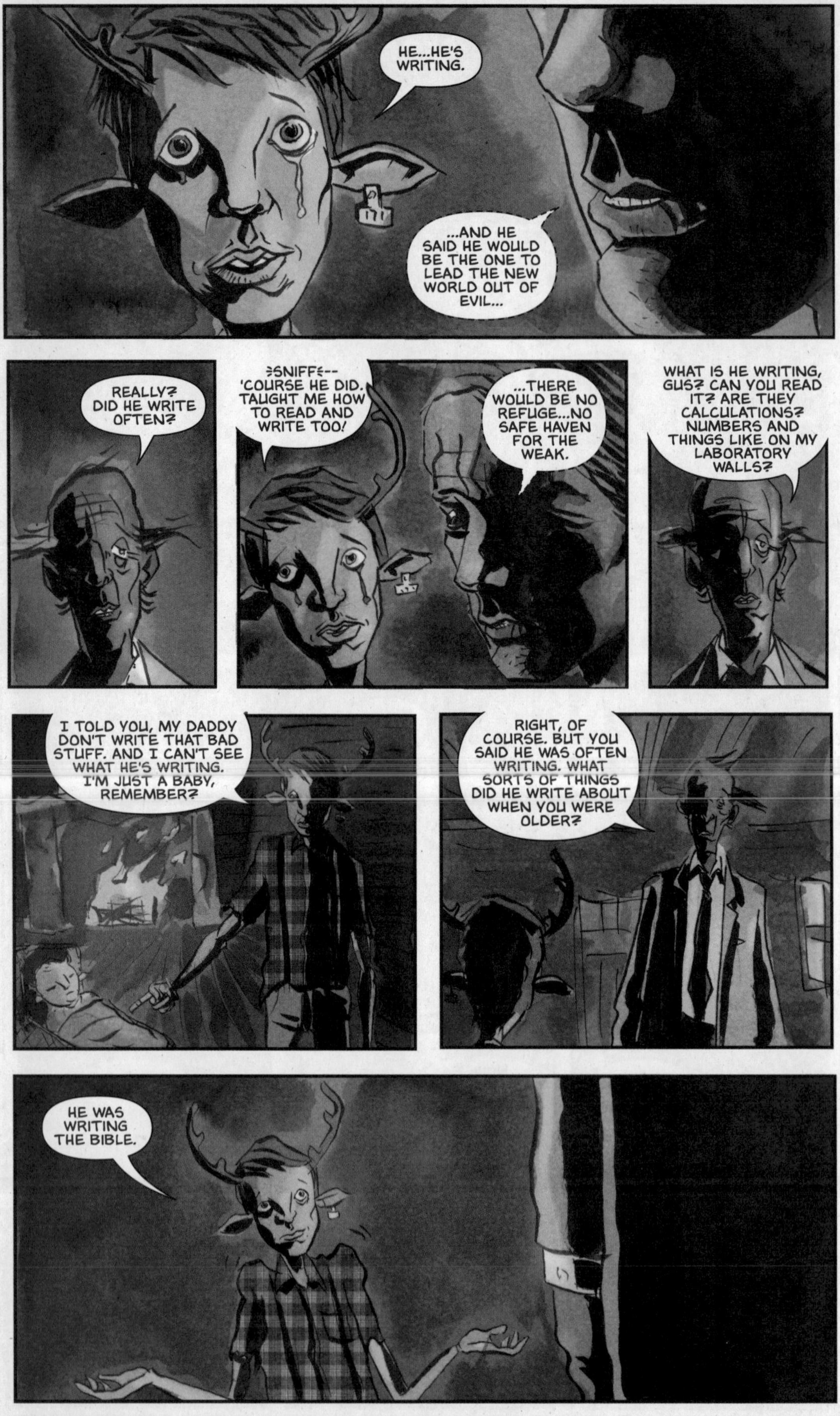
HE...HE'S WRITING.
...AND HE SAID HE WOULD BE THE ONE TO LEAD THE NEW WORLD OUT OF EVIL...
REALLY? DID HE WRITE OFTEN?
≶SNIFF≶-- 'COURSE HE DID. TAUGHT ME HOW TO READ AND WRITE TOO!
...THERE WOULD BE NO REFUGE...NO SAFE HAVEN FOR THE WEAK.
WHAT IS HE WRITING, GUS? CAN YOU READ IT? ARE THEY CALCULATIONS? NUMBERS AND THINGS LIKE ON MY LABORATORY WALLS?
I TOLD YOU, MY DADDY DON'T WRITE THAT BAD STUFF. AND I CAN'T SEE WHAT HE'S WRITING. I'M JUST A BABY, REMEMBER?
RIGHT, OF COURSE. BUT YOU SAID HE WAS OFTEN WRITING. WHAT SORTS OF THINGS DID HE WRITE ABOUT WHEN YOU WERE OLDER?
HE WAS WRITING THE BIBLE.

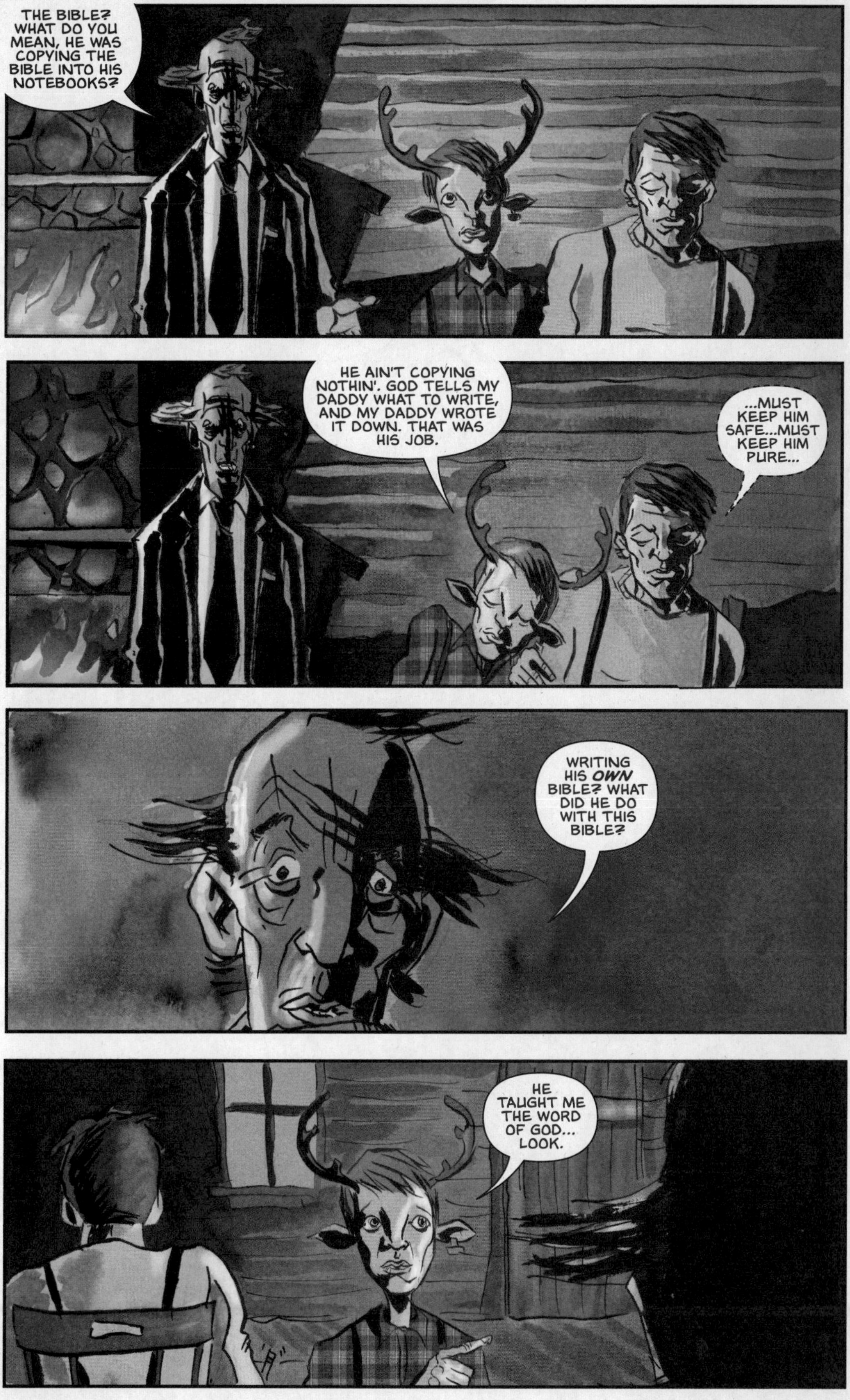
THE BIBLE? WHAT DO YOU MEAN, HE WAS COPYING THE BIBLE INTO HIS NOTEBOOKS?
HE AIN'T COPYING NOTHIN'. GOD TELLS MY DADDY WHAT TO WRITE, AND MY DADDY WROTE IT DOWN. THAT WAS HIS JOB.
...MUST KEEP HIM SAFE...MUST KEEP HIM PURE...
WRITING HIS *OWN* BIBLE? WHAT DID HE DO WITH THIS BIBLE?
HE TAUGHT ME THE WORD OF GOD... LOOK.

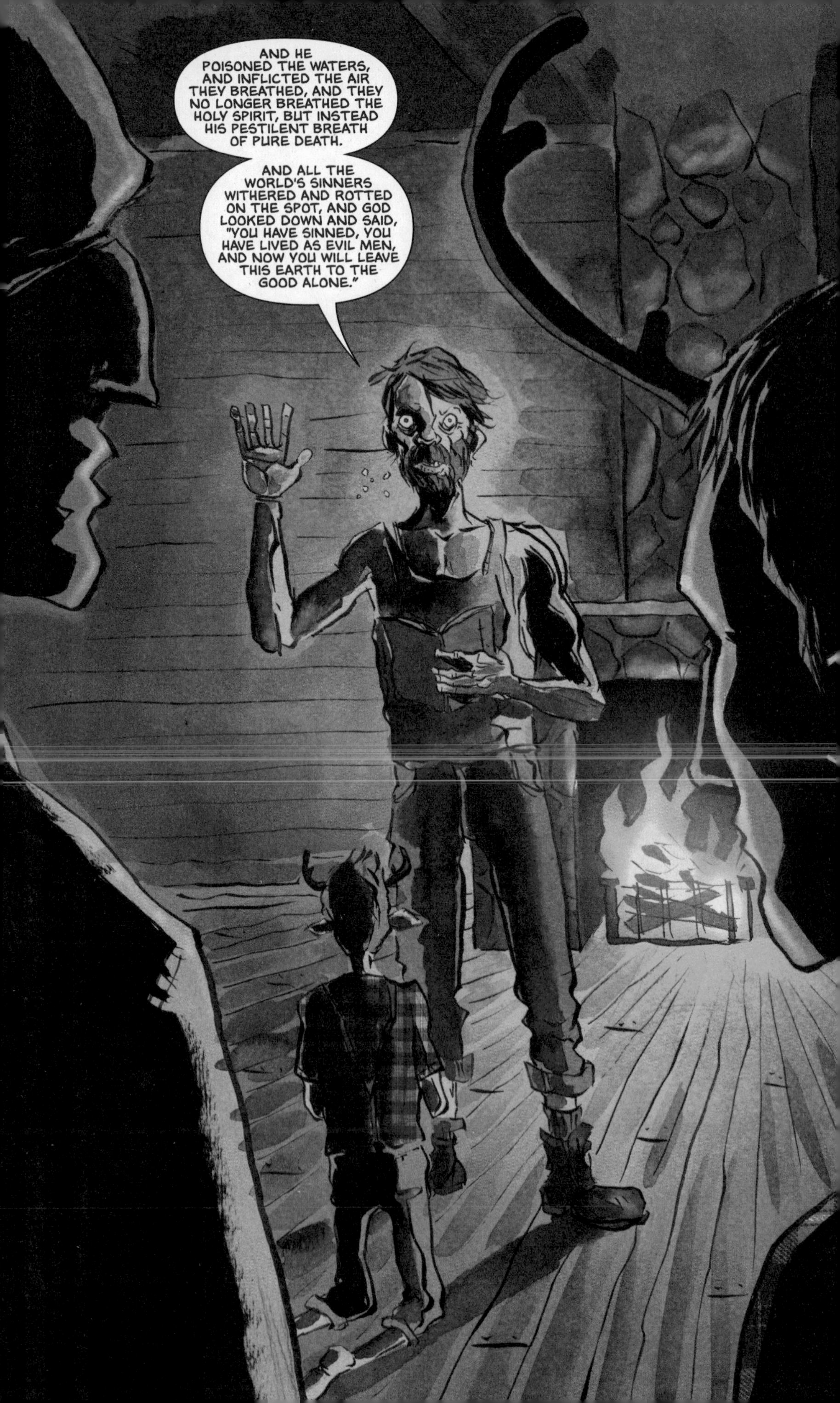
AND HE POISONED THE WATERS, AND INFLICTED THE AIR THEY BREATHED, AND THEY NO LONGER BREATHED THE HOLY SPIRIT, BUT INSTEAD HIS PESTILENT BREATH OF PURE DEATH.
AND ALL THE WORLD'S SINNERS WITHERED AND ROTTED ON THE SPOT, AND GOD LOOKED DOWN AND SAID, "YOU HAVE SINNED, YOU HAVE LIVED AS EVIL MEN, AND NOW YOU WILL LEAVE THIS EARTH TO THE GOOD ALONE."

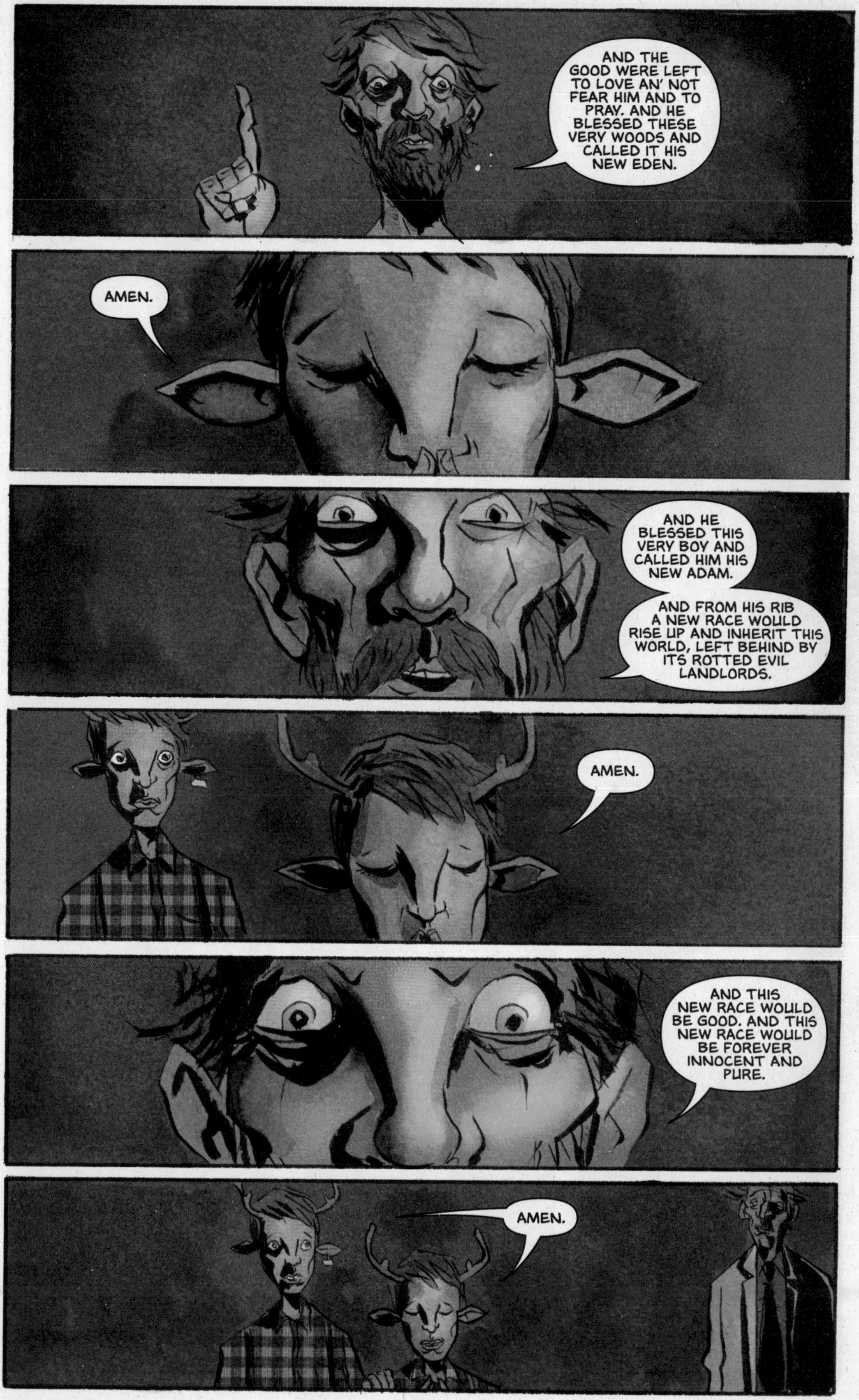
AND THE GOOD WERE LEFT TO LOVE AN' NOT FEAR HIM AND TO PRAY. AND HE BLESSED THESE VERY WOODS AND CALLED IT HIS NEW EDEN.
AMEN.
AND HE BLESSED THIS VERY BOY AND CALLED HIM HIS NEW ADAM.
AND FROM HIS RIB A NEW RACE WOULD RISE UP AND INHERIT THIS WORLD, LEFT BEHIND BY ITS ROTTED EVIL LANDLORDS.
AMEN.
AND THIS NEW RACE WOULD BE GOOD. AND THIS NEW RACE WOULD BE FOREVER INNOCENT AND PURE.
AMEN.

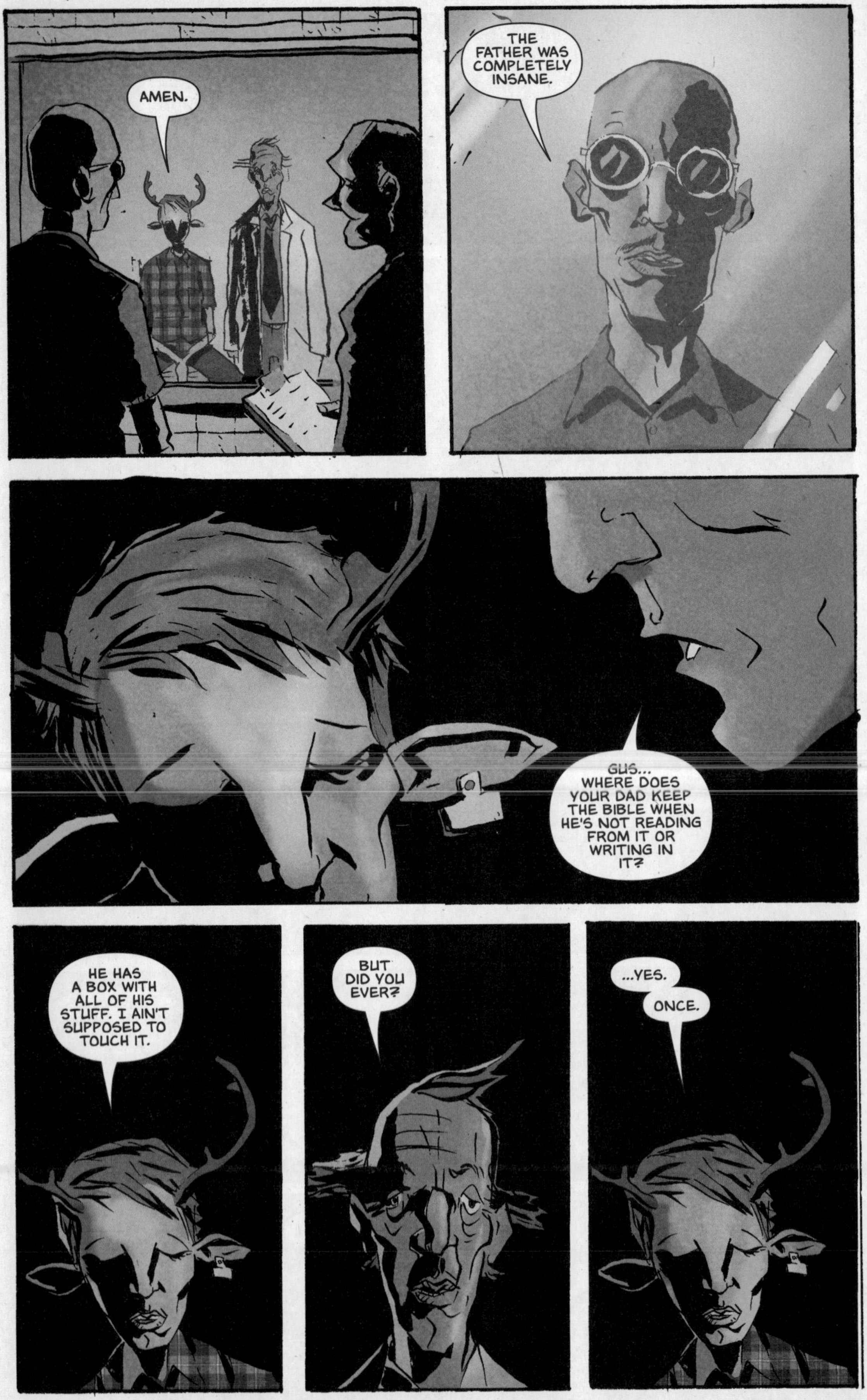
AMEN.
THE FATHER WAS COMPLETELY INSANE.
GUS... WHERE DOES YOUR DAD KEEP THE BIBLE WHEN HE'S NOT READING FROM IT OR WRITING IN IT?
HE HAS A BOX WITH ALL OF HIS STUFF. I AIN'T SUPPOSED TO TOUCH IT.
BUT DID YOU EVER?
...YES.
ONCE.

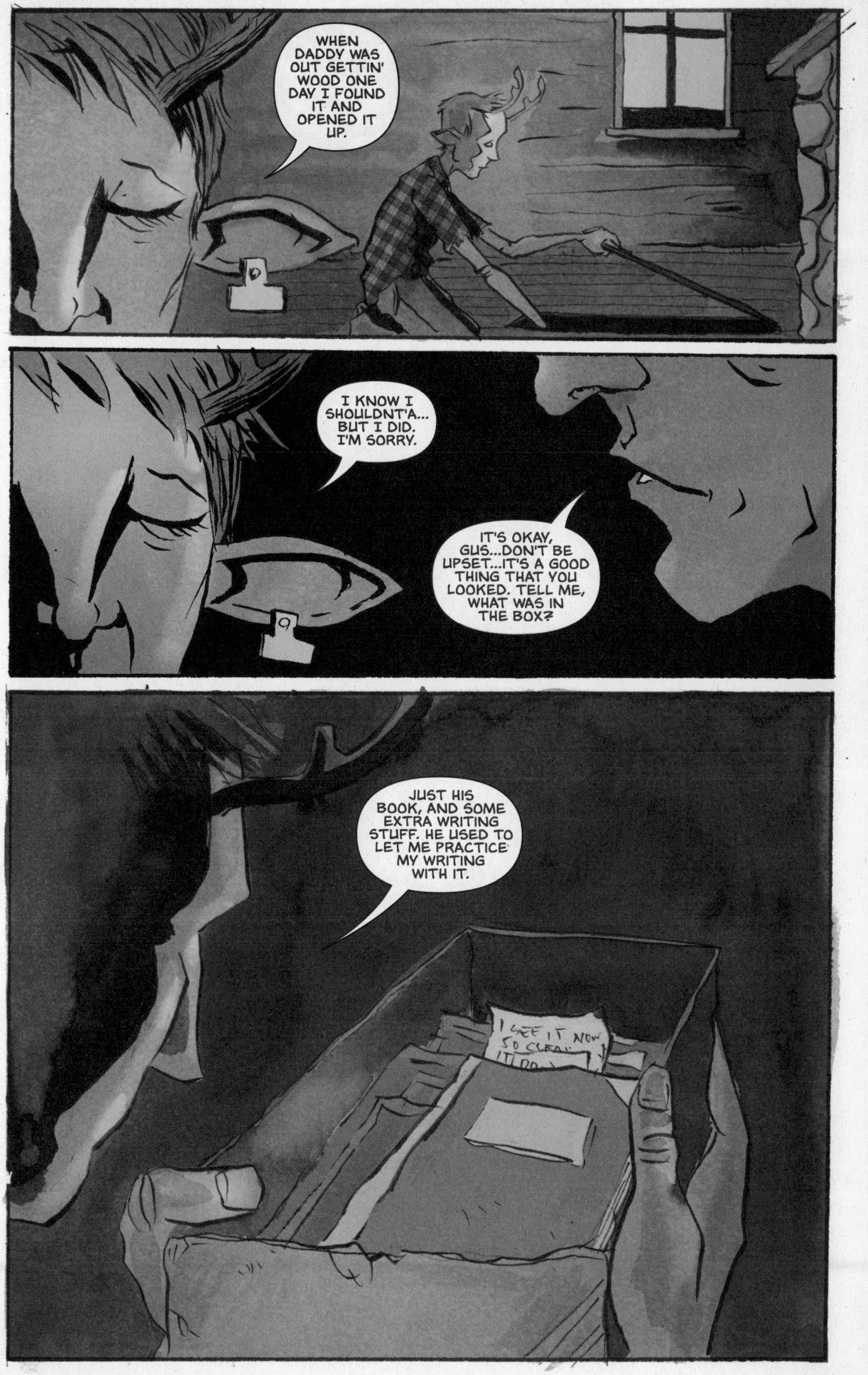
WHEN DADDY WAS OUT GETTIN' WOOD ONE DAY I FOUND IT AND OPENED IT UP.
I KNOW I SHOULDNT'A... BUT I DID. I'M SORRY.
IT'S OKAY, GUS...DON'T BE UPSET...IT'S A GOOD THING THAT YOU LOOKED. TELL ME, WHAT WAS IN THE BOX?
JUST HIS BOOK, AND SOME EXTRA WRITING STUFF. HE USED TO LET ME PRACTICE MY WRITING WITH IT.

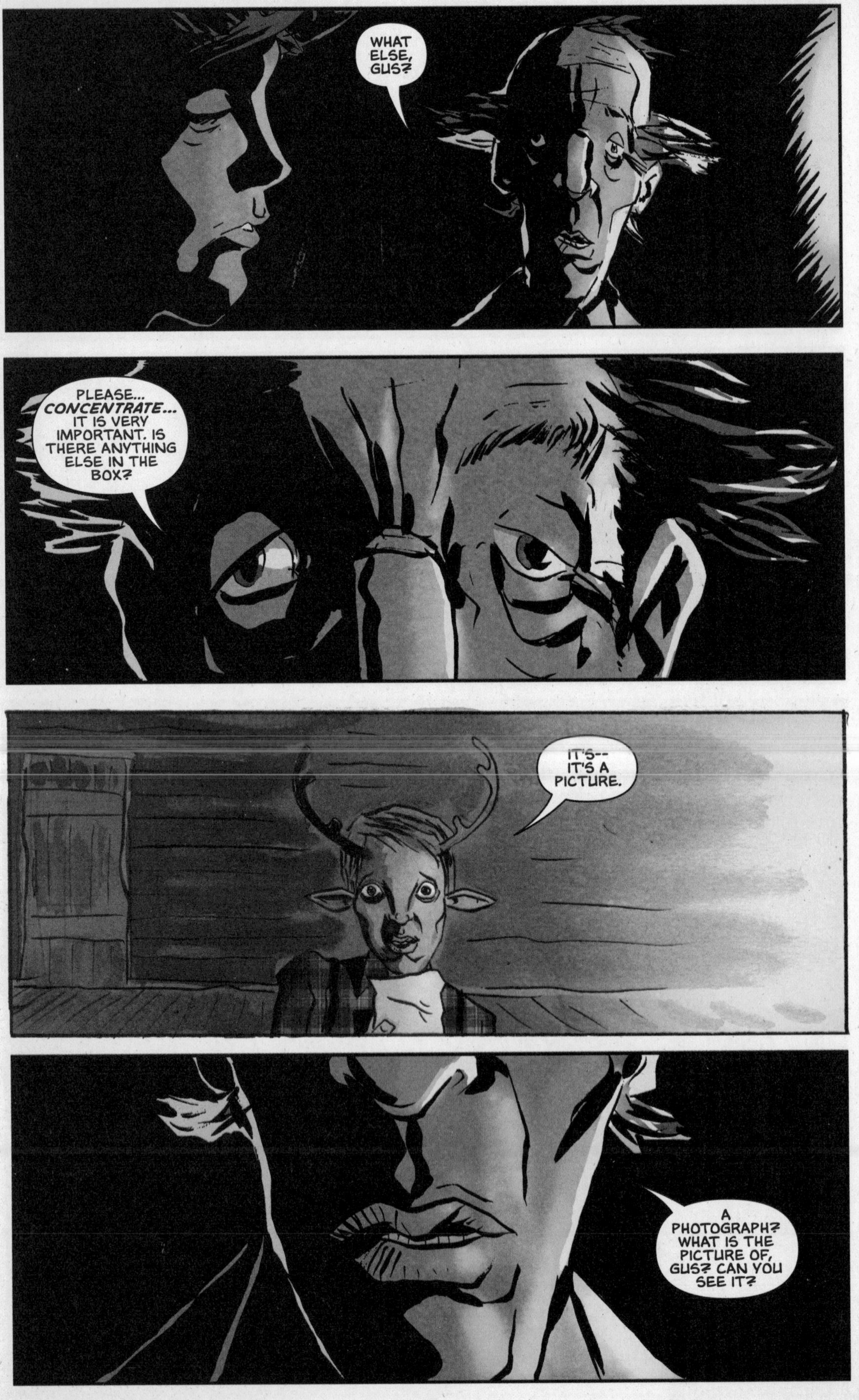
WHAT ELSE, GUS?
PLEASE... **CONCENTRATE...** IT IS VERY IMPORTANT. IS THERE ANYTHING ELSE IN THE BOX?
IT'S-- IT'S A PICTURE.
A PHOTOGRAPH? WHAT IS THE PICTURE OF, GUS? CAN YOU SEE IT?

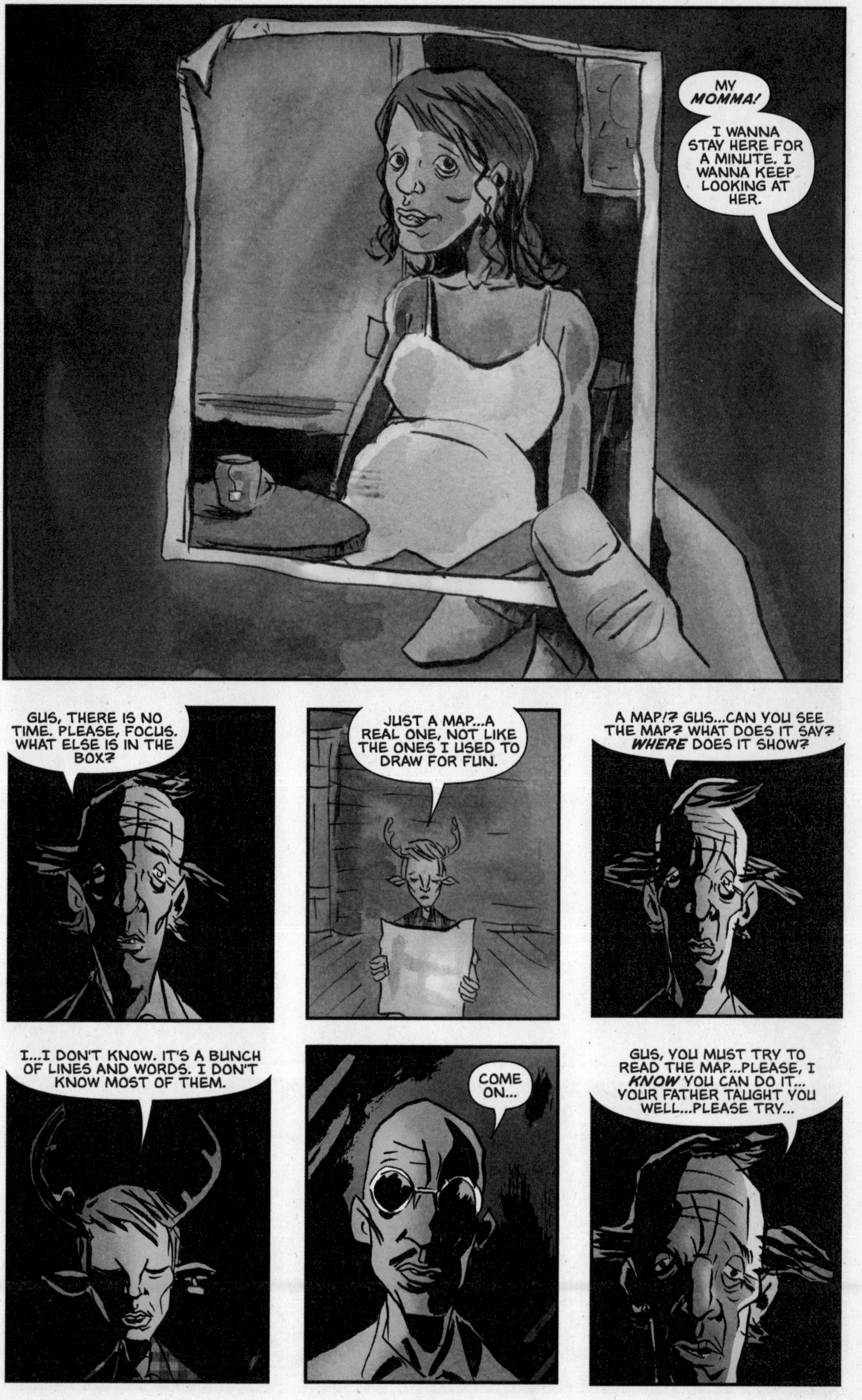
MY *MOMMA!*
I WANNA STAY HERE FOR A MINUTE. I WANNA KEEP LOOKING AT HER.
GUS, THERE IS NO TIME. PLEASE, FOCUS. WHAT ELSE IS IN THE BOX?
JUST A MAP...A REAL ONE, NOT LIKE THE ONES I USED TO DRAW FOR FUN.
A MAP!? GUS...CAN YOU SEE THE MAP? WHAT DOES IT SAY? *WHERE* DOES IT SHOW?
I...I DON'T KNOW. IT'S A BUNCH OF LINES AND WORDS. I DON'T KNOW MOST OF THEM.
COME ON...
GUS, YOU MUST TRY TO READ THE MAP...PLEASE, I *KNOW* YOU CAN DO IT... YOUR FATHER TAUGHT YOU WELL...PLEASE TRY...

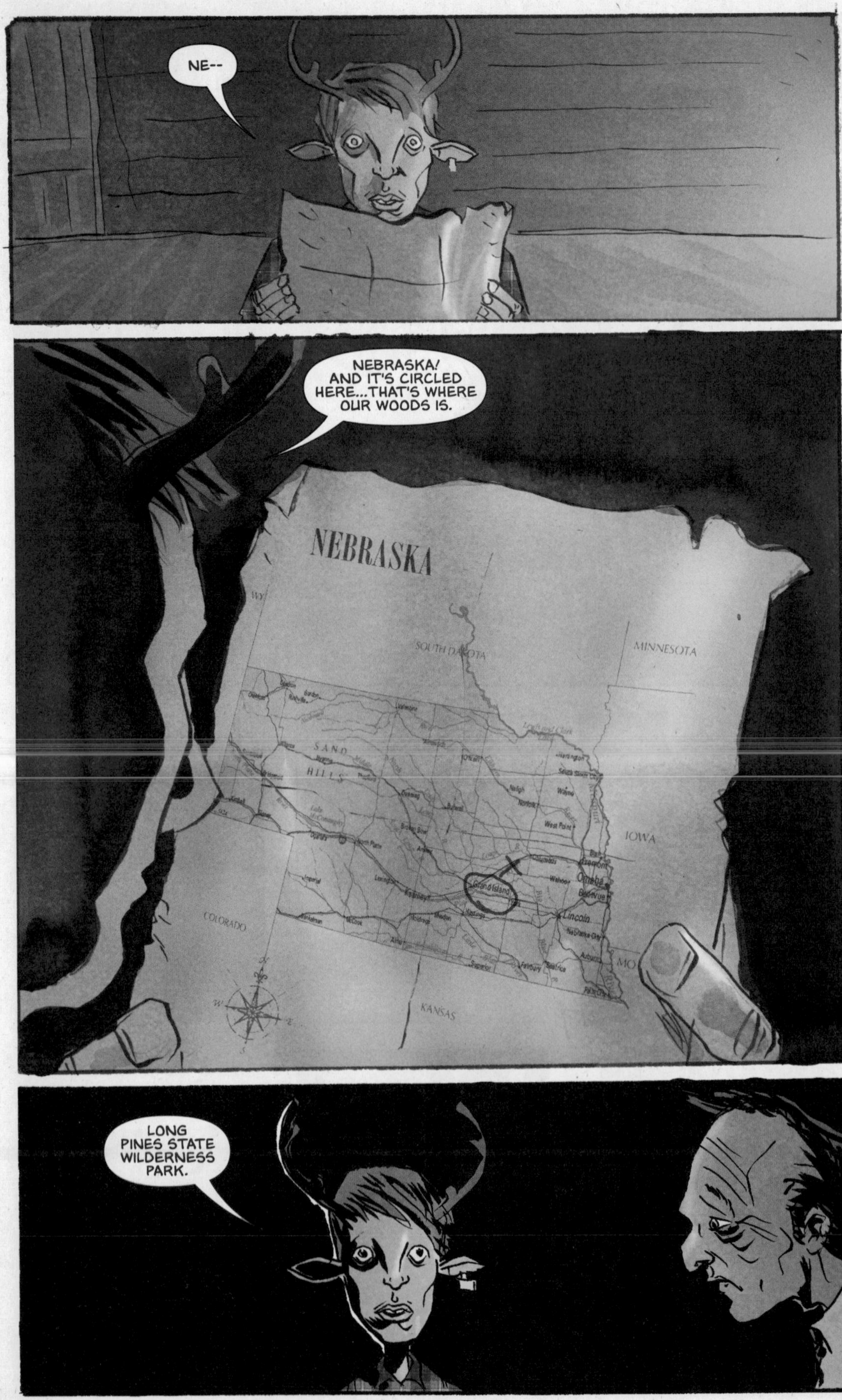
NE--
NEBRASKA! AND IT'S CIRCLED HERE...THAT'S WHERE OUR WOODS IS.
NEBRASKA
SOUTH DAKOTA
MINNESOTA
IOWA
COLORADO
KANSAS
MO
SAND HILLS
Grand Island
Lincoln
Omaha
West Point
LONG PINES STATE WILDERNESS PARK.

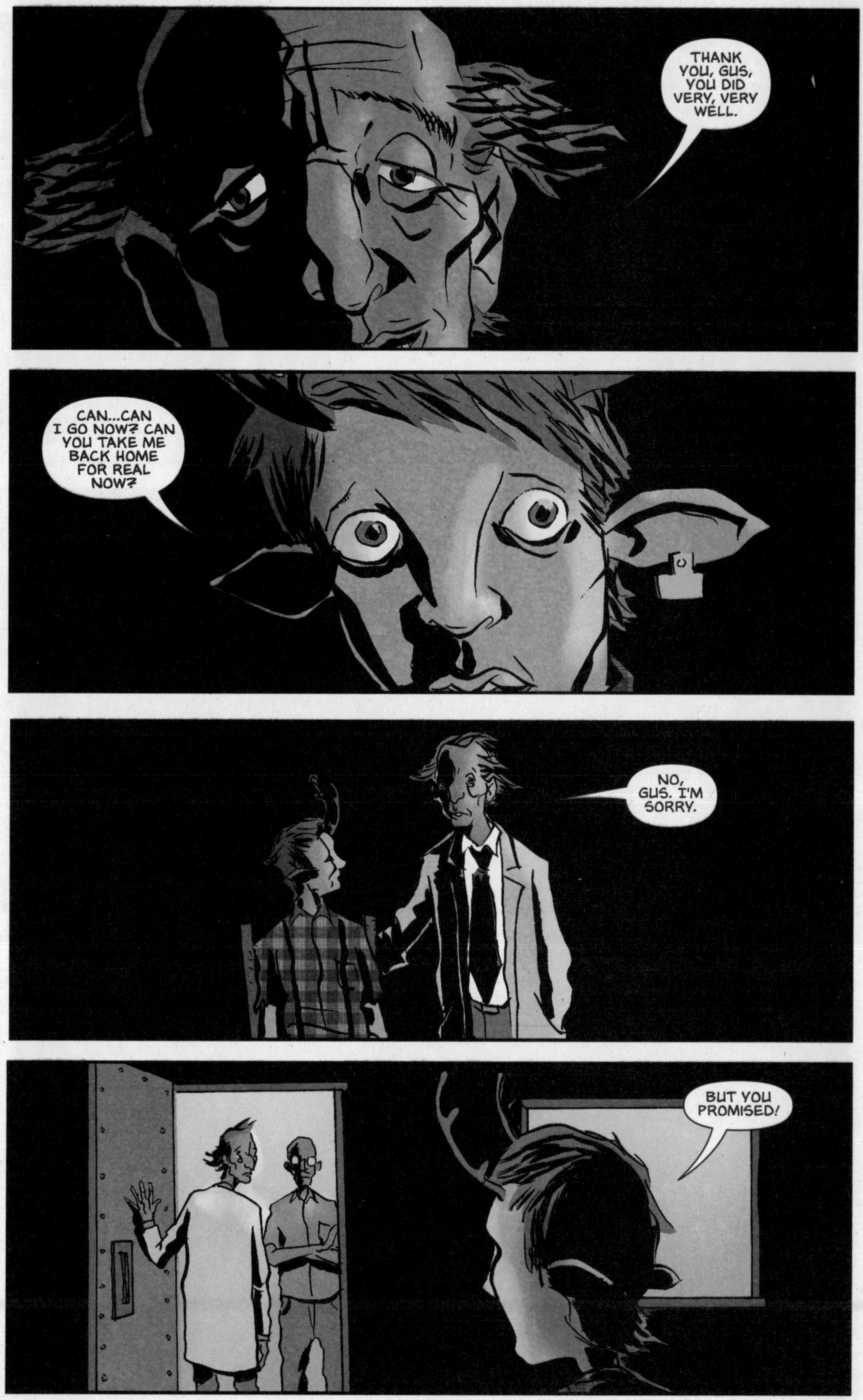
THANK YOU, GUS, YOU DID VERY, VERY WELL.
CAN...CAN I GO NOW? CAN YOU TAKE ME BACK HOME FOR REAL NOW?
NO, GUS. I'M SORRY.
BUT YOU PROMISED!

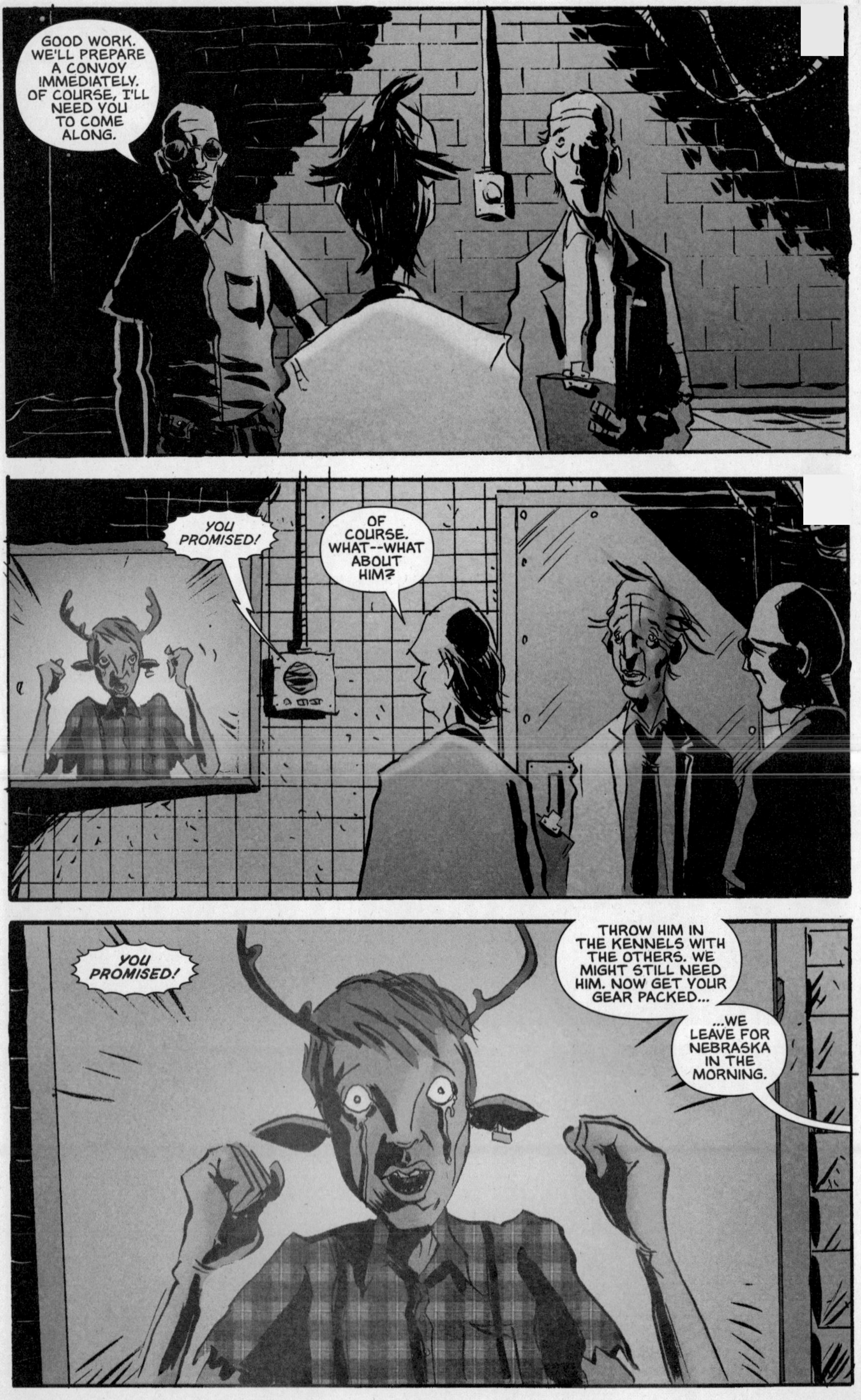
GOOD WORK. WE'LL PREPARE A CONVOY IMMEDIATELY. OF COURSE, I'LL NEED YOU TO COME ALONG.
YOU PROMISED!
OF COURSE. WHAT--WHAT ABOUT HIM?
YOU PROMISED!
THROW HIM IN THE KENNELS WITH THE OTHERS. WE MIGHT STILL NEED HIM. NOW GET YOUR GEAR PACKED...
...WE LEAVE FOR NEBRASKA IN THE MORNING.

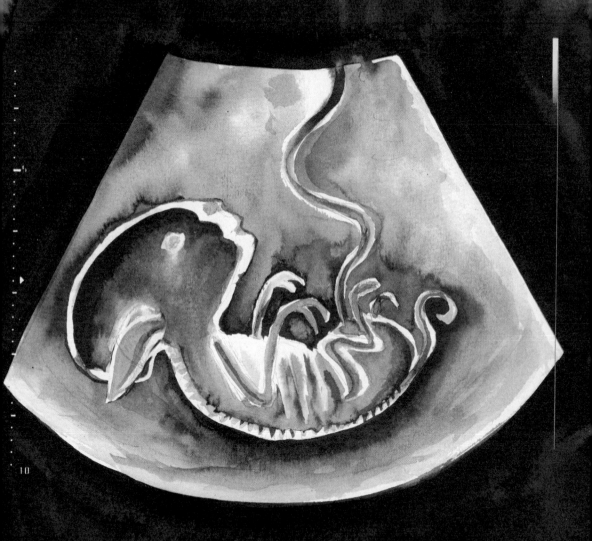

(2d) G16 105dB TA10/p90/HAR/FST 1

133421   SCIENCE CAMP 4-C   FPS38D   6.5 cm   MI 0.86   12-1C
Jepperd, Louise   09/16/2019   C3-EP   Gen.   TIs 0.4   09:35

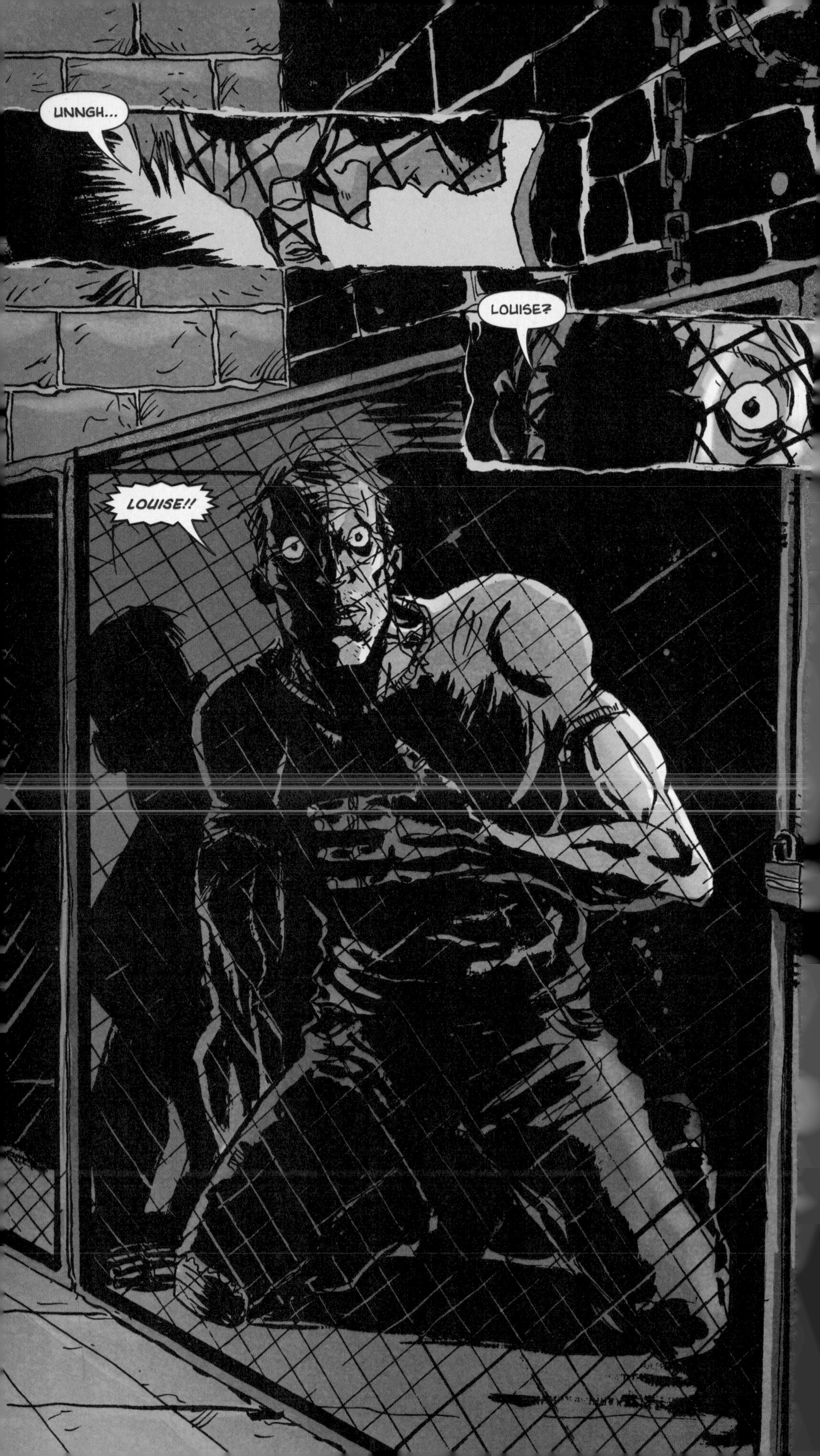
UNNGH...
LOUISE?
LOUISE!!

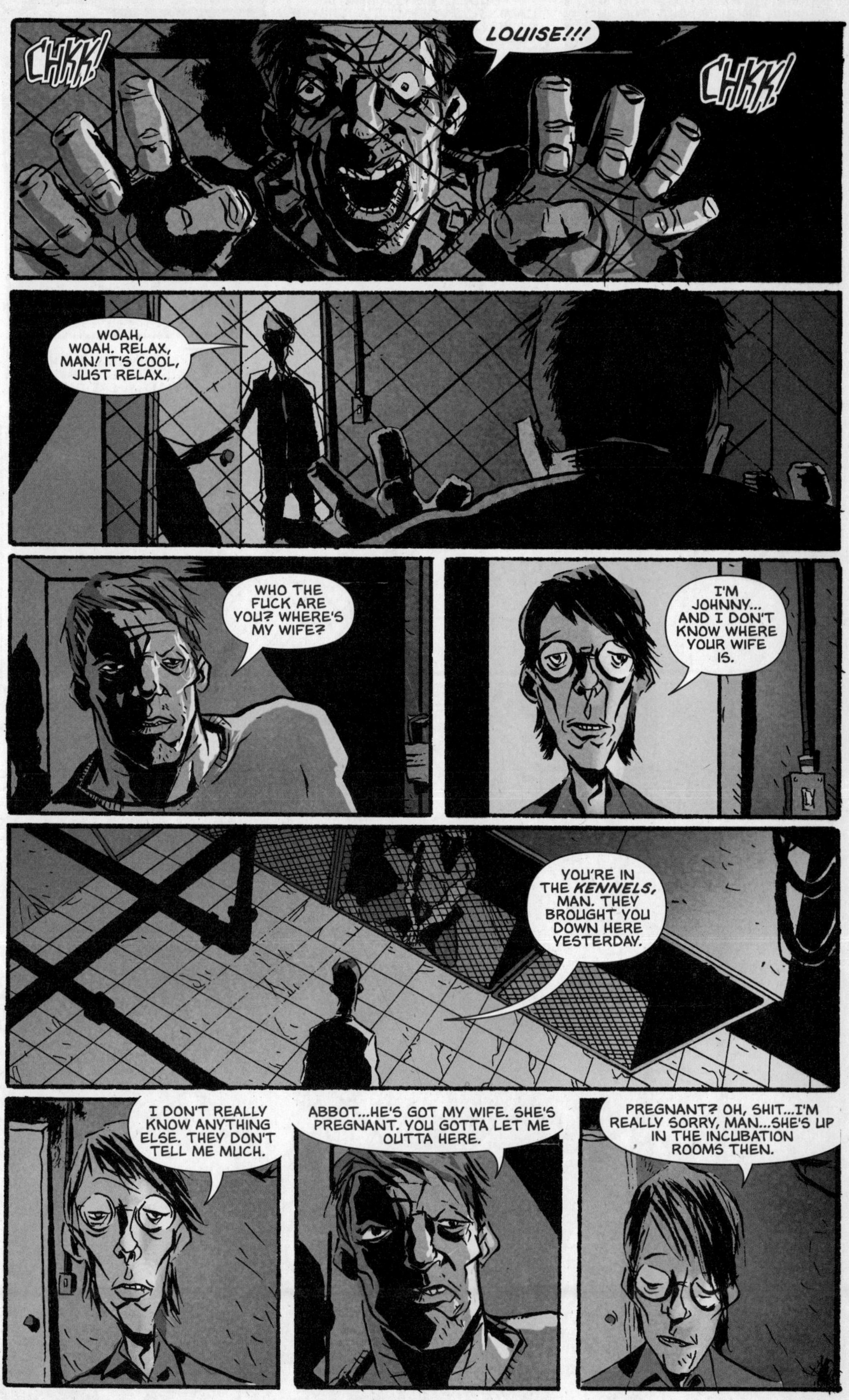
CHKK!
LOUISE!!!
CHKK!
WOAH, WOAH. RELAX, MAN! IT'S COOL, JUST RELAX.
WHO THE FUCK ARE YOU? WHERE'S MY WIFE?
I'M JOHNNY... AND I DON'T KNOW WHERE YOUR WIFE IS.
YOU'RE IN THE KENNELS, MAN. THEY BROUGHT YOU DOWN HERE YESTERDAY.
I DON'T REALLY KNOW ANYTHING ELSE. THEY DON'T TELL ME MUCH.
ABBOT...HE'S GOT MY WIFE. SHE'S PREGNANT. YOU GOTTA LET ME OUTTA HERE.
PREGNANT? OH, SHIT...I'M REALLY SORRY, MAN...SHE'S UP IN THE INCUBATION ROOMS THEN.

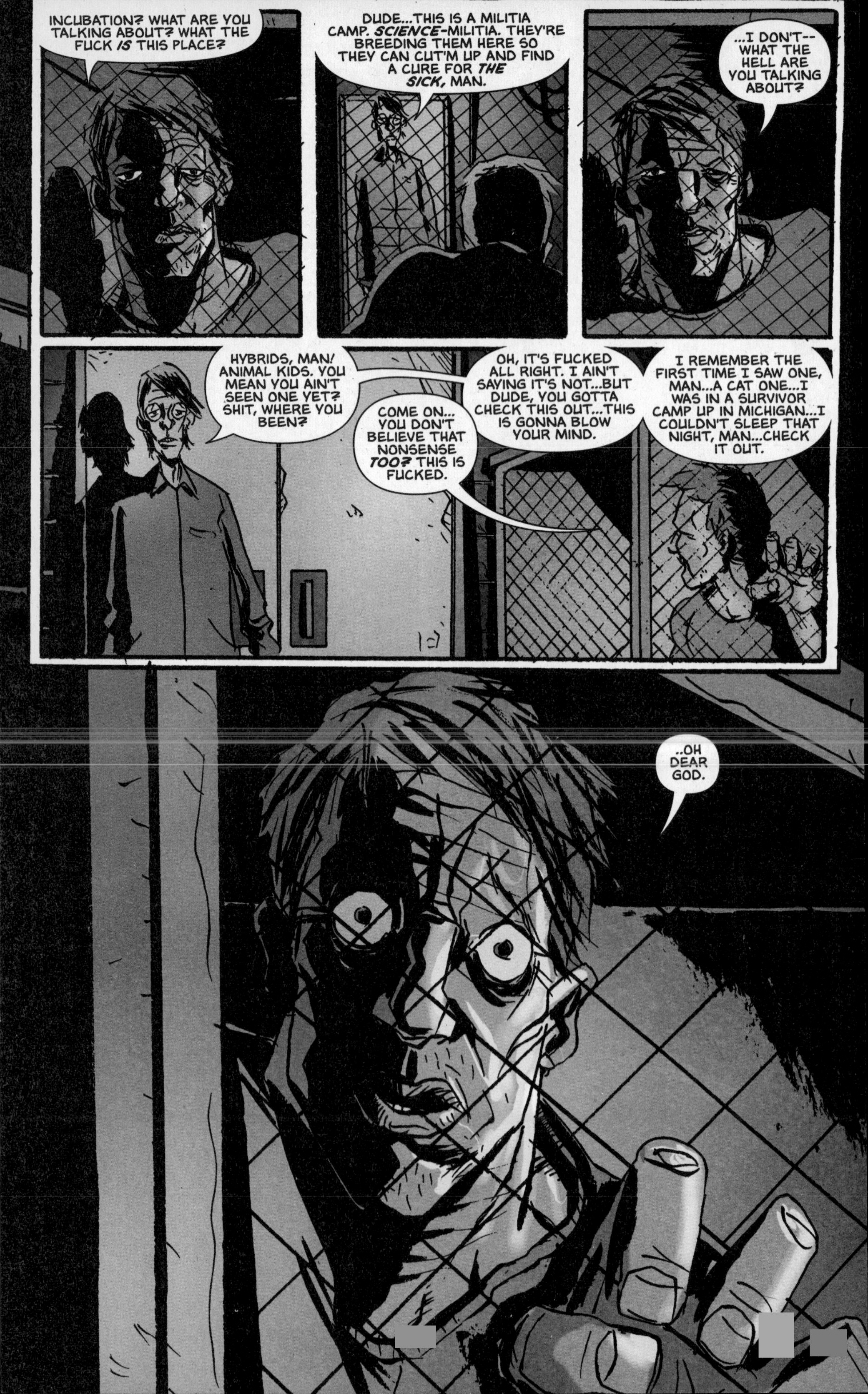
INCUBATION? WHAT ARE YOU TALKING ABOUT? WHAT THE FUCK *IS* THIS PLACE?
DUDE...THIS IS A MILITIA CAMP. *SCIENCE*-MILITIA. THEY'RE BREEDING THEM HERE SO THEY CAN CUT'M UP AND FIND A CURE FOR *THE SICK,* MAN.
...I DON'T-- WHAT THE HELL ARE YOU TALKING ABOUT?
HYBRIDS, MAN! ANIMAL KIDS. YOU MEAN YOU AIN'T SEEN ONE YET? SHIT, WHERE YOU BEEN?
COME ON... YOU DON'T BELIEVE THAT NONSENSE *TOO?* THIS IS FUCKED.
OH, IT'S FUCKED ALL RIGHT. I AIN'T SAYING IT'S NOT...BUT DUDE, YOU GOTTA CHECK THIS OUT...THIS IS GONNA BLOW YOUR MIND.
I REMEMBER THE FIRST TIME I SAW ONE, MAN...A CAT ONE...I WAS IN A SURVIVOR CAMP UP IN MICHIGAN...I COULDN'T SLEEP THAT NIGHT, MAN...CHECK IT OUT.
..OH DEAR GOD.

I KNOW, MAN, I KNOW.
YEAH, MAN... ALL THE BABIES BORN SINCE THE SICK ARE LIKE THAT. IT'S CRAZY. AND THEY GOT DOCTORS AND SCIENTISTS HERE TRYING TO FIGURE IT ALL OUT.
SWEET TOOTH
IN CAPTIVITY CONCLUSION

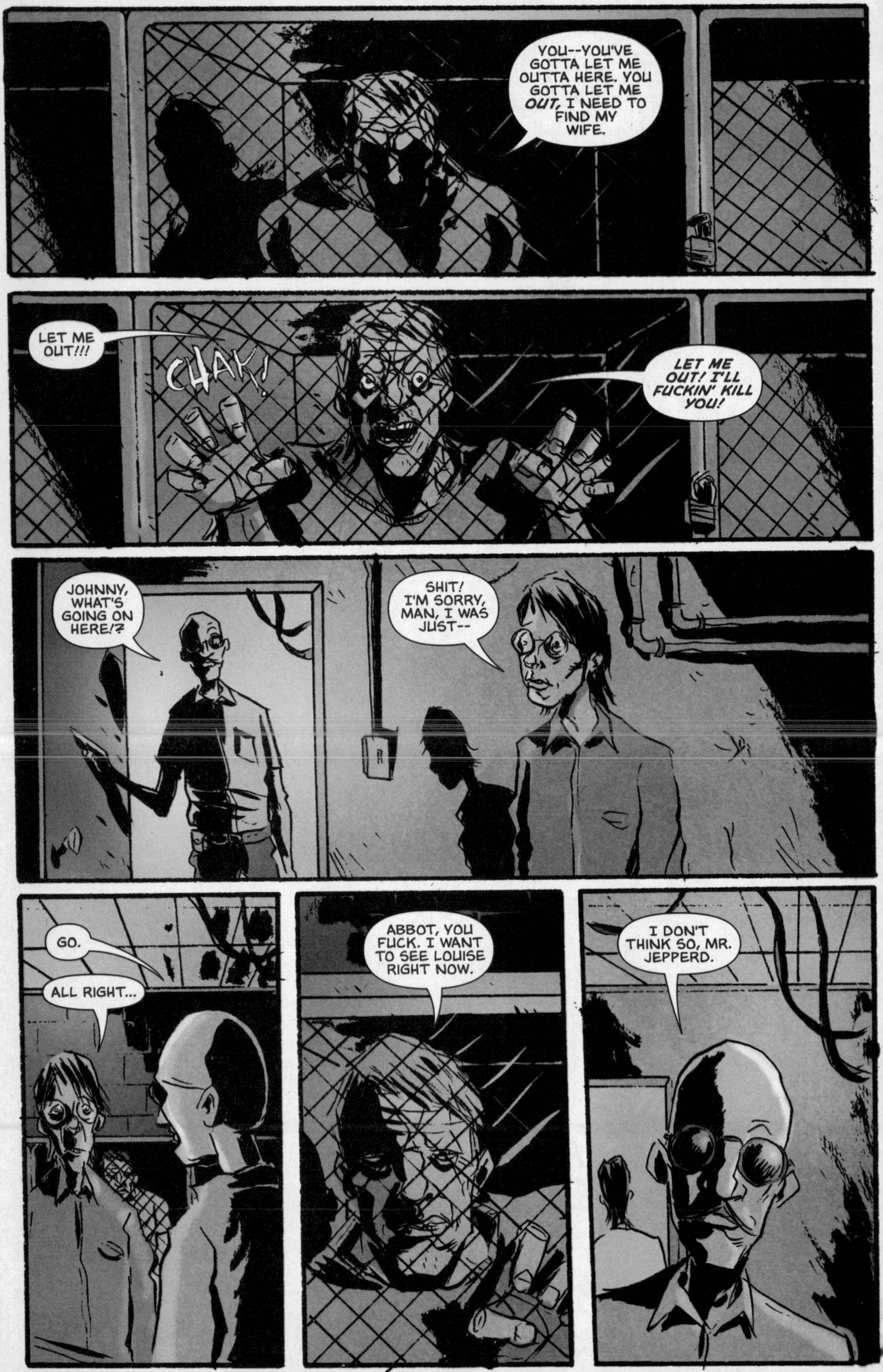

YOU--YOU'VE GOTTA LET ME OUTTA HERE. YOU GOTTA LET ME OUT, I NEED TO FIND MY WIFE.
LET ME OUT!!!
CHAK!
LET ME OUT! I'LL FUCKIN' KILL YOU!
JOHNNY, WHAT'S GOING ON HERE!?
SHIT! I'M SORRY, MAN, I WAS JUST--
GO.
ALL RIGHT...
ABBOT, YOU FUCK. I WANT TO SEE LOUISE RIGHT NOW.
I DON'T THINK SO, MR. JEPPERD.

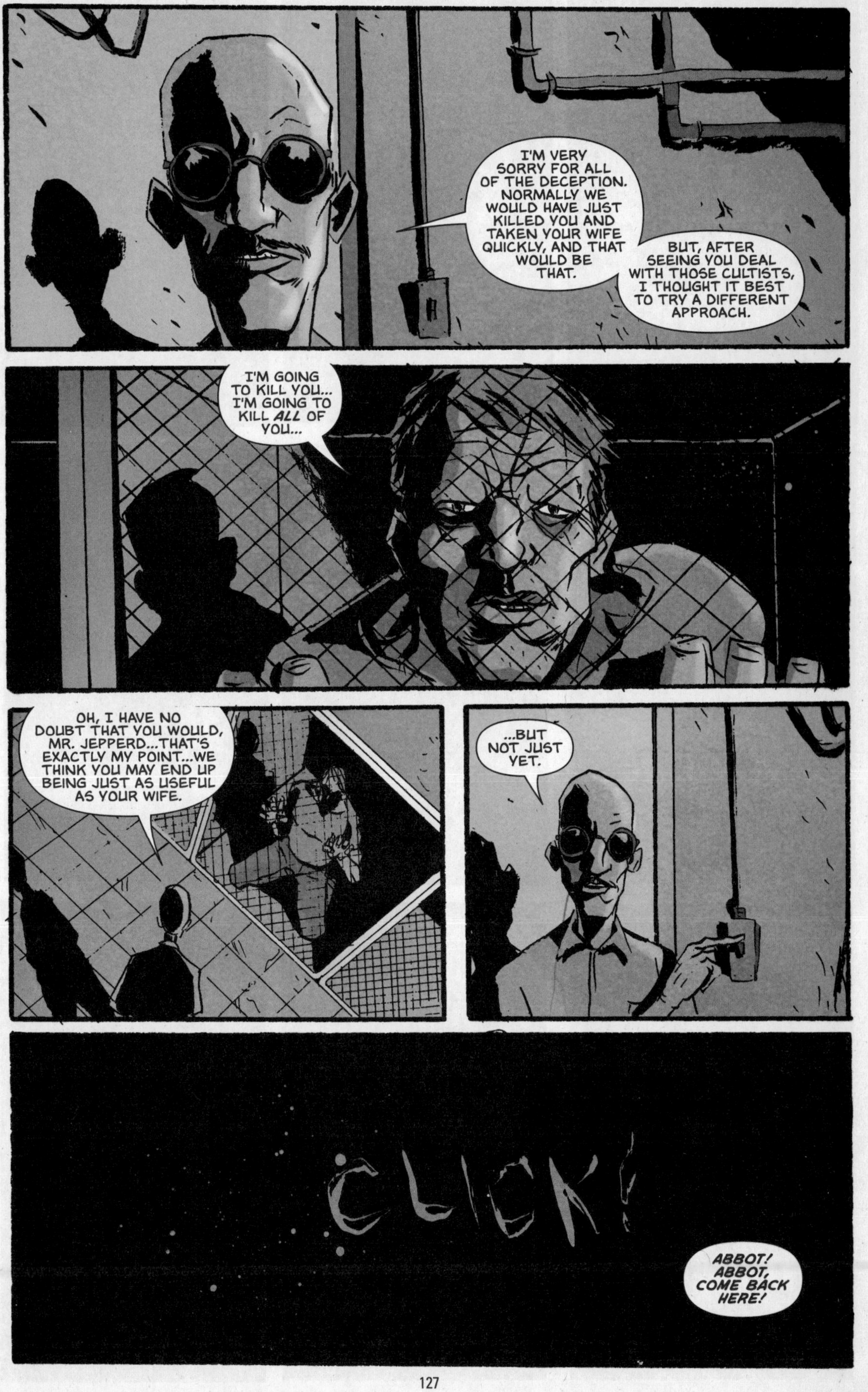
I'M VERY SORRY FOR ALL OF THE DECEPTION. NORMALLY WE WOULD HAVE JUST KILLED YOU AND TAKEN YOUR WIFE QUICKLY, AND THAT WOULD BE THAT.
BUT, AFTER SEEING YOU DEAL WITH THOSE CULTISTS, I THOUGHT IT BEST TO TRY A DIFFERENT APPROACH.
I'M GOING TO KILL YOU... I'M GOING TO KILL *ALL* OF YOU...
OH, I HAVE NO DOUBT THAT YOU WOULD, MR. JEPPERD...THAT'S EXACTLY MY POINT...WE THINK YOU MAY END UP BEING JUST AS USEFUL AS YOUR WIFE.
...BUT NOT JUST YET.
CLICK!
ABBOT! ABBOT, COME BACK HERE!

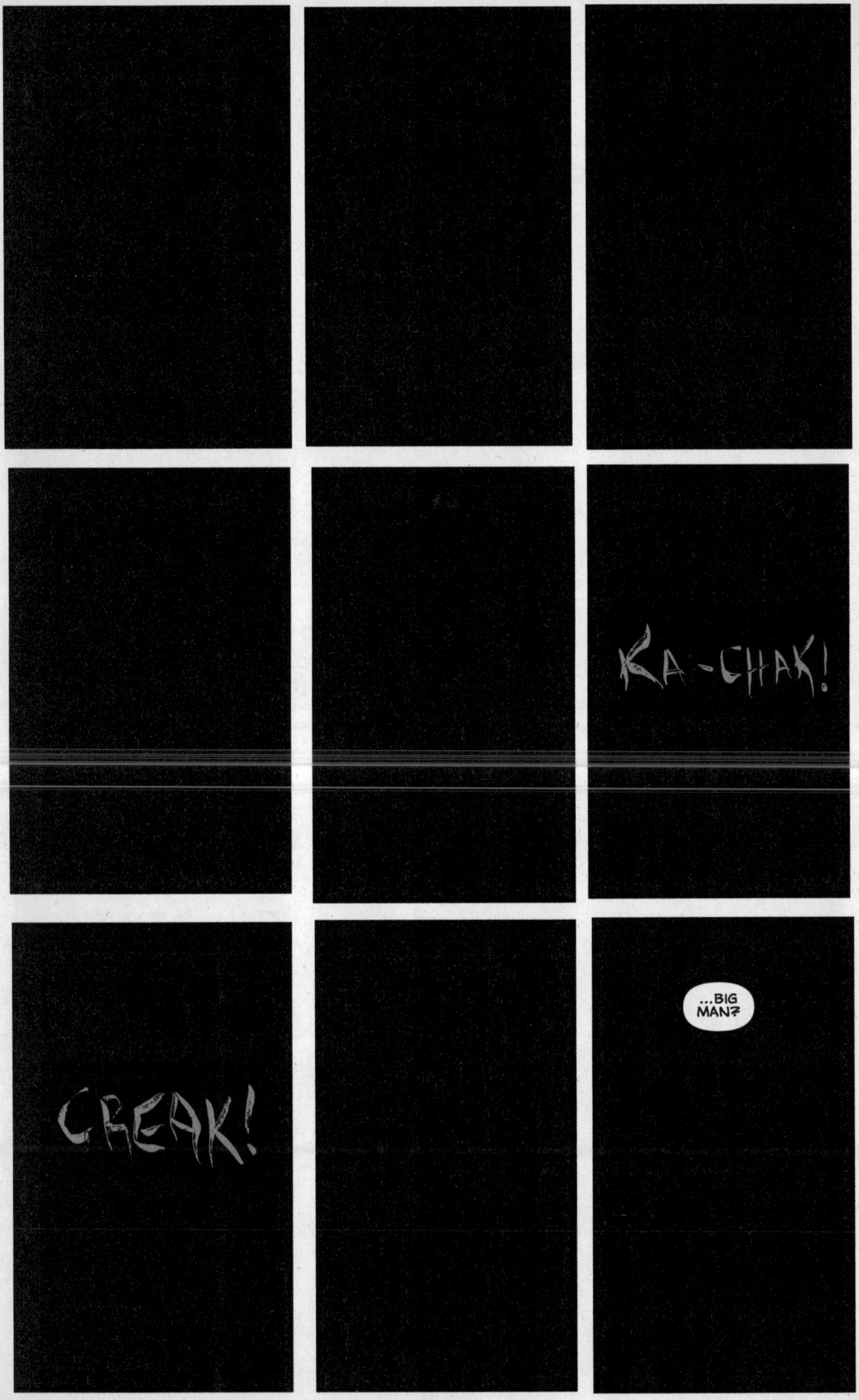

KA-CHAK!
CREAK!
...BIG MAN?

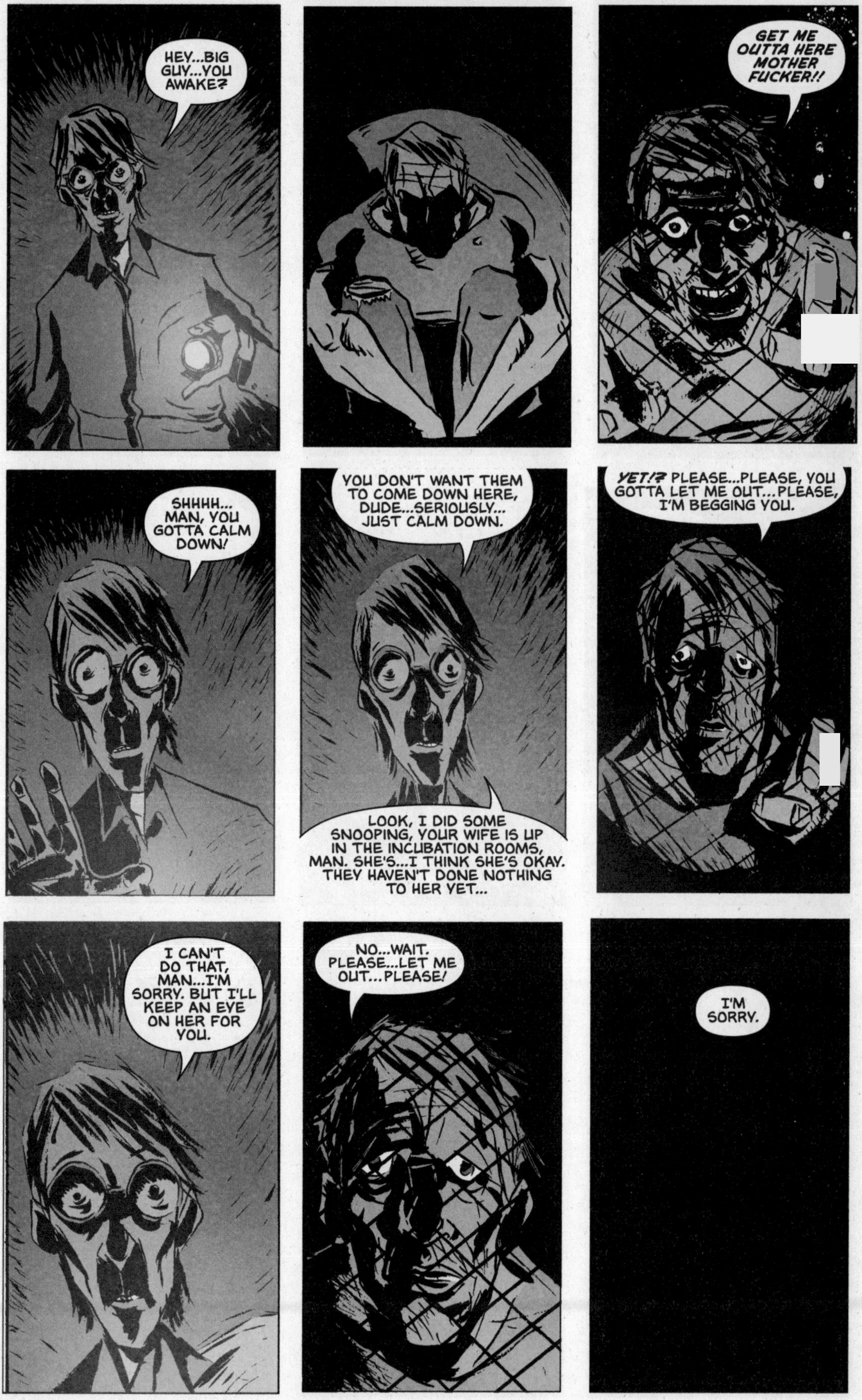
HEY...BIG GUY...YOU AWAKE?
GET ME OUTTA HERE MOTHER FUCKER!!
SHHHH... MAN, YOU GOTTA CALM DOWN!
YOU DON'T WANT THEM TO COME DOWN HERE, DUDE...SERIOUSLY... JUST CALM DOWN.
LOOK, I DID SOME SNOOPING, YOUR WIFE IS UP IN THE INCUBATION ROOMS, MAN. SHE'S...I THINK SHE'S OKAY. THEY HAVEN'T DONE NOTHING TO HER YET...
YET!? PLEASE...PLEASE, YOU GOTTA LET ME OUT...PLEASE, I'M BEGGING YOU.
I CAN'T DO THAT, MAN...I'M SORRY. BUT I'LL KEEP AN EYE ON HER FOR YOU.
NO...WAIT. PLEASE...LET ME OUT...PLEASE!
I'M SORRY.

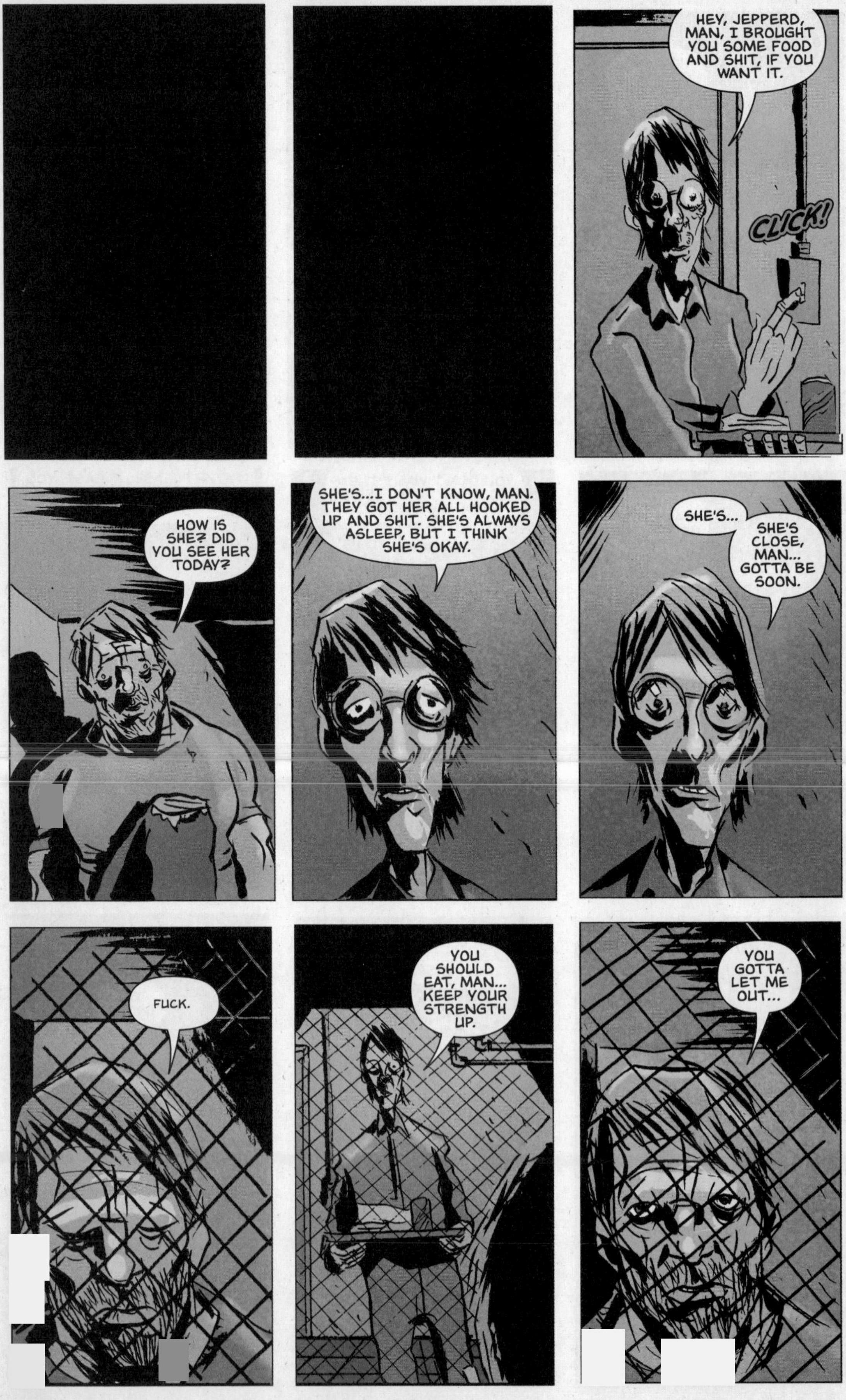
HEY, JEPPERD, MAN, I BROUGHT YOU SOME FOOD AND SHIT, IF YOU WANT IT.
CLICK!
HOW IS SHE? DID YOU SEE HER TODAY?
SHE'S...I DON'T KNOW, MAN. THEY GOT HER ALL HOOKED UP AND SHIT. SHE'S ALWAYS ASLEEP, BUT I THINK SHE'S OKAY.
SHE'S...
SHE'S CLOSE, MAN... GOTTA BE SOON.
FUCK.
YOU SHOULD EAT, MAN... KEEP YOUR STRENGTH UP.
YOU GOTTA LET ME OUT...

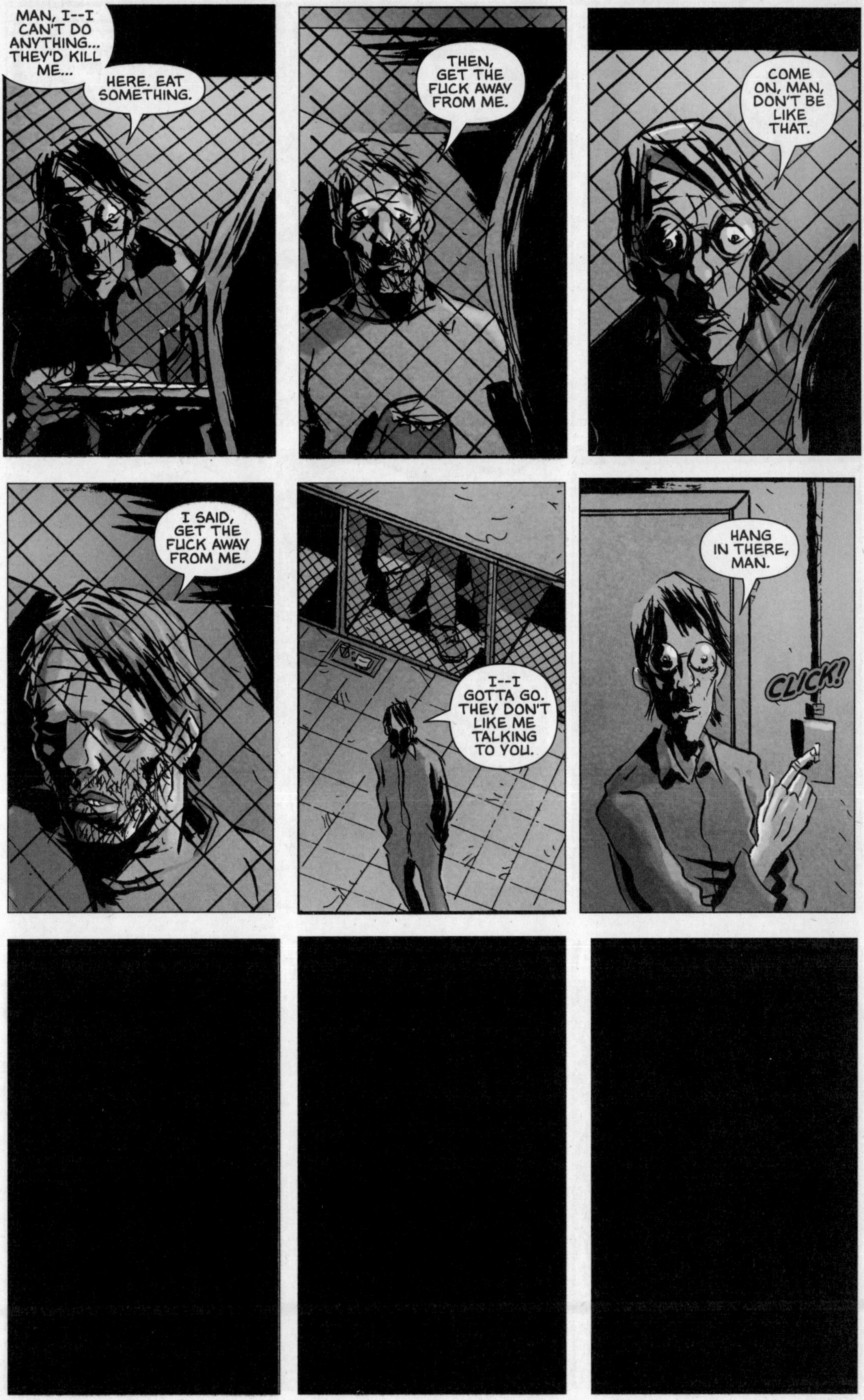
MAN, I--I CAN'T DO ANYTHING... THEY'D KILL ME...
HERE. EAT SOMETHING.
THEN, GET THE FUCK AWAY FROM ME.
COME ON, MAN, DON'T BE LIKE THAT.
I SAID, GET THE FUCK AWAY FROM ME.
I--I GOTTA GO. THEY DON'T LIKE ME TALKING TO YOU.
HANG IN THERE, MAN.
CLICK!

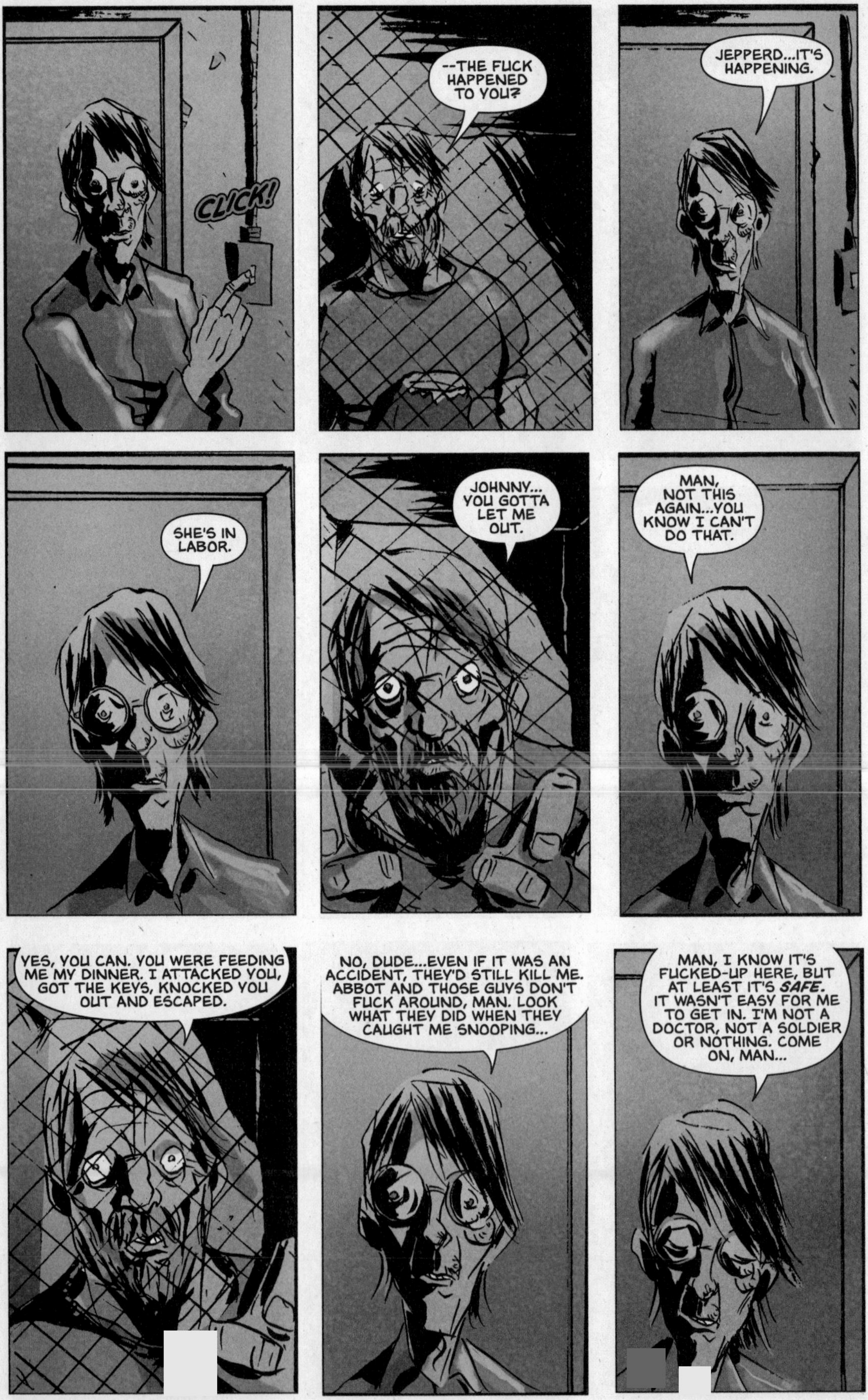
CLICK!
--THE FUCK HAPPENED TO YOU?
JEPPERD...IT'S HAPPENING.
SHE'S IN LABOR.
JOHNNY... YOU GOTTA LET ME OUT.
MAN, NOT THIS AGAIN...YOU KNOW I CAN'T DO THAT.
YES, YOU CAN. YOU WERE FEEDING ME MY DINNER. I ATTACKED YOU, GOT THE KEYS, KNOCKED YOU OUT AND ESCAPED.
NO, DUDE...EVEN IF IT WAS AN ACCIDENT, THEY'D STILL KILL ME. ABBOT AND THOSE GUYS DON'T FUCK AROUND, MAN. LOOK WHAT THEY DID WHEN THEY CAUGHT ME SNOOPING...
MAN, I KNOW IT'S FUCKED-UP HERE, BUT AT LEAST IT'S *SAFE*. IT WASN'T EASY FOR ME TO GET IN. I'M NOT A DOCTOR, NOT A SOLDIER OR NOTHING. COME ON, MAN...

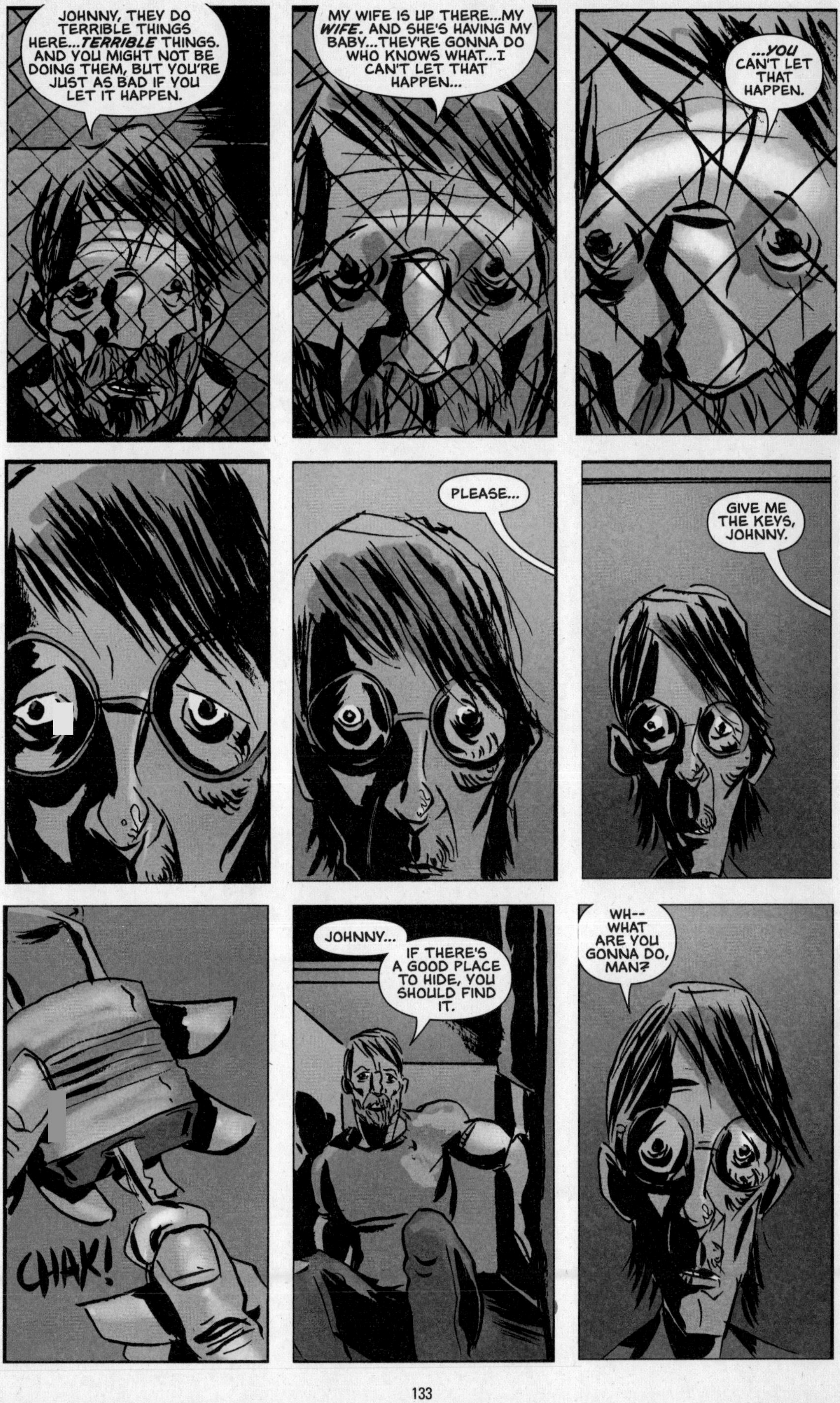
JOHNNY, THEY DO TERRIBLE THINGS HERE...TERRIBLE THINGS. AND YOU MIGHT NOT BE DOING THEM, BUT YOU'RE JUST AS BAD IF YOU LET IT HAPPEN.
MY WIFE IS UP THERE...MY WIFE. AND SHE'S HAVING MY BABY...THEY'RE GONNA DO WHO KNOWS WHAT...I CAN'T LET THAT HAPPEN...
...YOU CAN'T LET THAT HAPPEN.
PLEASE...
GIVE ME THE KEYS, JOHNNY.
CHAK!
JOHNNY...
IF THERE'S A GOOD PLACE TO HIDE, YOU SHOULD FIND IT.
WH-- WHAT ARE YOU GONNA DO, MAN?

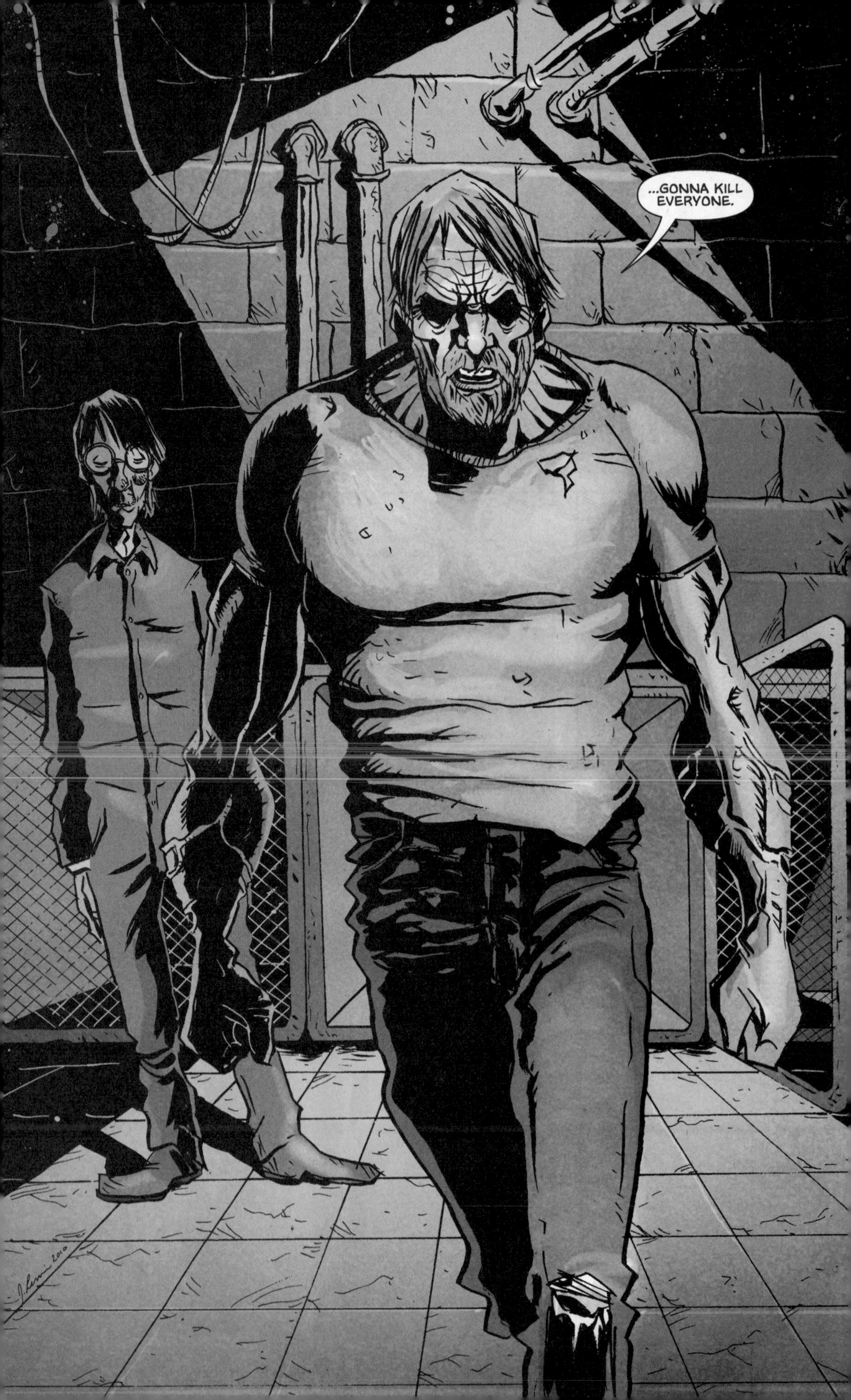
...GONNA KILL EVERYONE.

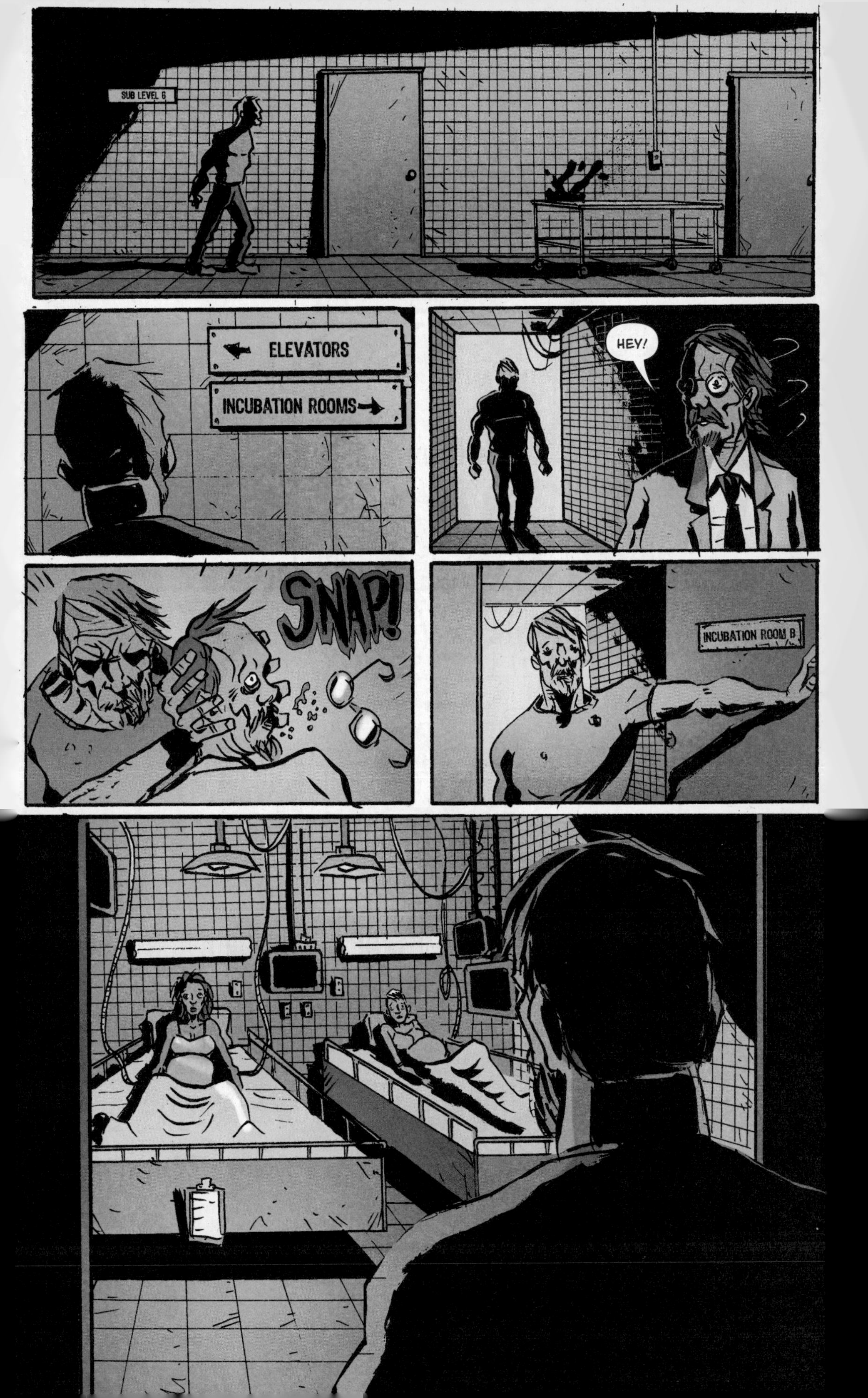
SUB LEVEL 6
ELEVATORS
INCUBATION ROOMS
HEY!
SNAP!
INCUBATION ROOM B

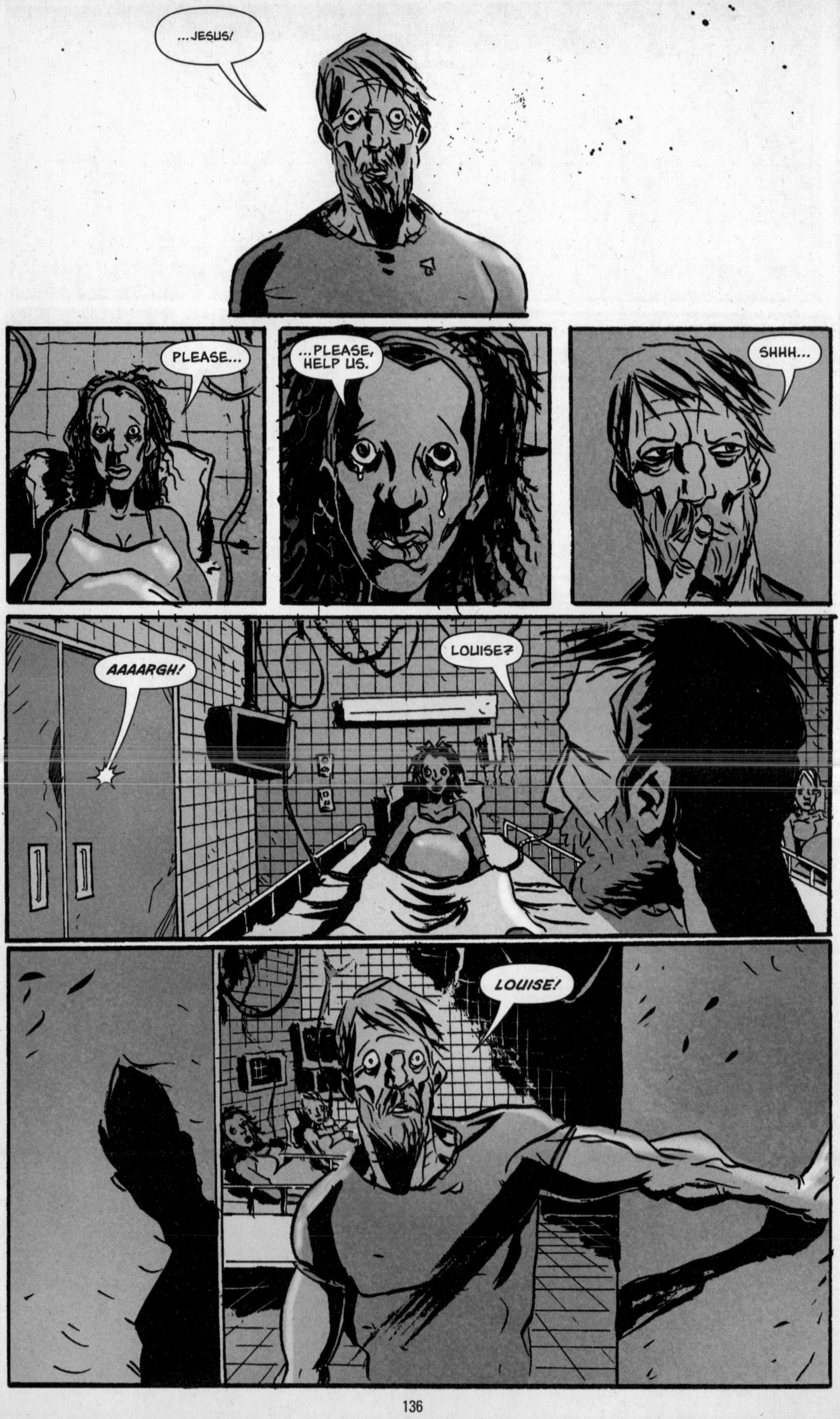
...JESUS!
PLEASE...
...PLEASE, HELP US.
SHHH...
AAAARGH!
LOUISE?
LOUISE!

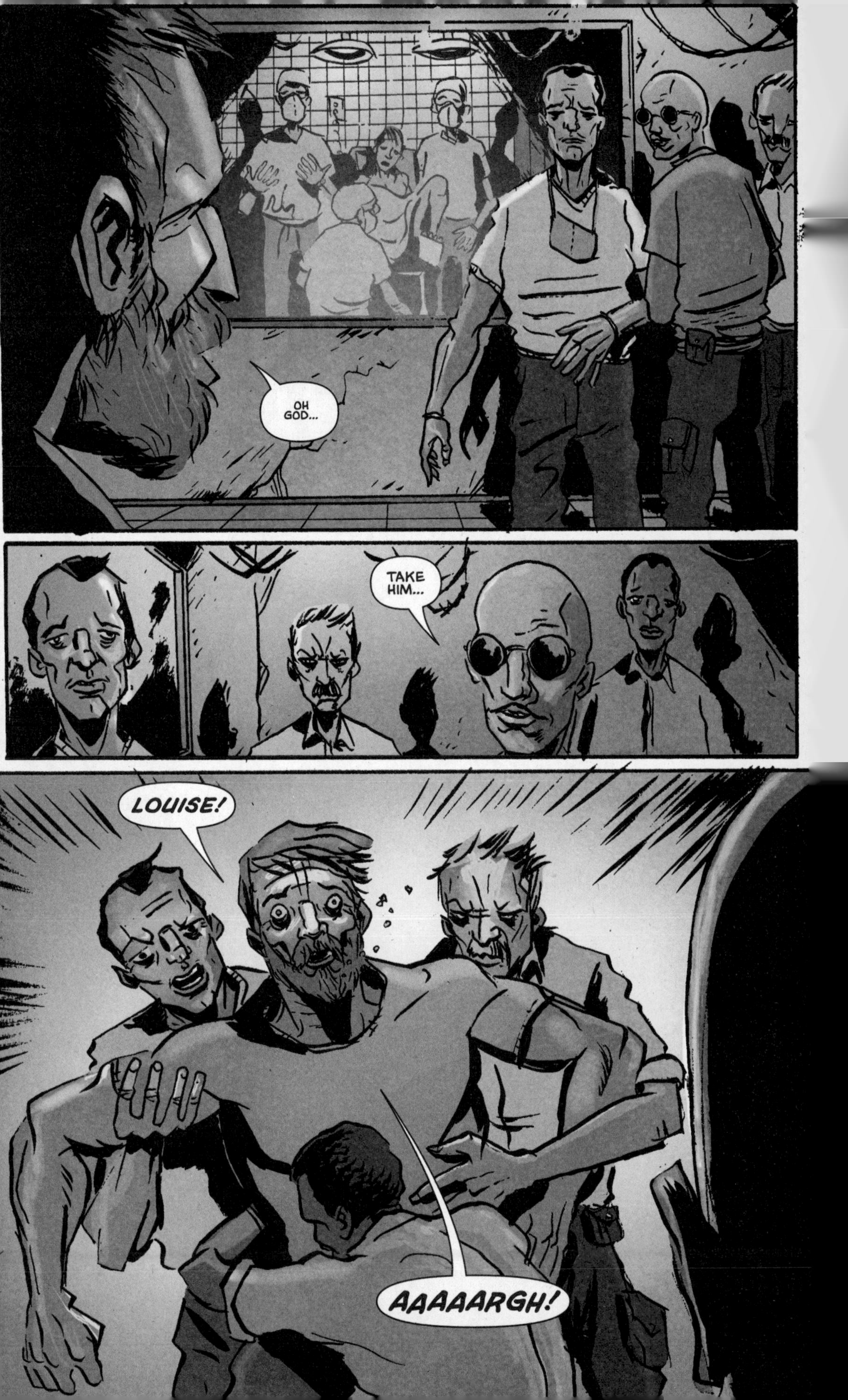
OH GOD...
TAKE HIM...
LOUISE!
AAAAARGH!

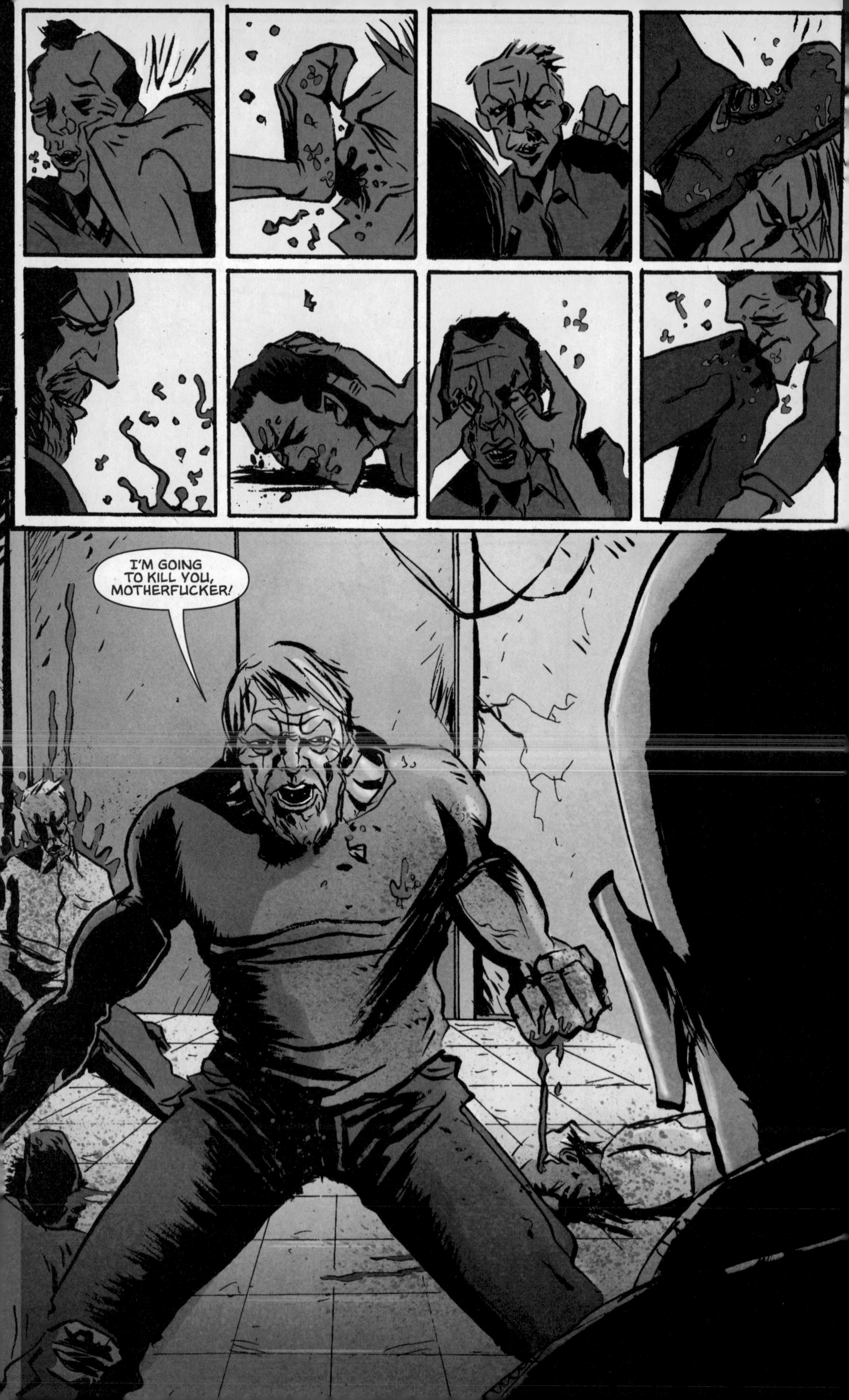
I'M GOING TO KILL YOU, MOTHERFUCKER!

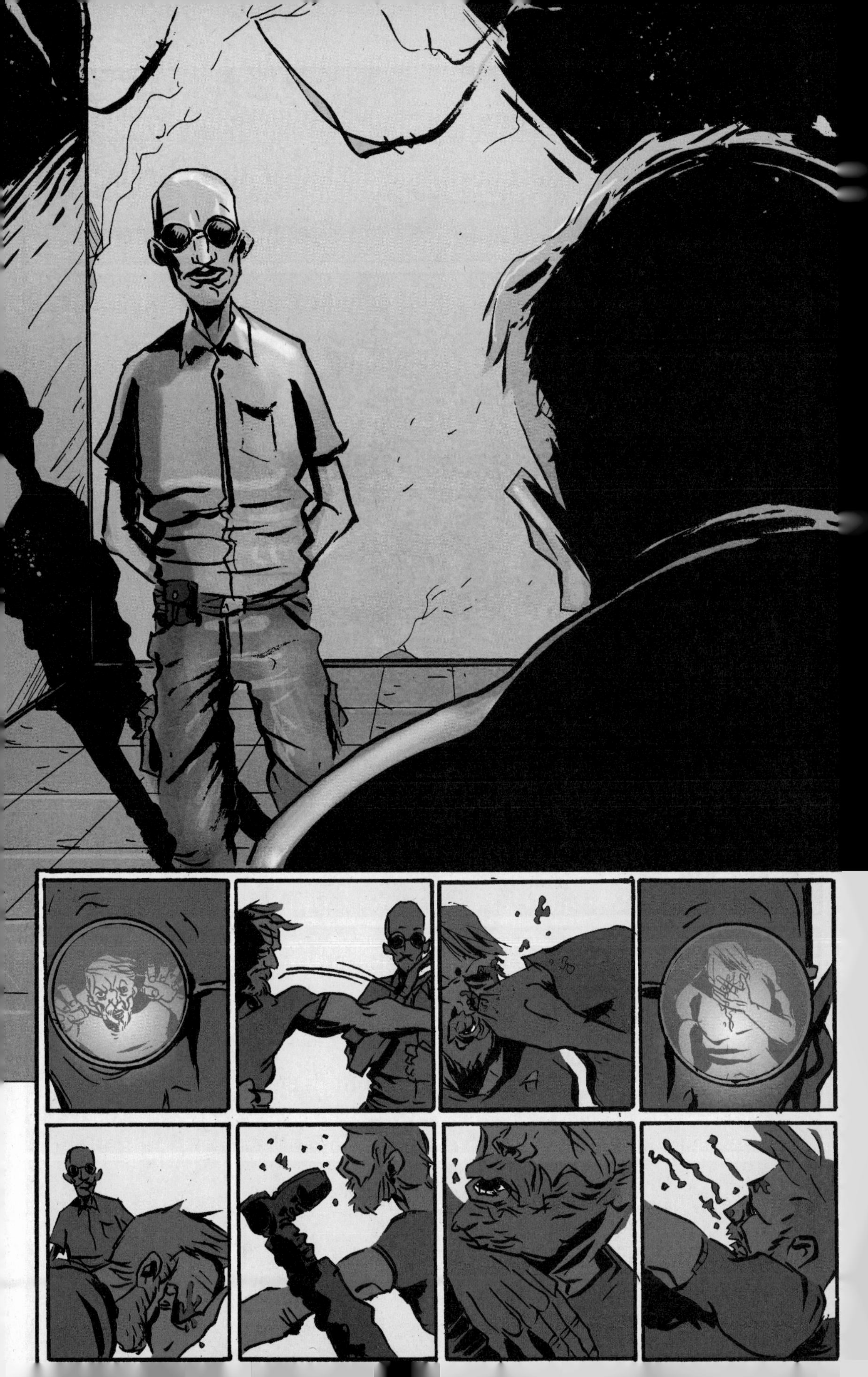

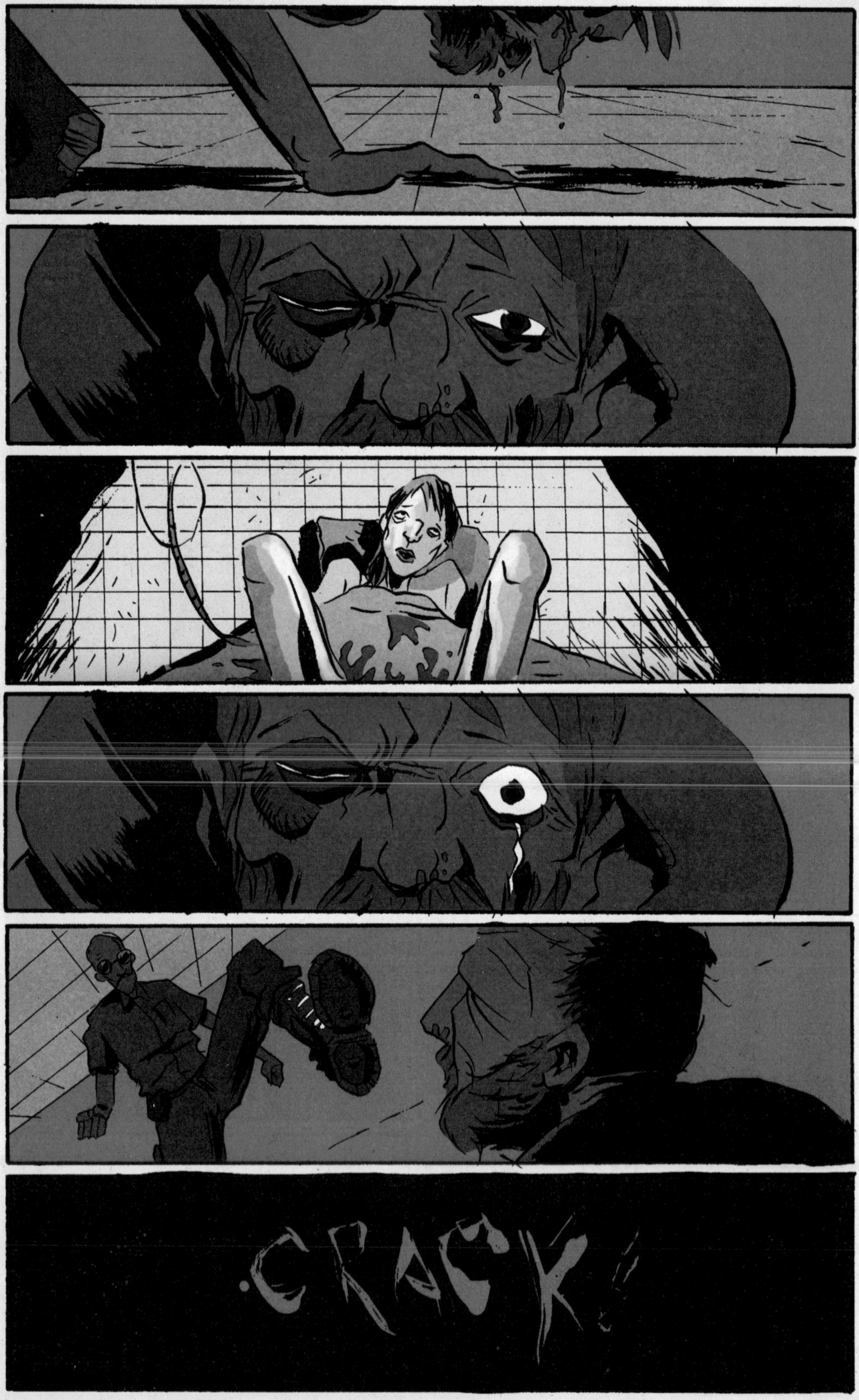
CRACK!

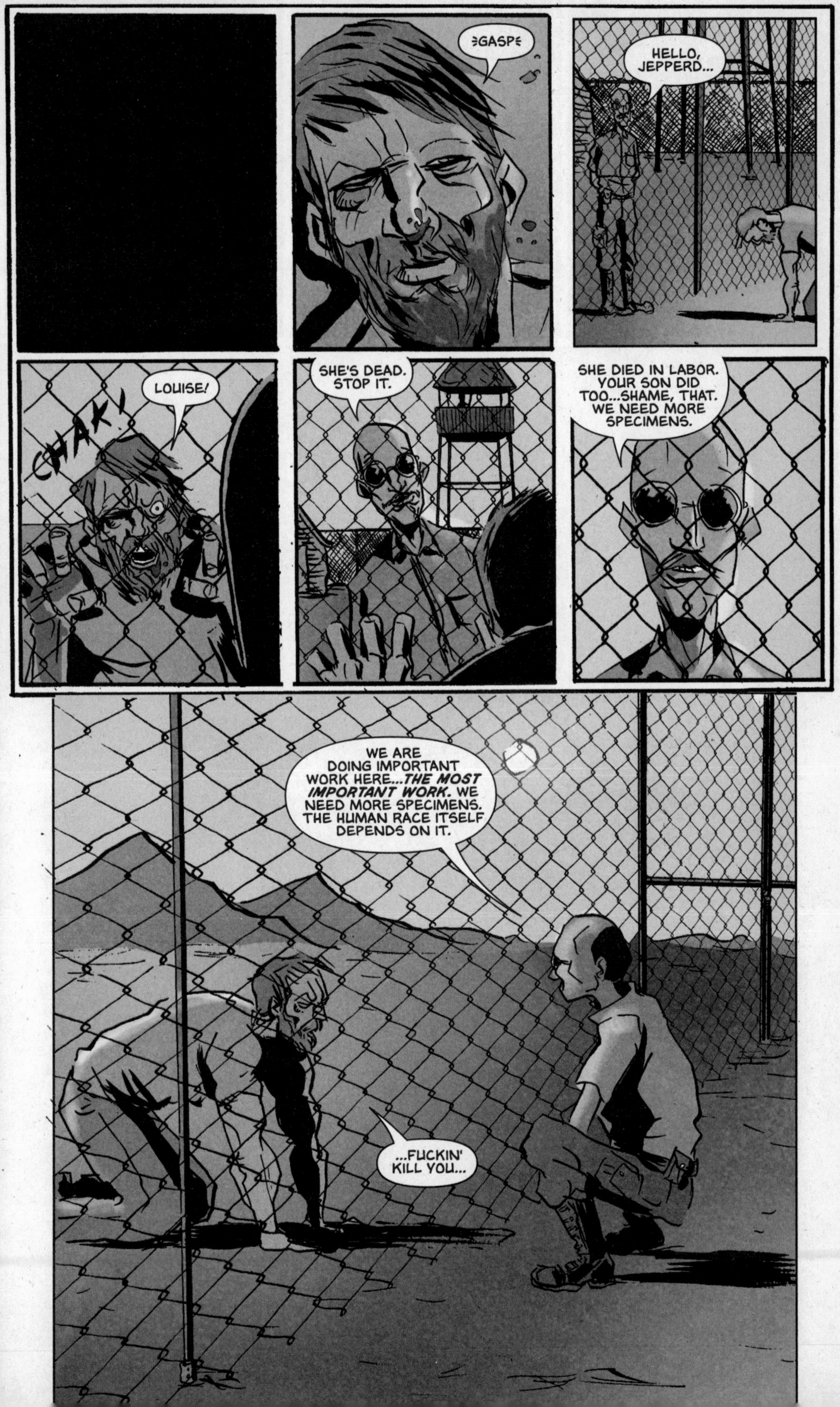
GASP
HELLO, JEPPERD...
CHAK!
LOUISE!
SHE'S DEAD. STOP IT.
SHE DIED IN LABOR. YOUR SON DID TOO...SHAME, THAT. WE NEED MORE SPECIMENS.
WE ARE DOING IMPORTANT WORK HERE...*THE MOST IMPORTANT WORK.* WE NEED MORE SPECIMENS. THE HUMAN RACE ITSELF DEPENDS ON IT.
...FUCKIN' KILL YOU...

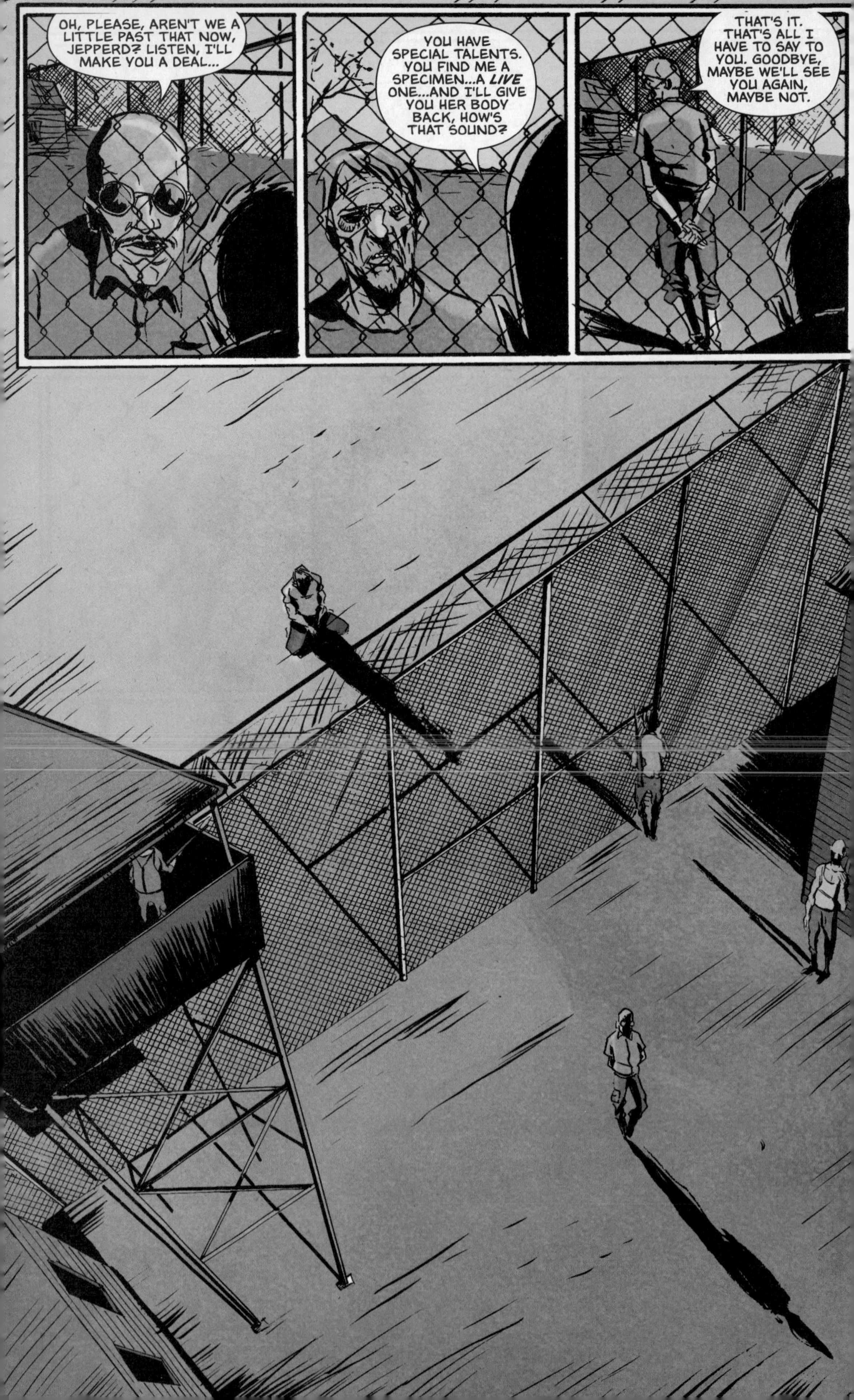
OH, PLEASE, AREN'T WE A LITTLE PAST THAT NOW, JEPPERD? LISTEN, I'LL MAKE YOU A DEAL...
YOU HAVE SPECIAL TALENTS. YOU FIND ME A SPECIMEN...A *LIVE* ONE...AND I'LL GIVE YOU HER BODY BACK, HOW'S THAT SOUND?
THAT'S IT. THAT'S ALL I HAVE TO SAY TO YOU. GOODBYE, MAYBE WE'LL SEE YOU AGAIN, MAYBE NOT.

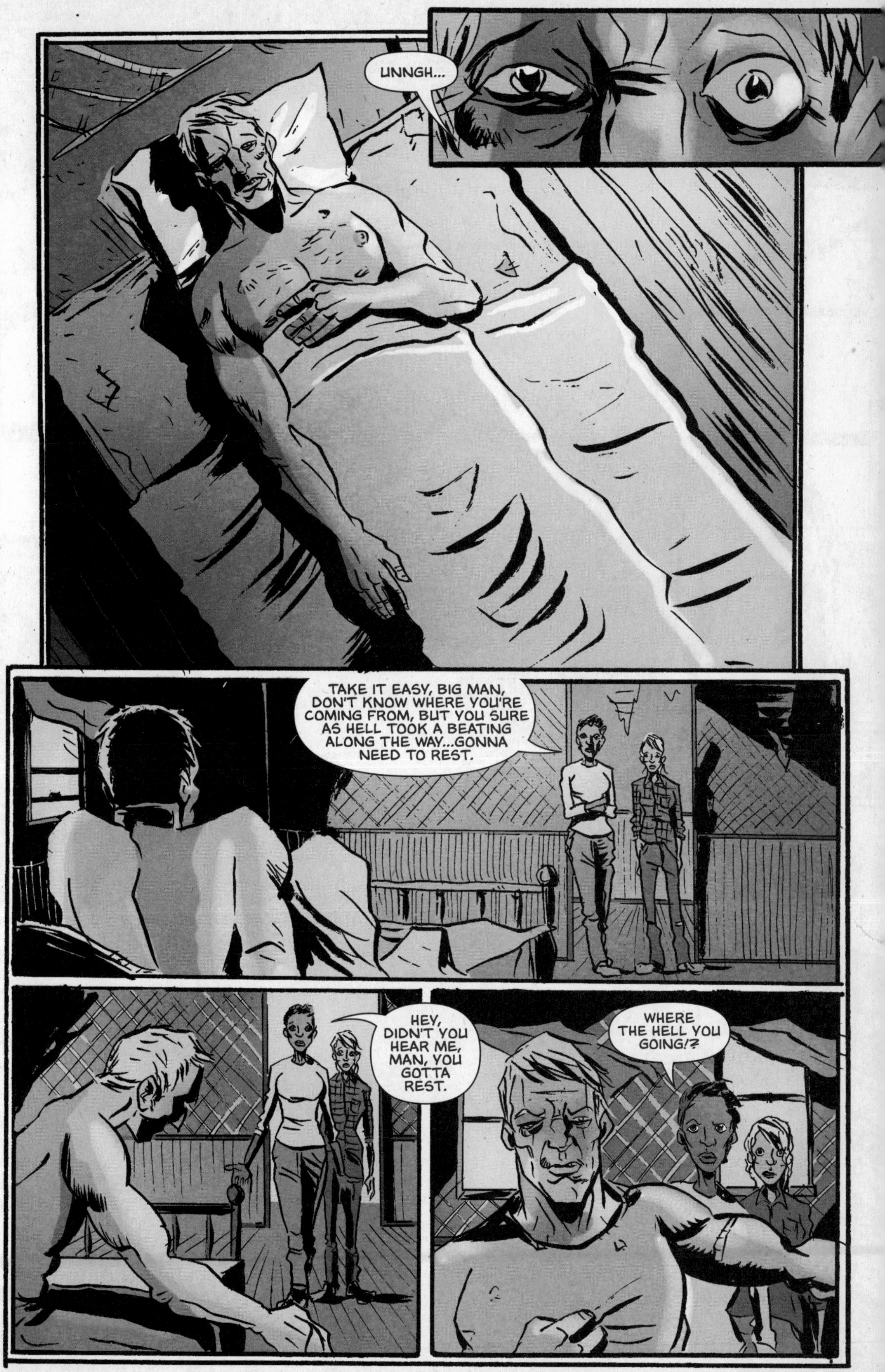
UNNGH...
TAKE IT EASY, BIG MAN, DON'T KNOW WHERE YOU'RE COMING FROM, BUT YOU SURE AS HELL TOOK A BEATING ALONG THE WAY...GONNA NEED TO REST.
HEY, DIDN'T YOU HEAR ME, MAN, YOU GOTTA REST.
WHERE THE HELL YOU GOING!?

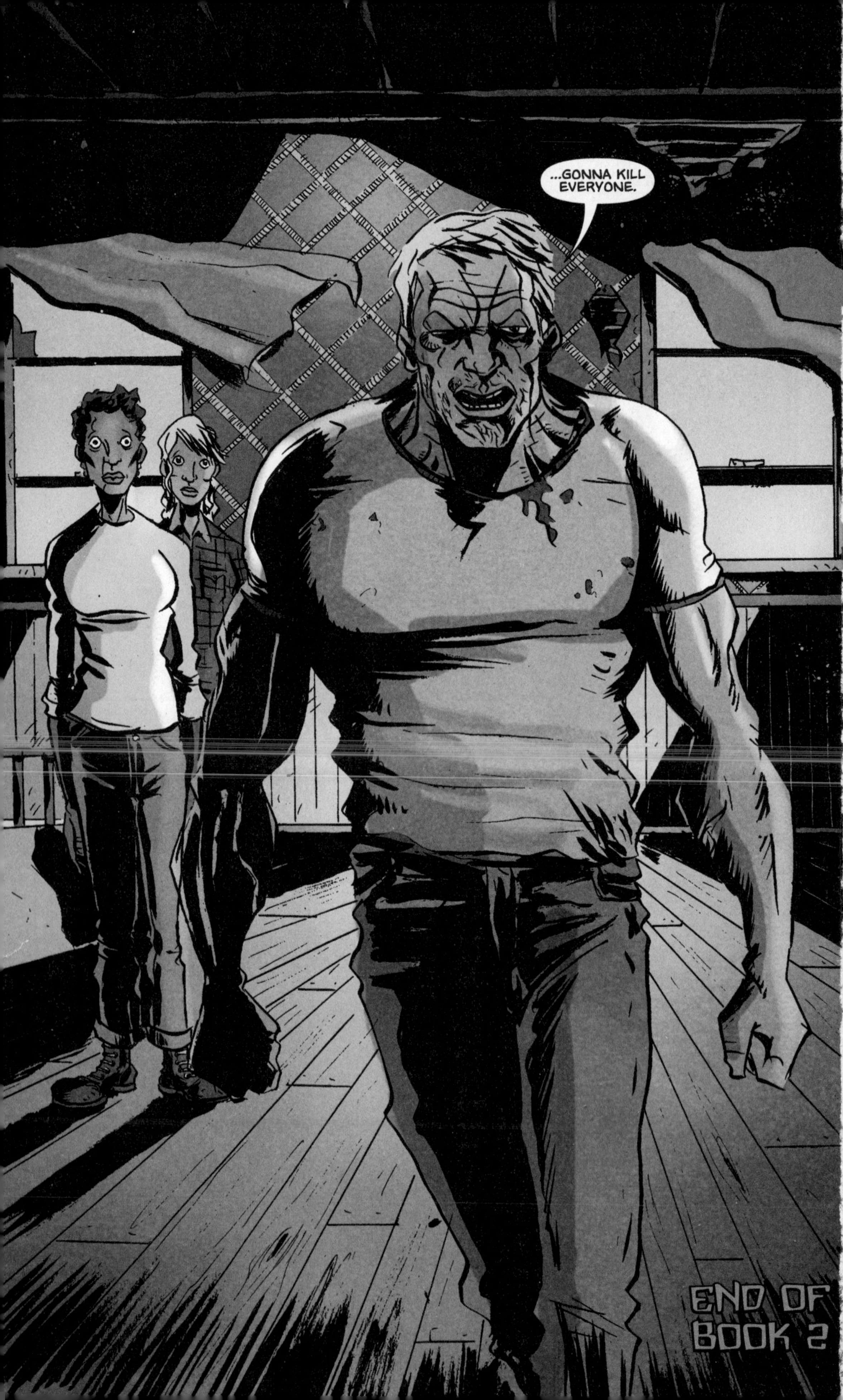
...GONNA KILL EVERYONE.
END OF BOOK 2